HERMENEUTICAL POLITICAL ECONOMY

An Introductory Textbook

Carmelo Ferlito

Monolateral

Hermeneutical Political Economy: An Introductory Textbook

Copyright © 2026 by Carmelo Ferlito

ISBN-13: 978-1-946374-33-2 (paperback)
ASIN: B0GGZCWTTK (Kindle)

Monolateral
monolateral.com

In today's political economy environment, the struggle over *humility* has arguably become the most important battleground. It pits those who believe in precisely measurable, quantitatively attainable policy targets—reflecting a pretence of knowledge—against those who recognise the limits of what can be known, echoing the insight that "*There are more things in heaven and Earth, Horatio, / Than are dreamt of in your philosophy*" (W. Shakespeare, Hamlet).

This divide now cuts more deeply than the traditional boundaries between schools of economic thought.

Carmelo Ferlito

CONTENTS

HERMENEUTICAL POLITICAL ECONOMY

AN INTRODUCTORY TEXTBOOK

Introduction

This book begins from a sense of unease. Not a casual dissatisfaction with particular policies or technical disagreements within the economics profession, but a deeper intellectual and civilizational unease concerning how modern societies understand economic life, political action, and the relationship between knowledge and power. Something fundamental has shifted in the way economics is practiced, taught, and mobilized for policy purposes—and that shift has consequences that reach far beyond academic debate.

At the centre of this transformation lies a profound reorientation of political economy away from understanding and toward control. Economics has increasingly come to be treated not as a discipline devoted to interpreting the logic of human cooperation under conditions of scarcity, time, and uncertainty, but as a toolbox for governance—a technology for managing outcomes, steering behaviour, and optimizing social performance. In parallel, public policy has been reconceived not as an art of prudential judgment exercised within institutional and moral constraints, but as a quasi-scientific activity whose legitimacy derives from models, indicators, and procedural correctness.

The result is a pervasive confusion between *knowing* and *doing*, between *explaining* and *commanding*, between *theory* and *rule*. Economics is asked to deliver certainty where only interpretation is possible; policy is expected to eliminate uncertainty where uncertainty is constitutive of human action itself. This book argues that this confusion is not merely a methodological error. It is a philosophical mistake with far-reaching ethical, institutional, and political consequences.

Hermeneutical Political Economy emerges as a response to this condition.

Economics as a Science of Meaning

At its core, hermeneutical political economy insists on a simple but demanding claim: economic life is meaningful before it is measurable. Markets, prices, capital, institutions, money, and policy are not neutral objects awaiting technical manipulation. They are social phenomena constituted by interpretation—by the expectations, beliefs, narratives, and imaginative projections of acting persons embedded in time and history.

Human beings do not merely respond to incentives; they interpret situations. They do not optimize within closed systems; they act within open horizons of uncertainty. They do not inhabit a world of fixed data; they continuously reinterpret past experience in light of imagined futures. Any economic theory that abstracts from this interpretative dimension does not merely simplify reality—it misrepresents it.

The hermeneutical tradition, from which this approach draws inspiration, begins with *verstehen*: understanding action from within the horizon of meaning in which it becomes intelligible. Applied to political economy, this implies that economics is not a natural science seeking invariant laws of motion, but a social science concerned with the intelligibility of coordination among free, creative, and fallible agents. Its task is not to predict outcomes with mechanical precision, but to clarify the constraints, tensions, and structural logics within which economic action unfolds.

This reorientation has decisive implications. It means that prices are not merely numerical equilibria, but communicative signals embedded in institutional contexts. Capital is not a homogeneous stock, but a temporal structure of expectations oriented toward an uncertain future. Money is not neutral, but interpretatively charged, shaping how economic actors distinguish relative scarcities from monetary distortions. Institutions are not technical devices, but repositories of social memory and shared meaning.

Economics, understood in this way, becomes a discipline of interpretation rather than control. It does not aspire to mastery over social processes, but to intelligibility. It does not eliminate uncertainty; it teaches us how to live with it.

Policy as an Art of Prudence

If economics is a science of understanding, public policy cannot be its mechanical application. Policy belongs to a different epistemic and moral category altogether. It is not a science in the strict sense, but an art—an art of judgment exercised under conditions of irreducible uncertainty.

This book therefore rejects both technocratic hubris and anti-theoretical pragmatism. On the one hand, it resists the idea that policy can be deduced from models or optimized through algorithms. On the other hand, it rejects the view that theory is dispensable in favour of ad hoc intervention. Between these extremes lies the classical notion of *prudence* (phronesis): the capacity to act responsibly in concrete circumstances without the illusion of certainty.

Prudential policy does not seek to engineer outcomes. It seeks to preserve and cultivate the institutional conditions under which coordination, learning, and discovery can occur. It recognizes that interventions reshape not only incentives but meanings; not only payoffs but expectations; not only behaviour but narratives. For this reason, policy cannot be evaluated solely through metrics and targets. Its deepest effects often unfold indirectly, over time, and beyond what can be measured.

To govern prudently is therefore to accept responsibility without guarantees. It is to acknowledge that error is not an accident of poor technique, but an unavoidable feature of action in an open-ended world. It is to resist both paralysis and overreach. And above all, it is to govern with humility.

AGAINST TECHNOCRACY AND SOCIAL ENGINEERING

A central theme of this book is the critique of technocracy—not understood simply as rule by experts, but as rule by measurement. Technocracy rests on the belief that what matters can be quantified, that values can be embedded in indicators, and that governance can be reduced to procedural compliance. In this worldview, judgment is replaced by algorithms, responsibility by systems, and moral deliberation by optimization routines.

Hermeneutical political economy exposes the limits and dangers of this approach. Measurement is not neutral. Indicators are not innocent. Algorithms do not abolish discretion; they conceal it. When governance is depersonalized, power becomes faceless and accountability dissolves. Injustice persists, but without authors. Decisions are made, but no one decides.

This book argues that such a transformation represents not progress, but an ethical crisis of governance. A society that governs without judgment governs without conscience. A political economy that treats persons as variables undermines the very foundations of legitimacy and freedom.

Against the dream of social engineering, the book advances a vision of society as a complex, emergent order—one that cannot be designed from above because the knowledge required for coordination is dispersed, tacit, and continuously evolving. Order arises not from command, but from interaction.

Stability emerges not from control, but from adaptive learning. Attempts to suppress uncertainty in the name of safety inevitably suppress creativity, entrepreneurship, and growth.

PLURALISM, HUMILITY, AND TRAGEDY

Hermeneutical political economy also entails a commitment to theoretical pluralism and intellectual humility. Social phenomena do not admit of monocausal explanations. Economic outcomes arise from the interaction of institutions, culture, technology, entrepreneurship, policy, and historical contingency. No single theory can exhaust this complexity without becoming ideological.

Disagreement, therefore, is not a defect of economic science. It is a resource. Competing interpretations act as mutual correctives, preventing premature closure and dogmatic certainty. This pluralism mirrors the market process itself, which coordinates not through consensus, but through compatibility among diverse perspectives.

At the deepest level, the book embraces a tragic vision of political economy. Tragedy here does not mean pessimism, but the recognition that human action unfolds under conditions of uncertainty, irreversibility, and moral risk. There are no final solutions, only provisional arrangements. There are no guarantees, only responsibilities. To act is always to risk error; to govern is always to choose without full knowledge.

This tragic condition is not a flaw to be corrected. It is the condition of freedom. A world without uncertainty would be a world without creativity. A society without risk would be a society without growth. The task of political economy is therefore not to abolish tragedy, but to navigate it wisely.

STRUCTURE AND PURPOSE OF THE BOOK

This book develops hermeneutical political economy as both a theoretical framework and a guide to disciplined judgment. It moves from foundational reflections on meaning, knowledge, and interpretation, through analyses of markets, institutions, money, capital, entrepreneurship, and policy, toward a sustained critique of technocracy and social engineering. Throughout, it insists on restoring proper distinctions: between economics and policy, theory and action, explanation and command, measurement and meaning.

The aim is not to offer a new blueprint for governance, but to recover a lost posture of thought—one grounded in humility, responsibility, and respect for the complexity of human cooperation. It is written for students, scholars, and practitioners who sense that something essential has been lost in contemporary political economy, and who seek not certainty, but understanding.

Hermeneutical political economy does not promise control. It promises clarity without illusion. And in a world increasingly governed by numbers yet starved of meaning, that promise is not modest—it is necessary.

Lesson 1

An Introduction To Hermeneutical Political Economy

1.1. The Great Confusion of Our Time: Economics, Policy, and the Eclipse of Understanding

The intellectual history of modern political economy is marked by a slow but decisive erosion of distinctions that once structured the relationship between knowledge and action, between explanation and governance, between understanding and command. Among these, none has been more consequential than the progressive confusion between economics and public policy. What were once recognized as two distinct yet dialogically related domains—one devoted to the interpretation of social reality, the other to prudential intervention within it—have increasingly been collapsed into a single technocratic practice. Economists are no longer expected merely to understand the economic order but to engineer it; policy makers no longer rely on economic theory as a grammar of constraints but treat it as an algorithm for social design.

This confusion is not merely conceptual. It is civilizational. It reshapes how societies understand power, responsibility, knowledge, and human agency itself. When economics is reimagined as a technology of control and policy as an exercise in applied engineering, the space for prudence, judgment, and moral responsibility narrows. The world becomes a system to be optimized rather than a reality to be understood. Human beings become variables rather than persons. Social coordination becomes a technical problem rather than a drama of interpretation unfolding through time.

At the root of this transformation lies a deeper epistemological shift: the replacement of understanding with measurement as the supreme criterion of knowledge. The older ambition of economics—to grasp the meaning of human action in conditions of scarcity, uncertainty, and time—has been displaced by the pursuit of formal precision. Mathematical tractability has increasingly been confused with truth. Statistical significance has come to substitute for causal intelligibility. The map has gradually been mistaken for the territory.

This shift has altered not only how economists see the economy, but also how policy makers imagine their own role. Once public policy was understood as an art of prudence—an activity rooted in judgment, institutional experience, and moral deliberation. Today it is increasingly modelled as a branch of applied science, governed by targets, indicators, optimization techniques, and algorithmic decision rules. The policy maker appears less as a custodian of institutional learning than as a technician of social performance.

Yet societies are not laboratories. Human beings are not particles. And history is not a controlled experiment. Economic life unfolds within a realm of meaning, expectation, trust, imagination, and error. Its order is not imposed from above but emerges through countless dispersed interpretations. To govern such a reality as if it were a machine is to mistake its very nature.

This is why the distinction between economics as a science of understanding and policy as an art of action is not an academic subtlety but a foundational requirement for any humane political economy. Economics seeks to interpret the conditions under which human cooperation becomes possible. Policy seeks to navigate within those conditions. Economics clarifies constraints. Policy assumes responsibility. The two belong together, but they are not the same.

To confuse them is as dangerous as confusing physics with aviation. Without physics, flight is impossible. But physics alone does not teach one how to fly. In the same way, economic theory is indispensable to sound policy, but it never replaces the art of governance. Theory reveals what cannot be done without cost; it does not dictate what must be done without exception. The moment theory is mistaken for a blueprint, it becomes ideology. The moment policy emancipates itself from theory, it becomes reckless improvisation.

The great confusion of our time lies precisely here. Economics has been tempted to become a technology of power. Policy has been tempted to become an application of formulas. Both temptations arise from the same source: the desire to eliminate uncertainty from human affairs. Yet uncertainty is not a defect of social life. It is its ontological condition.

Human action is necessarily interpretative. Each individual acts within a horizon of meaning shaped by memory, expectation, cultural inheritance, and creative imagination. No central intelligence can replicate this distributed interpretative faculty. No model can substitute for it. The economic order, for this reason, is not a static structure but a living process of continuous re-coordination. It evolves through discovery, error, adaptation, and institutional learning. It is always provisional, never complete.

Public policy intervenes within this process. It does not stand outside it. Every intervention reshapes not only incentives but meanings, not only costs and benefits but expectations and beliefs. A tax is never just a fiscal instrument; it is also a signal about what a society values. A regulation is never merely a constraint; it is also an interpretative frame imposed upon entrepreneurial imagination. Monetary policy is never only a technical adjustment; it is also a message about trust, stability, and the intertemporal structure of coordination.

To recognize this is already to abandon the dream of social engineering. For engineering presupposes a stable object whose behaviour can be predicted, controlled, and optimized. The social world offers no such object. It offers instead a field of interacting interpretations whose future cannot be deduced from present conditions. What has not yet been imagined cannot be modelled. What has not yet been discovered cannot be optimized.

And yet, the modern technocratic imagination persists in its refusal to accept this limit. It promises that with sufficient data, sufficient computing power, sufficient regulatory reach, the future can be rendered predictable and manageable. It seeks salvation in indicators and dashboards. It measures not because measurement serves understanding, but because what resists measurement resists control.

In this epistemological climate, economics is pressured to justify itself not by the depth of its interpretative insight but by the accuracy of its forecasts. Policy is evaluated not by its institutional wisdom but by its numerical performance. The result is a tragic inversion: the more precisely we measure, the less we understand; the more aggressively we intervene, the less we govern.

What is lost in this inversion is not merely theoretical subtlety. What is lost is the very space of human freedom. For freedom is inseparable from uncertainty. To act freely is to act without guarantees. To create is to venture into the unknown. A society that seeks to abolish uncertainty through control abolishes freedom in the process.

The task of a hermeneutical economics is therefore not to offer better tools for social engineering, but to dissolve the very illusion that social engineering is possible. It reminds us that economic life is not a mechanism but a drama of meaning. It teaches us that prices speak before they calculate, that institutions remember before they constrain, that markets discover before they optimize. It restores to economics its original vocation: understanding.

And by restoring economics to understanding, it restores public policy to prudence.

1.2. Verstehen, Meaning, and the Ontology of Economic Action

If economics is to be restored to its original vocation as a science of understanding, then the first discipline it must recover is the discipline of meaning. The economic world is not given as a set of neutral data points awaiting statistical treatment. It is given as a field of interpreted reality, shaped by the intentions, expectations, fears, hopes, and creative projections of acting persons. Human beings do not move through economic life as passive objects subjected to impersonal forces; they participate in it as interpreting agents who continuously assign significance to what they perceive and who shape their actions accordingly.

The German tradition captured this insight with the word *verstehen*: understanding not as external explanation, but as interpretative participation. To understand an action is not merely to correlate it with an outcome; it is to re-enter the horizon of meaning within which that action became intelligible to the actor. Economics, in this classical sense, is not the study of things but the interpretation of purposeful conduct unfolding in time.

This insight stands in radical tension with the dominant methodological posture of contemporary economics. The modern discipline increasingly models itself on the natural sciences, where the observer stands outside the object of inquiry and seeks invariant laws governing repeatable processes. But no such epistemic detachment is possible in the study of human action. The economist is himself an acting being embedded within the very order he studies. The observer belongs to the observed world. This creates what may be called the double hermeneutic of economics: individuals interpret reality in their actions, and economists interpret those interpretations in their theories.

This reflexivity has no analogue in physics. Planets do not revise their trajectories in response to theories of gravitation. Entrepreneurs do revise their plans in response to economic forecasts. Workers adjust their behaviour based on perceived opportunities. Consumers reinterpret their preferences in light of social meanings and institutional frames. Economic theories do not merely describe reality; they enter it, reshape expectations, and sometimes become self-fulfilling or self-defeating prophecies. The economy is therefore not only an object of interpretation but also a medium through which interpretations circulate and interact.

To deny this hermeneutical structure of economic life is to reduce human beings to automata responding to stimuli. It is to imagine that preferences are given, information is complete, and choices are mechanical optimizations. But such a reduction destroys the very phenomenon it pretends to explain.

For what defines economic action is not reaction but intention; not data but meaning; not equilibrium but discovery.

Every act of exchange is already an interpretation. When two individuals meet in the market, they bring with them not merely goods and money but understandings of value, expectations of future conditions, trust in institutional arrangements, and narratives about what the exchange signifies in their broader life projects. A price, in this context, is never a mere number. It condenses a constellation of interpretations about scarcity, desire, opportunity, risk, and time. To treat price solely as a quantitative datum is to abstract from the very meaning that gives it coordinating power.

The same holds for capital. In conventional economic modelling, capital is treated as a measurable factor of production, homogeneous and substitutable. In reality, capital is a deeply interpretative phenomenon. A piece of equipment becomes capital only because an entrepreneur sees in it the possibility of future use. Its "capital character" does not reside in its physical properties but in the meaning ascribed to it within a plan oriented toward the future. Capital is therefore not a stock of things but a structure of expectations. It exists in the tense of the future perfect: what will have been useful if certain plans succeed.

This temporal dimension is decisive. Human action is always oriented toward a future that does not yet exist. It is guided not by certainty but by conjecture. The entrepreneur acts on the basis of imagined states of the world. The consumer purchases on the basis of anticipated satisfaction. The worker trains on the basis of projected opportunities. Economic life is therefore suspended between memory and expectation, between what has been learned and what is hoped for. It unfolds in a time that is not the mechanical ticking of a clock but the existential time of waiting, risk, disappointment, surprise, and discovery.

This is why uncertainty is not a secondary complication to be managed by better information. It is an ontological feature of economic reality itself. The future cannot be known in advance because it is not merely hidden; it is open. It will be shaped by innovations that have not yet occurred, by interpretations that have not yet been formed, by creative acts that cannot be deduced from existing data. To imagine that uncertainty can be eliminated through probabilistic refinement is to confuse risk with novelty. Risk refers to known distributions of outcomes. Novelty refers to the emergence of what had not yet been conceived.

In this light, the attempt to model economic action as if it were governed by stable probability distributions becomes a metaphysical claim masquerading as technical convenience. It assumes, without argument, that the future is structurally identical to the past. It denies the open-endedness of human creativity. It replaces entrepreneurial imagination with stochastic variation. But a world in which genuine innovation occurs is a world that cannot be fully probabilized.

The hermeneutical nature of economic action therefore places a fundamental limit on prediction. One can identify tendencies, patterns, vulnerabilities, and institutional regularities. One cannot deduce future configurations of meaning. The acts that shape tomorrow's economy have not yet been interpreted, and therefore cannot yet be described.

It is precisely here that the contrast between understanding and control becomes most acute. To understand an action is to grasp its meaning within a world of intentions. To control a system is to manipulate variables within a closed mechanical structure. The social world belongs to the former category, not to the latter. It is not closed but open. It is not mechanically determined but interpretatively shaped.

Yet the modern technocratic imagination insists on treating the economy as if it were a controllable machine. It seeks stable coefficients where only shifting expectations exist. It searches for invariant laws where only evolving regularities prevail. It promises optimization where only provisional coordination is possible. In doing so, it does not merely misrepresent reality; it transforms the self-understanding of those who act within it.

When policy makers and economic advisers begin to believe that the economy is a machine, they act as engineers. They seek levers to pull, dials to adjust, protocols to implement. They imagine that causal chains are linear, feedback is predictable, and outcomes are programmable. But the very act of treating the economy as a machine alters the interpretative environment within which agents form their expectations. Interventions change not only incentives but beliefs. They modify not only constraints but imaginations. They reshape not only payoffs but narratives. And because meaning itself shifts, the system that emerges after intervention is not the system that was modelled before it.

This is why the relationship between theory and reality in economics can never be one of simple correspondence. Theory does not mirror a fixed object. It enters a living process. It becomes one of the interpretative forces that shape that process. Economic knowledge is therefore not neutral in the way physical measurement aims to be. It is performative. It participates in the outcomes it describes.

The recognition of this performative dimension of economic theory deepens, rather than weakens, the call for interpretative humility. For if theories shape expectations, and expectations shape action, then the dissemination of economic ideas becomes a moral act as well as a scientific one. The economist is no longer merely a detached observer but an indirect participant in the social drama she theorizes.

This insight brings into focus the ethical dimension of economic knowledge. To propose a model is not merely to offer an analytical tool; it is to offer an interpretative frame through which agents may come to see themselves and their possibilities. When economic discourse presents individuals as self-interested maximizers, it subtly reshapes how they perceive their own motives. When it represents markets as zero-sum arenas of competition rather than as discovery processes, it alters entrepreneurial imagination. When it reduces social coordination to incentive alignment, it risks flattening the moral texture of economic life.

A hermeneutical economics cannot ignore this reflexive dimension. It must ask not only whether a model predicts, but what kind of self-understanding it engenders. It must examine not only correlations but meanings. It must remain attentive to the interpretative consequences of its own language.

From this perspective, the concept of rationality itself must be reinterpreted. Modern economic theory tends to reduce rationality to instrumental optimization: the efficient selection of means to given ends. But human action rarely begins with fully specified ends. Ends themselves are often discovered through action. Preferences evolve. Aspirations change. What appears rational at one moment becomes folly at another as the interpretative field shifts.

Rationality, in this deeper sense, is not a computational algorithm but a dialogical openness to reality. It consists in the capacity to revise one's understanding in light of experience, to learn from failure, to recognize surprise, and to reinterpret the meaning of one's goals. This is an Aristotelian rationality rather than a Cartesian one: reason as participation in intelligibility rather than domination over it.

Economic learning, in this view, is not the convergence toward a pre-given optimum but an open-ended process of mutual adjustment among interpreting agents. Coordination is not imposed from above but emerges through countless decentralized revisions of plans. Markets do not solve equations; they host conversations. Prices are not solutions; they are sentences spoken in a language of scarcity and expectation. Profits and losses are not verdicts of a mechanical tribunal; they are messages inviting revision and realignment.

This interpretative structure of coordination also explains why economic order is always fragile. Because it depends on the continuous alignment of expectations, it can unravel when those expectations are disrupted. Monetary instability, for example, is not merely a technical disturbance of nominal magnitudes. It is a disruption of the interpretative framework through which entrepreneurs read price signals. It introduces noise into the conversation of the market. It blurs the distinction between relative and absolute changes. It alters the grammar of economic meaning.

In such moments, economic life becomes opaque to its own participants. The very signals that once guided action become ambiguous. Plans lose their anchors. Coordination falters. The resulting disorder is not mechanical chaos but interpretative crisis: a loss of shared meanings that once sustained cooperative expectations.

The same hermeneutical logic applies to institutions. Institutions are not merely formal rules enforced by sanctions. They are stabilized interpretations of how cooperation is possible. Property rights, contracts, money, corporate forms, and legal procedures are all crystallizations of shared understandings about legitimate action. They encode social memory. They transmit expectations across generations. They reduce uncertainty by making certain patterns of interpretation reliable.

But because institutions are interpretations, they are not immutable. They evolve as meanings evolve. They can be distorted by power, hollowed out by neglect, or reimagined through innovation. Institutional change is therefore not merely an administrative redesign; it is a transformation of the interpretative horizons within which action becomes intelligible.

This brings us back to public policy. If economic action is interpretative, then policy intervention is also interpretative intervention. It does not merely alter constraints; it reshapes meaning. It influences how agents understand what is permitted, encouraged, rewarded, or discouraged. It enters the hermeneutical fabric of society. For this reason, the policy maker is not merely a regulator of behaviour but an indirect author of social narratives.

To ignore this is to operate blindly within the realm of meaning. To legislate without attending to interpretation is to underestimate the depth at which policy intervenes. Laws do not merely bind; they speak. Regulations do not merely constrain; they signify. Taxes do not merely extract; they express priorities. Monetary regimes do not merely stabilize or destabilize prices; they communicate trust or mistrust in the future.

A purely technical conception of policy cannot capture this symbolic and interpretative dimension. It treats agents as if they responded only to incentives, not to meanings. It imagines that behaviour can be engineered without interrogating the narratives within which that behaviour becomes sensible. But societies do not move through equations. They move through stories.

The meanings people attach to policy often matter as much as the material consequences of policy itself.

This is why the art of policy cannot be reduced to applied economics. It requires not only structural literacy but interpretative sensitivity. It requires not only analytical competence but cultural and institutional intelligence. It requires not only models but prudence.

In this sense, the restoration of economics as a science of understanding is not an inward-looking academic enterprise. It is a civilizational necessity. A society that loses the capacity to interpret its own economic life inevitably seeks refuge in numbers. It clings to indicators as substitutes for meaning. It entrusts governance to algorithms as substitutes for judgment. It mistakes control for comprehension.

But to do so is to govern in the dark. For numbers without narratives cannot tell us what matters. Optimization without interpretation cannot tell us whom it serves. Precision without meaning cannot tell us what it destroys.

The rebirth of economics as an interpretative science therefore prepares the ground for the rebirth of public policy as an art. It reminds us that knowledge begins not with measurement but with wonder. It restores to reason its original posture of openness. It teaches us to see economic life not as a machine to be tuned but as a drama to be understood.

And only a society that understands itself can hope to govern itself wisely.

1.3. Policy as Prudence: Judgment, Institutions, and Action Under Uncertainty

If economics, understood hermeneutically, studies the meaning of human action, then public policy may be understood as the attempt to act meaningfully within that already interpreted world. Yet this acting is never the application of scientific laws to neutral material. It is always an intervention into a field of expectations, narratives, institutional memories, and power relations. Policy is therefore not a science in the strict sense. It is an art—an art of prudent judgment exercised under conditions of radical uncertainty.

The classical name for this art is *phronesis*. It designates not technical skill, which can be taught through procedures, nor pure theoretical knowledge, which can be codified into propositions, but a form of practical wisdom that grows through experience. Prudence is the capacity to judge what is fitting in concrete circumstances whose full structure cannot be known in advance. It deals not with what is necessary, but with what is contingent. It does not operate through universal rules alone, but through situational discernment.

This is why public policy can never be fully routinized. No rulebook can exhaust the complexity of social life. No algorithm can substitute for judgment. No model can capture the full meaning of the context into which a decision intervenes. The more one attempts to govern by rigid procedures alone, the more one displaces responsibility onto mechanisms that cannot bear it.

Yet modern governance increasingly proceeds as if prudence could be replaced by technique. The policy maker is recast as a technician of incentives. The statesman yields to the manager. Deliberation gives way to dashboards. Responsibility is diffused across models, indicators, and compliance protocols. In this transformation, policy loses its ethical core. It becomes an activity without subject, action without author, governance without accountability.

The technocratic imagination arises not because of malicious intent, but because of fear—fear of uncertainty, fear of discretion, fear of fallibility. It promises that if only the right procedures are established, decisions will become objective, neutral, and risk-free. But such a promise is illusory. Rules do not eliminate discretion; they merely relocate it. Models do not abolish judgment; they conceal it behind formalism. Algorithms do not dissolve responsibility; they obscure it.

Prudence, by contrast, begins with the acknowledgment that decisions must be taken without full knowledge. It embraces the tragic dimension of action: the fact that to act is always to risk, to choose is always to exclude, to intervene is always to alter the very field one seeks to improve. It accepts that error is not an accident of poor technique but a structural feature of human agency.

This insight places public policy in a fundamentally different epistemic category from engineering. Engineering presupposes stable materials governed by invariant laws. Once the specifications are correct, execution is largely a matter of technique. But social life offers no such stability. The "materials" of policy—expectations, beliefs, trust, norms, institutional loyalties—are themselves mutable, reflexive, and responsive to intervention. Each act of governance reshapes the very substrate upon which future governance must operate.

This explains why good policy is never merely a matter of choosing the right instruments. Instruments gain meaning only within institutional contexts. A tax imposed within a culture of civic trust does not mean the same thing as the same tax imposed within a culture of mutual suspicion. A regulation introduced into a stable institutional environment does not function in the same way as the same regulation imposed upon a fragile or corrupt system. The formal identity of a policy instrument conceals the diversity of its institutional meanings.

Institutions, as we have seen, are not inert frameworks. They are sedimented interpretations of social cooperation. They embody historical learning. They encode expectations about what is normal, legitimate, and trustworthy. They stabilize meaning across time. For this reason, institutional disruption is never merely a technical adjustment. It is an interpretative earthquake.

Prudence in policy therefore requires institutional memory. It requires attention to the histories embedded in rules, routines, legal forms, and administrative practices. It demands sensitivity to what may appear inefficient in the abstract but is functional in sustaining social trust. Technocratic models, by abstracting from history, tend to classify such institutional inertia as irrational. But in many cases, what appears as inertia is the visible trace of tacit wisdom accumulated through experience.

This is not to sanctify all existing institutions. Institutions can ossify. They can drift away from their original purposes. They can become vehicles of privilege and domination. But the critique of institutions must itself be prudent. It must distinguish between those features that preserve meaning and those that merely preserve power. To reform institutions without understanding their interpretative role is to risk destroying what one cannot rebuild.

Public policy, then, must always navigate between two symmetrical dangers. On one side lies the danger of blind conservatism: the refusal to change institutions even when they no longer serve human flourishing. On the other side lies the danger of reckless rationalism: the belief that institutions can be redesigned from scratch according to abstract models. Prudence is the virtue that inhabits the space between these extremes. It changes with restraint and preserves with intelligence.

In this light, the relationship between policy and uncertainty becomes clearer. Uncertainty is not an external obstacle that better information will eventually dissolve. It is internal to the very structure of social existence. The outcomes of interventions cannot be fully anticipated because they depend on future interpretations that have not yet taken shape. Agents will react in ways that surprise designers precisely because they are not programmable units but creative interpreters.

Every policy therefore initiates a cascade of second-order effects that escape its original intent. It changes not only payoffs but narratives, not only incentives but identities. When monetary policy alters interest rates, it does not merely reprice time; it reshapes entrepreneurial imagination, household aspirations, and the symbolic meaning of saving and debt. When industrial policy subsidizes certain sectors, it does not merely allocate resources; it reorients cultural expectations about what forms of work are desirable and legitimate. When welfare policy restructures social support, it does not merely redistribute income; it redefines the relationship between individual agency and collective responsibility.

Technocratic governance tends to focus on first-order effects because they are measurable. Prudence, by contrast, remains attentive to second-order and third-order consequences precisely because they are often unmeasurable yet decisive. It understands that what matters most in policy is often what appears only later, indirectly, and through channels no model had anticipated.

This temporal asymmetry between intervention and consequence creates a tragic dimension in public action. The policy maker acts today on the basis of necessarily incomplete knowledge, while the full implications of her action will unfold across years and generations. Responsibility therefore extends beyond contemporaneous evaluation. It demands an ethical orientation toward the future that cannot be reduced to current performance metrics.

Here again, the dominance of short-term indicators undermines prudence. When governance is evaluated primarily through quarterly outcomes, electoral cycles, or annual budget targets, the horizon of responsibility contracts. Policy becomes reactive rather than reflective. It chases visible effects rather than cultivating invisible conditions. It optimizes flows while neglecting structures.

Prudential policy, by contrast, is structural before it is instrumental. It asks not only what should be done now, but what kind of institutional environment should be sustained over time. It attends not only to outputs but to the robustness of the processes that generate them. It recognizes that certain goods—trust, legal predictability, entrepreneurial confidence, civic cooperation—cannot be produced by decree. They must be grown.

This is why the art of policy cannot be severed from the art of institution-building. Institutions are not merely containers for policy; they are its most important medium. They constrain and enable, distort and stabilize, amplify and dampen. To intervene wisely in social life is therefore to intervene first and foremost in the interpretative architecture of institutions.

At this point, the contrast between technocratic governance and prudential governance becomes stark. Technocracy seeks to govern outcomes. Prudence seeks to govern conditions. Technocracy fixes targets. Prudence cultivates contexts. Technocracy manages variables. Prudence attends to meanings. The former presupposes control. The latter accepts fragility.

This fragility is not merely epistemic but moral. To govern is to affect the life chances of others. It is to intervene in the drama of human flourishing and failure. No policy choice is ethically neutral. Even inaction is a form of action when it preserves existing distributions of opportunity and power.

Prudence therefore includes not only cognitive humility but moral deliberation. It demands that the policy maker weigh not only efficiency but dignity, not only cost–benefit calculations but justice, not only growth targets but the integrity of social relationships.

The technocratic imagination resists this moral thickness. It seeks refuge in numbers precisely because numbers appear to absolve responsibility. If a policy fails, the model can be blamed. If harm occurs, the data were imperfect. Judgment is displaced onto procedure. But no algorithm can bear moral accountability. Only persons can.

The attempt to replace prudence with technique therefore leads not to more responsible governance but to the erosion of responsibility itself. Policy becomes anonymous. Power becomes impersonal. Decisions are executed without authors. This institutional anonymity is one of the defining pathologies of modern administration. It creates a system in which no one decides, yet everything is decided.

A hermeneutical reconstruction of public policy insists on restoring the personal dimension of judgment to the centre of governance. It refuses to treat uncertainty as a technical defect to be eliminated. It recognizes it as an existential condition to be inhabited wisely. It reclaims the idea that to govern is not to engineer but to interpret, not to optimize but to discern, not to program but to respond.

This does not entail abandoning analysis. Prudence does not mean arbitrariness. It means ordered openness. It means the disciplined integration of theoretical insight, empirical observation, institutional memory, and ethical reflection. It means knowing that even the most rigorous analysis must ultimately be appropriated by judgment if it is to inform action.

In this sense, the art of policy stands in the same relationship to economics as the art of medicine stands to physiology. Knowledge of the body is indispensable, but healing is never the mechanical application of biological laws. The physician treats not a generic organism but a concrete person. The physician must interpret symptoms within a broader narrative of life, habits, environment, and vulnerability. Likewise, the policy maker acts not upon abstract aggregates but within a living social body whose responses will always exceed calculation.

To confuse medicine with pharmacology would be a grave error. To confuse policy with applied economics is no less so.

The recovery of prudence as the central virtue of public policy therefore marks not a retreat from rationality but a deepening of it. It recognizes that reason is not exhausted by calculation. It includes judgment, imagination, memory, and ethical responsibility. It is reason as openness rather than reason as domination.

Only within this conception of policy does the distinction between economics as understanding and policy as action regain its full significance. Economics clarifies the invisible grammars of coordination. Policy navigates within those grammars. Economics interprets the social order. Policy participates in its ongoing creation.

To forget this is to mistake governance for command. To remember it is to rediscover governance as a dialogical practice embedded in the fragile fabric of interpretation.

1.4. COMPLEXITY, EMERGENCE, AND THE COLLAPSE OF SOCIAL ENGINEERING

The hermeneutical conception of economics and the prudential conception of public policy converge upon a single ontological insight: society is not a machine. It is an evolving order of meanings, expectations, institutions, and creative adjustments that exceeds the grasp of any single intelligence. The modern science of complexity has given formal expression to this ancient philosophical intuition. Yet its deepest significance is not technical but civilizational. It shatters, once and for all, the dream of social engineering.

Complexity is not merely a matter of scale. A system is not complex simply because it contains many components. It is complex because the interactions among those components are non-linear, because feedback loops are unstable, because small causes can generate large effects and large interventions can dissolve into irrelevance, because order emerges without design and disorder can arise from excessive control. In complex systems, causality is dispersed, not centralized. Outcomes are emergent, not imposed. Control is partial, not total.

This description applies with particular force to social and economic life. The economy is not an object constructed by policy; it is a constantly evolving field of interaction among interpreting agents. Each actor responds not only to physical constraints but to symbols, narratives, memories, expectations, and institutional framings. The social order is therefore doubly complex: it is complex in its interactions and hermeneutical in its constitution.

This double complexity places a decisive limit upon the ambition of governance. It means that the social order cannot be optimized in the way an engine can be optimized. There is no social equivalent of a closed system in thermodynamic equilibrium. There is only an open-ended process of coordination that forever escapes final stabilization.

The failure to grasp this has haunted political economy since the nineteenth century. From the rationalist utopias of early socialism to the technocratic dreams of modern macroeconomic management, the persistent temptation has been to treat society as if it were an object of design rather than a subject of historical becoming. The image of the social planner stands as the emblem of this illusion: a solitary intelligence surveying the totality of social relations from above and rearranging them according to a master plan.

Complexity renders this image not merely naïve but incoherent. There is no vantage point from which society can be seen as a whole, because the knowledge required to coordinate social life is not given in totality anywhere. It is dispersed across millions of minds, embedded in tacit knowledge, transmitted through practices, and constantly revised through experience. The social order coordinates precisely because no one controls it.

This is the paradox at the heart of emergence. Order arises not from command but from interaction. Coordination emerges not because agents intend it, but because their interpretations respond to one another through institutional filters. The market, in this sense, is not a mechanism for allocating resources alone; it is a continuous discovery procedure through which society learns what is possible.

Emergence shatters the linear imagination of policy. In linear systems, effects are proportional to causes. In complex systems, they rarely are. A small regulatory adjustment can generate massive structural distortions. A minor tax change can reconfigure entire production chains. A marginal modification in monetary policy can destabilize expectations across generations. Conversely, sweeping legislative reforms can be absorbed with little visible effect if they fail to resonate with the interpretative fabric of society.

This disproportion between action and outcome reveals the deepest fragility of the social engineering mentality. It is not merely that planners lack sufficient data; it is that the structure of social causation itself resists centralization. The belief that enough information will one day make total control possible is therefore not a scientific hypothesis but a metaphysical commitment to a world without creativity.

Complexity also transforms the meaning of failure. In mechanical systems, failure is often attributable to faulty design or defective execution. In complex systems, failure is often inseparable from learning. Each attempt to intervene generates new information that had not been available before the intervention. Mistakes become sources of knowledge. Unintended consequences become signals for institutional revision. The very process of trial and error through which markets coordinate is the same process through which institutions evolve.

To attempt to eliminate failure from social life is therefore to attempt to eliminate learning itself. A society that cannot err cannot innovate. A policy regime that immunizes itself against feedback becomes brittle. It grows increasingly detached from the reality it seeks to govern. Resilience requires not perfection but adaptability. And adaptability presupposes openness to surprise.

The technocratic imagination, however, tends to interpret surprise as a design defect rather than as an ontological feature. When models fail, the response is not to question the ambition of control but to demand more refined models. When policy outcomes diverge from forecasts, the divergence is attributed to insufficient data rather than to the openness of the future. Complexity is thus acknowledged rhetorically but denied practically.

This denial is ethically consequential. For it leads to interventions that are increasingly aggressive in their attempt to compensate for past failures. The more control slips through one's fingers, the more forcefully one grips. What begins as regulation becomes micromanagement. What begins as coordination becomes coercion. What begins as stabilization becomes domination.

Yet domination cannot stabilize a complex system. It can only suppress its visible expressions while accumulating invisible tensions. When feedback is blocked rather than absorbed, it does not disappear. It migrates. It mutates. It re-emerges elsewhere in forms that are more violent and less manageable.

This is why complexity dissolves not only the illusion of omniscient planning but also the illusion of infinite policy escalation. There are structural limits to intervention that cannot be crossed without transforming the very nature of the system being governed. A market subjected to omnipresent control ceases to function as a discovery process. A monetary system subjected to unlimited manipulation ceases to communicate intertemporal meaning. A society subjected to total regulation ceases to be a society of free actors and becomes a bureaucratic artifact.

At this point, the meaning of emergence acquires its full philosophical depth. Emergence does not merely describe how patterns arise from interactions. It describes how meaning arises from freedom. New structures appear not because they were programmed, but because human beings reinterpret existing structures in novel ways. Innovation, in this sense, is not a technological event alone. It is an act of re-signification. The entrepreneur does not merely combine factors of production; he reimagines their meaning.

This act of re-signification lies beyond the reach of policy control. One can subsidize research. One cannot command discovery. One can regulate markets. One cannot manufacture entrepreneurial vision. One can fund education. One cannot decree imagination. Every attempt to force creativity produces its opposite: conformity.

This is why true emergence always surprises power. It arises at the margins, not at the centre. It bursts forth from below, not from above. It cannot be summoned by blueprint. It can only be made possible by institutions that protect freedom, property, exchange, and learning.

The modern state, however, increasingly conceives itself not as the guardian of emergence but as its architect. This shift represents one of the great civilizational reversals of the past century. The state no longer merely frames the conditions under which social energies unfold; it increasingly seeks to determine their direction, pace, and objectives. In doing so, it takes upon itself a cognitive burden that no centralized authority can bear.

Complexity theory exposes the impossibility of this burden. It shows that knowledge in social systems is not merely incomplete but structurally dispersed. It shows that coordination does not require shared knowledge of the whole, but shared rules of interaction. It shows that order does not require command, but compatibility. It shows that stability is not a product of control, but of adaptive feedback.

From this perspective, the true function of public institutions appears in a new light. Institutions do not exist to design outcomes. They exist to structure interactions. They are not engines of allocation. They are grammars of coordination. They do not produce prosperity. They make prosperity intelligible and possible.

This redefinition has decisive implications for economic policy. Monetary institutions, for example, cannot be treated as instruments for steering growth as if growth were a hydraulic variable. Their deeper function is to stabilize the intertemporal language of the market. When that language is distorted, entrepreneurs lose the ability to distinguish relative price changes from monetary noise. Investment becomes speculative guesswork rather than interpretative judgment. Capital structure becomes fragile.

Similarly, fiscal institutions cannot be reduced to redistribution mechanisms alone. They encode social understandings about responsibility, solidarity, and reciprocity. Taxation is not merely a transfer of resources; it is an interpretative signal about what society deems legitimate to appropriate and what it deems legitimate to retain. When this symbolic dimension is ignored, fiscal policy produces not cooperation but resistance.

Regulatory institutions, likewise, do not merely constrain behaviour. They reshape imagination. They determine which entrepreneurial projects appear possible, respectable, or desirable. An overly dense regulatory environment does not merely increase compliance costs; it narrows the horizon of what agents can even conceive.

In all these domains, complexity and emergence reveal a single lesson: policy cannot govern outcomes without destroying the processes that generate outcomes. It can only govern conditions. And conditions, to be fertile, must remain open rather than closed.

This is why the myth of social engineering persists alongside its repeated failures. It promises what no complex system can deliver: certainty. It nourishes the longing for a world in which risk can be abolished, crises prevented, innovation programmed, and conflict optimized away. Yet such a world would no longer be a human world. It would be a static artifact.

Human flourishing requires not stability alone but creative instability. It requires not security alone but the possibility of surprise. It requires not order alone but the freedom to challenge order. A society that eliminates uncertainty in the name of safety eliminates growth in the name of control. It purchases the illusion of security at the price of stagnation.

Complexity therefore restores tragedy to political economy. It reminds us that there are no final solutions, only provisional arrangements. It dissolves the fantasy of permanent equilibrium. It reinstates time as an open horizon rather than as a parameter to be optimized. It teaches us that the future cannot be engineered because it has not yet been interpreted.

This return of tragedy is not pessimistic. On the contrary, it is the condition of meaning. Only in a world where outcomes are not guaranteed can responsibility matter. Only in a world where failure is possible can learning occur. Only in a world where the future is open can creativity flourish.

The collapse of social engineering is therefore not a loss for liberal civilization. It is its rescue. It liberates policy from the burden of omniscience. It liberates economics from the illusion of control. It restores both to their proper tasks: understanding and prudence.

And in doing so, it prepares the ground for a renewed political economy in which humility is not weakness, uncertainty is not chaos, and complexity is not an obstacle to order but its deepest source.

1.5.   COMPETING EXPLANATIONS, PLURAL CAUSATION, AND THEORETICAL HUMILITY

Once complexity and emergence are taken seriously, the very idea of a single, sovereign explanation of social phenomena becomes untenable. Economic life does not unfold along a single causal line but within a dense web of interacting forces: institutional, cultural, psychological, entrepreneurial, political, technological, and historical. Each of these dimensions possesses a certain autonomy.

None can be reduced to the others without distortion. The economy, therefore, does not admit of a final explanatory key. It admits only of partial, layered, and context-bound interpretations.

Yet the modern scientific imagination has been repeatedly tempted by the dream of monocausality. It has sought to identify the fundamental variable behind all social outcomes—capital accumulation, class struggle, incentives, information asymmetries, productivity, technology, ideology, or expectations—only to discover, with each failed attempt, that reality exceeds the grasp of any single principle. What has persisted, however, is not the success of monocausality but its seduction. The longing for one true cause reflects not the structure of the social world but the psychological need for intellectual closure.

Plural causation, by contrast, is not a methodological compromise: it is an ontological demand. The social order is multi-layered because human beings themselves are multi-dimensional. They act not only as profit-seekers but as bearers of traditions, as members of communities, as moral agents, as political actors, as creators of meaning. Their motivations intersect. Their interpretations overlap. Their actions reverberate across multiple planes simultaneously. Any theory that seeks to compress this richness into a single explanatory dimension commits, at the outset, a violence against reality.

Economic phenomena therefore arise not from isolated causes but from constellations of interacting interpretations. A financial crisis cannot be explained solely by monetary policy, nor solely by regulation, nor solely by animal spirits, nor solely by inequality. It emerges at the intersection of institutional incentives, narratives of risk, technological instruments, political decisions, cultural attitudes toward debt, and global interdependencies. Each explanation captures something real. None captures the whole.

This plurality of causes generates a corresponding plurality of theories. And this theoretical plurality is not a sign of immaturity in the social sciences. It is the natural reflection of the complexity of their object. In a world of emergent orders, no single model can dominate without becoming ideological. The demand for theoretical uniformity is therefore not a scientific demand; it is a political one masquerading as methodology.

Monocausal theories possess an irresistible rhetorical power. They offer clarity in a confusing world. They promise predictive mastery. They reduce complexity to a single narrative that can be mobilized for political action; but this very clarity is their danger: by suppressing competing explanations, they suppress the feedback through which understanding corrects itself; they convert provisional interpretations into dogmatic certainties.

The great ideologies of the modern age have all been built upon mono-causal economic narratives. Marxism reduced social order to class struggle. Neoclassical technocracy reduces it to optimization under constraints. Certain strands of monetary activism reduce it to liquidity management. Certain strands of institutional determinism reduce it to legal formalism. In each case, a fragment of reality has been raised to the status of total explanation. And in each case, the suppression of complexity has eventually produced theoretical breakdown and political disillusion.

The hermeneutical conception of economics resists this temptation at its root. Because it understands economic life as a world of meanings rather than as a mechanical system of forces, it recognizes that explanation must always remain interpretative, not exhaustive. To explain is not to exhaust reality, but to illuminate one of its dimensions. Every explanation is therefore also a concealment. It reveals by focusing and distorts by excluding.

Theoretical humility begins precisely here: in the recognition that no explanation can claim a monopoly on truth. This humility is not relativism. It does not deny that some explanations are better than others. It insists, however, that even the best explanations remain partial. They must remain open to revision. They must remain vulnerable to competing interpretations. They must remain porous to empirical surprise.

This epistemic posture stands in sharp contrast to the technocratic style of policy advice. Technocracy thrives on monocausality because it requires a single lever of control: if one variable governs the system, then the policy maker need only adjust that variable. Complexity and plural causation dissolve this fantasy; rather, they reveal a world in which interventions propagate across multiple channels, interact with cultural expectations, and generate feedback that no controller can master.

Plural causation therefore transforms the meaning of expertise. The expert is no longer the one who knows the single decisive variable. He is the one who understands the limits of her own domain, who knows how her partial knowledge intersects with other forms of knowledge, who resists the temptation to universalize her own perspective. Expertise becomes dialogical rather than authoritarian. It becomes a contribution to collective understanding rather than a command over it.

This dialogical conception of knowledge is deeply congruent with the market process itself. Markets coordinate not because all agents share the same explanation of reality, but precisely because they do not. Each participant sees something different. Each acts on localized, partial, and often tacit knowledge. The system coordinates not through consensus but through compatibility.

Prices do not impose a single narrative upon the market. They translate multiple narratives into a common language of exchange.

The tragedy of technocratic policy is that it seeks to govern society as if it required consensus on explanation rather than compatibility of action. It seeks to impose a unitary narrative where a plurality of interpretations would suffice. It tries to replace the spontaneous conversation of the market with the monologue of authority. In doing so, it suppresses precisely the diversity of perspectives that generates discovery.

Plural causation also reshapes the meaning of disagreement in economic discourse. If no single theory can exhaust reality, then disagreement is not a defect to be eliminated but a resource to be cultivated. Competing explanations reveal different facets of the same process. They act as mutual correctives. They prevent premature closure. They sustain the openness of inquiry.

When disagreement is suppressed in the name of scientific authority, theory hardens into doctrine. When doctrine hardens into policy, governance becomes ideology. And when ideology encounters resistance from reality, the result is not learning but escalation. Each failure is interpreted not as a signal of theoretical limitation but as evidence that the policy has not yet gone far enough.

The history of economic planning in the twentieth century offers tragic confirmation of this dynamic. Each deviation from the plan was interpreted as sabotage rather than as information. Each market signal was dismissed as noise rather than as meaning. The refusal to acknowledge plural causation transformed error into guilt. And guilt demanded punishment rather than revision.

The hermeneutical approach to economics dissolves this tragic spiral at its root. It understands that reality always "talks back" to theory. It treats unintended consequences not as anomalies but as messages. It sees resistance not as hostility to be crushed but as meaning to be interpreted. It replaces the logic of domination with the logic of dialogue.

This dialogical posture transforms not only how economics is practiced but also how public policy is conceived. If social outcomes arise from plural causes, then no single policy instrument can be sovereign. If meanings are layered, then interventions must be cautious. If institutions encode historical learning, then reform must proceed experimentally. If agents interpret policy through diverse cultural lenses, then governance must remain attentive to narrative as well as to incentives.

Policy, in this framework, becomes an activity of interpretative engagement. It does not impose a final explanation upon society. It inserts tentative hypotheses into the social conversation and listens for the replies that reality returns.

Each reform becomes an experiment in meaning. Each outcome becomes a commentary upon the assumptions that guided action. Governance becomes a learning process rather than an implementation protocol.

This learning process, however, requires a political culture capable of tolerating ambiguity. It requires citizens willing to accept that no policy is final, no reform decisive, no institution immune from revision. It requires political actors willing to admit fallibility without surrendering responsibility. These are demanding virtues. They run against the grain of mass politics, which thrives on certainty, slogans, and enemies.

Monocausal narratives are politically attractive precisely because they simplify moral imagination. If there is one cause of social suffering, then there is one enemy. If there is one enemy, then there is one solution. Politics becomes a crusade rather than a conversation. Policy becomes a weapon rather than a craft.

Plural causation, by contrast, complicates moral imagination. It forces us to confront the fact that social evils often arise from the interaction of many well-intended actions. It undermines the fantasy of pure victims and pure villains. It reveals the tragic structure of social life: the fact that suffering often emerges not from malice but from miscoordination.

This tragic vision does not paralyze action. It disciplines it. It calls for interventions that are proportional, revisable, institutionally sensitive, and morally cautious. It resists both cynical resignation and messianic zeal. It affirms responsibility without absolutizing power.

Theoretical humility, in this sense, is not a weakness of scholarship but its highest virtue. It preserves the openness of inquiry. It guards against ideological capture. It keeps economics anchored to the complexity of life rather than to the symmetry of its own models. It reminds the economist that her task is not to rule reality but to listen to it.

And it reminds the policy maker that governance is not the execution of an algorithm but the interpretation of an evolving social text whose meaning is never fully given in advance.

1.6. TIME, NOVELTY, AND THE TRAGIC LIMITS OF PREDICTION

At the deepest level of economic and political life lies a category that no model has ever succeeded in domesticating: time. Not time as a neutral dimension measured by clocks, but time as the existential horizon of becoming within which human action unfolds. Economic life is not suspended in a static present. It stretches between remembered pasts and imagined futures. Every act of production, every exchange, every investment, every policy decision is situated within this temporal tension between what has been and what might be.

Modern economic theory, however, has persistently attempted to neutralize time. It has translated it into a variable to be discounted, a parameter to be optimized, a sequence of dated equilibria connecting timeless states. In doing so, it has transformed historical becoming into geometric succession. But real time is not geometrical. It is creative. It does not merely transmit effects; it generates novelty.

Novelty is the decisive scandal for prediction. If the future were merely the unfolding of what already exists, if every possible state of the world were already contained within the data of the present, then meaningful forecasting might in principle be achievable. But the future of human societies is not merely hidden; it is open. It will be shaped by discoveries that have not yet been made, by interpretations that have not yet been formed, by innovations that cannot be deduced from existing configurations of knowledge.

The entrepreneur embodies this openness of time in its most concentrated form. Entrepreneurial action is not the execution of an algorithm over known data. It is the projection of a meaning into an uncertain future. The entrepreneur does not merely respond to a known price vector; he imagines a configuration of reality that does not yet exist and acts as if it might come to be. She wagers on a future that is not statistically calculable because it has not yet entered the space of articulated possibilities.

In this sense, entrepreneurship is not merely a category of production. It is an ontological act: the insertion of the new into the fabric of the real. Every genuine innovation redefines the space of what is possible. It does not merely rearrange known elements; it creates new meanings, new goods, new desires, new institutional challenges. No probability distribution can assign a likelihood to what has not yet been conceived.

The same holds, in a different register, for policy action. When public authorities intervene in the social order, they also project meanings into the future. A reform is not merely a rearrangement of rules; it is an attempt to redefine the horizon of expectations according to which people will act tomorrow. Yet the reception of this projection is never fully controllable. Agents will interpret policy through their own narratives, interests, memories, and cultural frames. Outcomes will diverge from intentions. Secondary and tertiary effects will unfold through pathways that no model can fully anticipate.

This is why prediction occupies such an ambiguous position in political economy. On the one hand, some degree of foresight is indispensable. To act without any expectation of consequences would be pure recklessness. On the other hand, the certainty promised by predictive mastery is fundamentally illusory. The more a theory claims to predict the social future with precision, the more it tacitly denies novelty, creativity, and freedom.

The tragic dimension of economic and political action emerges precisely here. Human beings must act without knowing. They must wager under conditions of radical uncertainty. They must take responsibility for decisions whose full implications will only be revealed after those decisions have irreversibly reshaped the field of possibilities. There is no retreat from this tragedy without retreating from freedom itself.

Modern technocracy seeks to resolve this tragic condition by transforming uncertainty into risk, and risk into probability. What cannot be probabilized is treated as negligible. What escapes modelization is ignored in policy design. Yet this strategy does not abolish uncertainty; it merely blinds itself to it. The unexpected does not disappear because it has been excluded from the model. It returns, often with destabilizing force, as what policy makers call "shocks".

The language of shocks already betrays the mechanical imagination at work. A shock is conceived as an external disturbance to a system otherwise assumed to be in orderly equilibrium. But in a genuinely historical world, novelty is not an external disturbance; it is the normal condition. The idea of a stable equilibrium punctuated by occasional shocks inverts the real structure of time. It treats order as primary and change as exceptional. In fact, it is change that is primary. Order is always provisional.

This inversion has profound implications for the meaning of crisis. In a mechanical worldview, crisis is a malfunction to be corrected so that the system may return to its normal state. In a historical-hermeneutical worldview, crisis is a revelation. It discloses hidden tensions, misinterpretations, and institutional rigidities that had been accumulating beneath the surface of apparent stability. It is not merely a failure of technique; it is an event of meaning.

Every economic crisis can therefore be read as a breakdown in mutual interpretation. Plans that once appeared compatible reveal themselves as incompatible. Expectations that once converged reveal themselves as illusory. Signals that once guided action reveal themselves as distorted. The tragedy of crisis lies not merely in material loss but in the collapse of intelligibility itself.

And yet, this same collapse is also the condition for renewed learning. Because it shatters inherited narratives, crisis opens space for reinterpretation. It forces agents to revise their understanding of risk, time, value, and coordination. It reveals the fragility of institutions that had been taken for granted. It exposes the moral and epistemic premises that had silently governed behaviour. Crisis, in this sense, is not merely destructive. It is also hermeneutically productive.

This dual character of crisis—at once catastrophic and revelatory—cannot be captured by models that reduce instability to stochastic deviation. It belongs to the realm of historical meaning rather than statistical fluctuation. It unfolds through time not as noise but as narrative rupture.

From this perspective, the recurring promise of crisis prevention through superior forecasting appears in a new light. It is not merely empirically implausible; it is conceptually incoherent. To prevent all crises would be to prevent novelty. To eliminate all breakdowns would be to eliminate learning. To stabilize the social order completely would be to freeze it into immobility.

This does not mean that societies should resign themselves to avoidable suffering. It means that the ambition of total prevention must be replaced by the cultivation of resilience. The question is not how to foresee every future state of the economy, but how to build institutions capable of absorbing surprise without collapsing. Not how to predict every disruption, but how to remain adaptive when disruptions occur.

Resilience is not a technical property alone. It is an interpretative virtue. It presupposes that agents understand instability as a normal feature of historical existence rather than as an anomalous failure. It requires institutional arrangements that allow error to be corrected without systemic breakdown. It requires cultural attitudes that tolerate uncertainty without succumbing to panic or authoritarian longing.

The longing for predictive certainty, by contrast, often generates the opposite of resilience. Because it underestimates novelty, it overcommits to rigid plans. Because it denies deep uncertainty, it erects fragile structures optimized for a world that exists only in the model. When reality diverges from expectation, the resulting dissonance is magnified rather than cushioned.

Here again, the contrast between prudence and technocracy becomes decisive. Prudence accepts that the future cannot be mastered. It therefore favours institutional diversity, decentralization, redundancy, and experimentalism. Technocracy seeks to minimize error through centralized coordination and uniform standards. It therefore maximizes the systemic consequences of error when central assumptions fail.

Historical experience consistently confirms this asymmetry. Systems built upon decentralized trial and error accumulate small, localized failures that foster learning. Systems built upon centralized design accumulate latent failures that erupt catastrophically. What appears inefficient in the short run often proves robust in the long run. What appears optimized often reveals itself as brittle.

The temporal structure of policy action therefore mirrors the temporal structure of economic action. Both operate under conditions of uncertainty that are not reducible to risk. Both must navigate between the Scylla of paralysis and the Charybdis of hubris. Both must act without guarantees. And both must remain open to revision.

This openness is not merely cognitive but moral. Because consequences unfold through time, responsibility cannot be discharged at the moment of decision alone. It extends across the arc of unfolding effects. To govern justly is therefore not merely to choose well today, but to remain responsive tomorrow when today's choices reveal their unintended meanings.

This temporal extension of responsibility cannot be captured by static accountability mechanisms. It requires a political culture oriented toward learning rather than self-justification. It demands institutions capable of revision rather than merely of enforcement. It calls for leaders willing to reinterpret their own past judgments in light of present consequences.

The tragedy of modern technocratic politics lies precisely in its resistance to such reinterpretation. Because legitimacy is grounded in expertise rather than in wisdom, failure is experienced as a threat to authority rather than as an opportunity for learning. Each error therefore provokes defensive rationalization rather than reflective correction. The system becomes locked into a cycle of escalation.

The hermeneutical understanding of time dissolves this defensive posture. It acknowledges that no decision exhausts its own meaning at the moment it is taken. Meaning unfolds through time. Consequences speak back to intentions. Reality responds to projection. Policy, no less than entrepreneurial action, is therefore a wager placed within a narrative whose next chapter cannot be written in advance.

To embrace this narrative structure of time is to recover the tragic dignity of public action. It is to recognize that governing is not a technical vocation alone but a moral drama in which choices reverberate beyond the horizon of immediate calculation. It is to abandon the fantasy of definitive solutions in favour of the discipline of provisional judgment.

In this sense, the tragic limits of prediction are not a defect of economic and political life. They are the very condition under which freedom, responsibility, and creativity remain possible. A world in which everything could be predicted would be a world in which nothing truly new could happen. It would be a world without entrepreneurship, without innovation, without historical meaning.

The price of freedom is uncertainty. The price of creativity is unpredictability. The price of responsibility is the impossibility of certainty. Public policy, when it forgets this price, transforms itself into an anti-historical force. Economics, when it forgets this price, transforms itself into an anti-human science. To remember the limits of prediction is therefore to remember what it means to be human in time.

1.7. Measurability, Technocracy, and the Ethical Crisis of Governance

The modern age is defined not only by its machines, its markets, or its institutions, but by a far more subtle transformation: the progressive enthronement of measurability as the supreme criterion of truth. What can be measured is treated as real. What cannot be measured is increasingly treated as marginal, subjective, or irrelevant. This transformation has reshaped not only the natural sciences but also the social sciences, public administration, and the very self-understanding of political authority.

In economics, this enthronement of measurability has taken the form of an ever-expanding apparatus of quantification. Models grow more intricate, datasets more massive, estimation techniques more refined. Yet with each step forward in technical sophistication, something else retreats: the language of meaning. Economic discourse becomes increasingly fluent in symbols and increasingly inarticulate in human terms. It speaks with extraordinary precision about correlations and with growing awkwardness about purpose, dignity, responsibility, and hope.

Public policy, in turn, mirrors this transformation. Governance becomes increasingly organized around targets, indicators, benchmarks, and performance metrics. The vocabulary of prudence, judgment, and political responsibility is displaced by the vocabulary of optimization, compliance, and output measurement. Ministers become managers. Civil servants become operators of procedural systems. The polity becomes an organization to be administered rather than a community to be governed.

This shift is often justified in the name of neutrality. Numbers appear impartial. Indicators appear objective. Algorithms appear free of bias. Yet this appearance is profoundly deceptive. Every act of measurement is already an act of interpretation. Every indicator embodies a theory of what matters. Every benchmark encodes a hierarchy of values. The dream of value-free governance through numbers is therefore not a scientific ideal but a political myth.

When measurability becomes the ultimate criterion of legitimacy, the unmeasurable does not disappear. It is simply silenced. Trust, civic responsibility, entrepreneurial imagination, moral courage, institutional memory, social cohesion—none of these can be captured by a metric without being distorted. Yet all of them are indispensable to a flourishing society. When policy attends only to what can be counted, it abandons what truly counts.

This abandonment has profound ethical consequences. The policy maker increasingly comes to see the world not as a field of human meanings but as a dashboard of variables. Success is defined not by the quality of social life but by the attainment of numerical targets. Failure is defined not by injustice or suffering but by the deviation of indicators from projected trajectories. Governance becomes a matter of hitting metrics rather than of sustaining meaning.

This is the deep structure of technocracy. Technocracy is not merely rule by experts. It is rule by measurement. It is the belief that social life can be governed through quantitative proxies without remainder. It is the conviction that once the correct indicators have been selected, collective values no longer need to be debated because they have been silently embedded in the metric itself.

Yet this silent embedding is precisely where the ethical danger lies. Values do not vanish when they are not named; they become unaccountable. When deliberation about ends is replaced by optimization of means, political responsibility dissolves into procedural correctness. The question "What ought we to do?" is replaced by the question "What does the indicator require?" Moral reasoning yields to algorithmic compliance.

The ethical crisis of governance therefore does not arise primarily from corruption or incompetence. It arises from depersonalization. Decisions are no longer owned by persons. They are executed by systems. Authority becomes anonymous. Accountability becomes diffused. Harm becomes unintended and therefore morally neutralized. The more rigorously policy adheres to procedure, the less anyone appears to be responsible for its consequences.

This depersonalization is nowhere more evident than in the growing reliance on algorithmic governance. Risk scores determine access to credit, employment, insurance, and even freedom. Predictive policing systems pre-classify individuals as threats before any crime has been committed. Automated welfare systems determine eligibility for support without recourse to narrative explanation. Machine learning models guide regulatory enforcement without being intelligible even to their designers.

What is presented as an advance in efficiency is in fact a radical contraction of moral space. The individual is no longer encountered as a person whose situation requires interpretation but as a data point whose classification triggers an automated response. The dialogical structure of governance collapses. There is no longer anyone to whom one can appeal, no one with whom one can argue, no one who can exercise discretion. Power becomes faceless.

This facelessness produces a new kind of injustice: injustice without a perpetrator. When harm occurs, there is no guilty agent—only a malfunctioning system. When exclusion is imposed, there is no oppressor—only an unfavourable score. When dignity is violated, there is no violator—only a procedural outcome. The very grammar of moral protest is thus eroded, because protest presupposes a person to whom one can speak.

The technocratic imagination greets this erosion with relief. It sees in depersonalization the end of arbitrariness. It imagines that by eliminating discretion it has eliminated injustice. But discretion is not the enemy of justice; irresponsibility is. A system without discretion is not just. It is merely rigid. And rigidity in the face of human diversity is itself a form of cruelty.

The hermeneutical conception of governance stands in radical opposition to this trend. It insists that public action always remains a morally burdened act. It cannot be discharged into a system. It cannot be dissolved into procedure. It cannot be outsourced to machines. To govern is to judge. To judge is to assume responsibility. To assume responsibility is to expose oneself to moral risk.

This exposure cannot be eliminated without eliminating the ethical core of political life. A society that seeks to govern without judgment becomes a society that governs without conscience. It may still be efficient. It may still be orderly. But it will no longer be just in any meaningful sense.

The obsession with measurability also reshapes the self-understanding of citizens. When public value is defined exclusively through metrics, individuals begin to see themselves as units of performance. Students become test scores. Workers become productivity indices. Patients become cost profiles. Entrepreneurs become recipients of incentives. The plural richness of human identity is flattened into numerical output.

This flattening has subtle but devastating consequences. Human beings begin to orient their self-worth toward externally imposed benchmarks rather than toward internally cultivated meaning. They learn not to ask what kind of life is worth living, but what performance will be rewarded. Moral aspiration withers into compliance optimization. Excellence is redefined as indicator maximization.

This transformation reaches its logical culmination in the culture of continuous evaluation. Every action becomes an object of assessment. Every role becomes a function to be scored. Every institution becomes a performance unit. Surveillance replaces trust. Auditing replaces responsibility. Reporting replaces narrative. The social order becomes a permanent examination.

And yet, paradoxically, the more intensely performance is measured, the more its meaning erodes. When education is governed by standardized testing, learning becomes instrumental. When healthcare is governed by cost metrics, care becomes transactional. When science is governed by citation indices, inquiry becomes strategic. When governance is governed by benchmarks, politics becomes administration.

The colonization of meaning by measurability thus produces a crisis not only of governance but of purpose. A society that can count everything risks believing in nothing. It becomes extraordinarily capable of calculation and increasingly incapable of wisdom.

This crisis also reshapes the relation between policy and legitimacy. In classical political thought, legitimacy arises from the orientation of power toward the common good as interpreted through public deliberation. In technocratic governance, legitimacy is redefined as procedural correctness and metric compliance. Power no longer needs to justify its ends. It need only demonstrate that it has followed the algorithm.

This redefinition transforms citizens from participants in collective judgment into objects of administration. Their consent is no longer sought through persuasion but inferred from compliance. Political agency withers into behavioural response. Freedom is reinterpreted as choice among administratively structured options.

The hermeneutical vision of political economy cannot accept this reduction without rejecting itself. For if economics is a science of understanding, and policy an art of prudence, then both presuppose subjects capable of meaning. A governance that treats persons as variables denies the very ontological basis upon which both economics and policy rest.

The ethical crisis of governance is therefore inseparable from the epistemological crisis of economics. When economics abandons meaning for measurement, policy abandons judgment for procedure. When theory reduces action to optimization, governance reduces responsibility to algorithmic execution. The same metaphysical decision—against meaning and for control—unfolds across both domains.

To confront this crisis is not to reject measurement as such. Measurement has its place. Numbers can illuminate. Indicators can inform. Data can discipline illusions. But measurement must remain a servant of understanding, not its master. Indicators must remain signs, not idols. Algorithms must remain tools, not sovereigns.

The restoration of this hierarchy is the central ethical task of contemporary political economy. It requires that we once again ask not only how much, how fast, and how efficiently, but why, for whom, and at what moral cost. It requires that we restore narrative, deliberation, and judgment to the centre of public life. It requires, above all, that we resist the seduction of a power that no longer has to answer to persons because it answers only to itself in the mirror of its own metrics.

The ultimate danger of technocracy is not tyranny in the classical sense. It is something subtler and perhaps more difficult to resist: a world in which no one commands and therefore no one can be held responsible. A world governed by systems in which power circulates without a face, decisions occur without authors, and injustice unfolds without villains.

Against this world, hermeneutical political economy raises a simple but demanding claim: that to govern is to judge, and to judge is to stand exposed before others. There is no humane governance without this exposure. There is no just policy without the risk of responsibility. There is no political order worthy of free persons that does not preserve space for interpretation, error, revision, and forgiveness.

To defend this space today is not nostalgia. It is resistance.

1.8. Theory as Grammar: Why Policy Cannot Fly Without Economics

If public policy is an art and not a science, it may nevertheless appear paradoxical that economic theory should still be indispensable to its practice. If policy cannot be deduced from models, if social reality resists algorithmic control, if uncertainty and novelty undermine predictive mastery, why insist so strongly on the primacy of theory? Why not abandon theory altogether in favour of pragmatic improvisation?

The answer is simple and demanding at once: because even an art requires a grammar. One cannot compose music without knowing harmony, even if harmony alone does not produce a symphony. One cannot practice medicine without understanding physiology, even if physiology alone does not heal the patient. And one cannot govern wisely without understanding the invisible structures that coordinate social life, even if that understanding never dictates a single policy choice in advance.

The relationship between economics and policy is therefore not one of command but of articulation. Economic theory does not tell the policy maker what to do. It tells him what kind of world he is acting within. It reveals the deep constraints, the structural tensions, the trade-offs that no amount of political will can abolish. It exposes the grammar of coordination that precedes and exceeds every intervention.

To return to the image already evoked: one cannot fly without knowing the laws of physics. But knowledge of physics alone does not generate flight. It merely makes flight intelligible and possible. In the same way, economic theory does not produce good policy. It merely prevents catastrophic illusion.

When policy emancipates itself from theory, it does not become freer. It becomes blind. It loses the capacity to distinguish between what is desirable and what is possible, between what is morally appealing and what is structurally sustainable. It begins to treat symptoms as if they were causes. It confuses redistribution with creation, liquidity with capital, demand with coordination, nominal magnitudes with real processes.

Blind policy is not a rare anomaly. It is the normal condition of governance whenever theory is dismissed as "ideological" or "academic". In such moments, urgency replaces understanding. Moral fervour replaces institutional literacy. The will to act displaces the need to interpret. And because the structural logic of the system remains unacknowledged, interventions often strike the surface of phenomena while leaving their deeper grammar untouched.

This is why so many well-intentioned policies generate perverse effects. Price controls intended to protect the poor generate shortages that harm the poor most. Credit expansions intended to stimulate growth generate capital misallocations that end in crises. Labour regulations intended to protect workers generate barriers that exclude the most vulnerable from employment. Trade restrictions intended to defend national industry generate rent-seeking structures that weaken innovation.

In each of these cases, the moral intuition is often understandable. What fails is not compassion but structural understanding. The policy maker acts upon the visible symptom without grasping the invisible coordination process beneath it. The grammar of the market is violated in the name of justice, and injustice is thereby amplified.

Yet the opposite danger is equally real. When theory is absolutized, it hardens into ideology. When models are treated as blueprints, policy becomes an exercise in abstract deduction. The policymaker begins to believe that if the assumptions hold on paper, they must be made to hold in reality. Human beings are then forced to adapt to the model rather than the model to human beings.

Here again, the physics analogy is instructive. The laws of physics describe how the world behaves. They do not prescribe how airplanes ought to fly. Engineers must translate physical principles into concrete designs using judgment, experimentation, and contextual adaptation. They must take into account materials, weather, human error, institutional constraints, and unforeseen contingencies. The same principle holds for the relationship between economic theory and policy. Economic theory describes coordination, not destinies. It reveals how prices communicate information, how incentives shape behaviour, how institutions stabilize expectations, how money structures intertemporal exchange, how capital embodies time and uncertainty. It does not stipulate what social goals ought to be pursued. It clarifies the cost of pursuing them in certain ways.

Once this clarifying function is understood, the false opposition between "theorists" and "pragmatists" dissolves. There is no genuine pragmatism without theory, because action without understanding is mere reaction. And there is no genuine theory without humility, because models without fallibility become instruments of domination rather than of insight. The real task of economic theory is therefore not to dominate policy but to discipline it. It restrains the political imagination where imagination threatens to become arbitrary. It reminds the policy maker that resources are scarce, that time cannot be reversed, that trade-offs cannot be abolished, that incentives matter, that coordination is fragile, that capital is time-bound, that monetary disturbances are not neutral, that institutions embody memory.

In doing so, theory performs a negative but indispensable task. It tells us what we cannot do without cost. It warns us against believing that noble ends exempt us from structural constraints. It dissolves the fantasy that we can change one variable in isolation without affecting the whole. This negative discipline of theory is more important than any positive prescription. For most policy disasters arise not because leaders did not know what to do, but because they believed that something could be done without consequence. They exceeded the limits of structural intelligibility in the name of urgency.

The role of theory is therefore to protect society from certain kinds of political intoxication. It tempers the will to act with the need to understand. It resists the inflation of moral certainty into technical omnipotence. It reminds power of its finitude. At the same time, theory also protects society from the opposite intoxication: the technocratic belief that because something is efficient it must be legitimate. Efficiency is not a moral category. A police state can be efficient. A surveillance regime can be optimized. A command economy can move masses of resources rapidly. None of this guarantees justice or human flourishing.

Economic theory alone cannot determine the ends of policy. It is silent on ultimate purposes. It does not tell us what kind of society we ought to desire. It only tells us that whatever we desire must pass through the grammar of scarcity, time, incentive, and coordination. Ends without this grammar become destructive even when they are ethically motivated.

This is why the deepest conflict of contemporary governance is not between left and right, market and state, freedom and equality. It is between two different images of reason. On one side stands instrumental reason, which understands rationality as optimization under constraints. On the other side stands interpretative reason, which understands rationality as participation in meaning under conditions of uncertainty.

Technocratic policy rests almost entirely on the first image. Hermeneutical political economy rests on the second. The first seeks to manage outcomes. The second seeks to understand processes. The first seeks control. The second seeks intelligibility. The first centralizes decision-making in the name of efficiency. The second disperses it in the name of learning.

Economic theory, when interpreted through a hermeneutical lens, becomes the bridge between these two forms of reason. It reminds us that optimization always takes place within meanings that cannot themselves be optimized. It shows that incentives work only because they are interpreted. It reveals that coordination is always more than calculation because it is also trust, expectation, and belief.

When policy is grounded in this deeper understanding of theory, it becomes neither ideological nor arbitrary. It becomes prudent. It accepts that some goals must be pursued indirectly, that some evils cannot be eradicated without generating worse ones, that some inequalities reflect scarcity rather than injustice, that some instabilities are the price of creativity.

This does not lead to resignation. It leads to responsibility properly understood. A responsible policy maker does not pretend to command the economy. He seeks to understand its language. He does not try to rewrite its grammar; rather, he tries to speak it more coherently.

In this sense, theory is not a tool of domination but of dialogue. It does not give orders to reality. It listens to it. And because it listens, it can speak to power in another register—not as an oracle of control, but as a witness of constraint. This witnessing function of theory is particularly vital in an age of permanent emergency. When every political issue is framed as an existential crisis, the temptation to suspend grammar in the name of urgency becomes overwhelming. Theory is dismissed as delay. Caution is denounced as complicity. Prudence is rebranded as cowardice.

Yet it is precisely in moments of emergency that grammar matters most. For it is when passion is highest that blindness is greatest. Theory does not paralyze action in such moments. It prevents it from becoming catastrophic. A policy that ignores the time-structure of capital will destroy investment in the name of growth. A policy that ignores the informational role of prices will create shortages in the name of justice. A policy that ignores the incentive structure of taxation will weaken initiative in the name of solidarity. A policy that ignores the institutional foundations of trust will corrode legitimacy in the name of efficiency.

In all these cases, theory acts as memory against amnesia. It recalls what politics is tempted to forget. It insists that the economy has a structure that cannot be bent at will without breaking. Yet theory must also remain vulnerable to reality. It must remain corrigible by experience. The grammar itself evolves as institutions, technologies, and cultural meanings evolve. What was once a stabilizing rule may become a rigid constraint. What was once an efficient coordination device may become a bottleneck. Theory must therefore interpret not only society but also itself.

This reflexivity of theory completes the hermeneutical circle. Economics is not a set of eternal laws imposed upon history. It is an evolving interpretation of how coordination has taken place under changing conditions. It speaks truth only insofar as it remains open to revision.

Policy, in turn, must remain in dialogue with this evolving grammar. It cannot fly by instinct alone. But it also cannot fly by formula. It flies by judgment—judgment informed by theory, disciplined by complexity, restrained by humility, and animated by purpose. To defend the primacy of theory in such a world is therefore not to defend abstraction against reality; it is to defend reality against fantasy. It is to insist that before we act upon the world, we must strive to understand the deep logic that makes action intelligible at all.

1.9. Human Flourishing, Entrepreneurship, and Interpretative Order

All the preceding reflections on meaning, prudence, complexity, time, plural causation, measurability, and theory converge upon a single, irreducible question: what kind of social order is compatible with human flourishing? If economics is indeed an interpretative science and policy an art of prudent action under uncertainty, then their ultimate criterion cannot be efficiency alone, nor stability alone, nor growth alone. It must be the capacity of a society to sustain the unfolding of meaningful human lives across time.

Human flourishing is not a technical state. It is not a measurable output. It does not coincide with any single indicator of welfare. It is a dynamic condition in which persons are able to interpret their own existence as worthwhile, to project meaningful futures, to assume responsibility for their actions, and to participate in social orders that they experience not as prisons but as enabling frameworks. Flourishing is therefore inseparable from freedom—not freedom as arbitrary choice, but freedom as the space within which interpretation, initiative, and responsibility become possible.

Within this space of freedom, entrepreneurship emerges not merely as an economic function among others, but as a primordial anthropological act. Entrepreneurship is the human capacity to see what is not yet visible, to imagine what does not yet exist, and to act as if it might come into being. It is the elective affinity between imagination and responsibility. It is the courage to wager on an uncertain future and the discipline to bear the consequences of that wager.

The entrepreneur is not defined by the size of her firm, the sector in which she operates, or the scale of her investment. He is defined by an interpretative posture toward reality. He reads the world not as a closed system of constraints but as an open field of possibilities. He perceives misalignments where others see equilibrium, latent meanings where others see given facts, unmet needs where others see saturation. He inhabits the world in the future tense.

In this sense, entrepreneurship is not reducible to innovation policy, research subsidies, or startup ecosystems, however important these may be. It is a form of human action that precedes and exceeds its institutional expressions. It is the anthropological engine of social change. Every flourishing society is, in this deeper sense, an entrepreneurial society—not because all become business owners, but because creative reinterpretation of reality permeates everyday life.

Markets, when understood hermeneutically, are the institutional form through which this entrepreneurial reinterpretation becomes socially coordinated. They are not merely mechanisms for allocating resources. They are arenas of communicative interaction in which countless projections of meaning encounter one another. Prices emerge as condensed narratives of scarcity, expectation, risk, and value. Profits and losses become a language of success and failure in the collective drama of coordination.

Within this drama, flourishing does not consist in the elimination of failure but in the possibility of learning from it. A society that forbids failure forbids discovery. A society that guarantees outcomes suffocates initiative. A society that insulates individuals from the consequences of their interpretations also deprives them of the dignity of responsibility.

Yet the opposite extreme is equally inhospitable to flourishing. A society that exposes individuals to unmediated uncertainty without institutional protection condemns them to existential precarity. Freedom without form dissolves into anxiety. Initiative without framework collapses into chaos. The art of institutional order therefore lies precisely in structuring uncertainty without abolishing it, in protecting vulnerability without neutralizing agency.

This is the point at which policy, when rightly understood, enters the architecture of flourishing. Policy does not create meaning, but it can nurture or suffocate the conditions under which meaning is generated. It does not command entrepreneurship, but it can either open or close the horizons within which entrepreneurial imagination operates. It does not impose responsibility, but it can either reinforce or corrode the link between action and consequence upon which responsibility depends.

Monetary institutions, for example, shape the temporal horizon of human projects. Where money is stable, time remains intelligible. Long-term planning becomes meaningful. The future remains a space of projection rather than a field of panic. Where money is systematically distorted, time disintegrates into short-term opportunism. The deep grammar through which present sacrifice is connected to future gain is corrupted. In such a world, flourishing contracts into survival, and entrepreneurship degenerates into speculation.

Legal institutions shape the narrative of trust. Where property and contract are reliably protected, individuals can interpret their actions as inviolable commitments. They dare to bind themselves through promises because the social world honours the binding force of meaning. Where legality becomes arbitrary or politicized, interpretation becomes defensive. Promises are discounted. Cooperation retreats into narrow circles of personal familiarity. Social complexity shrinks.

Fiscal institutions shape the narrative of reciprocity. Where taxation is perceived as a fair contribution to common goods, solidarity becomes credible. Where it is perceived as arbitrary extraction, resistance becomes rational. The same numeric rate can thus generate either cooperation or evasion depending on its interpretative embedding.

Regulatory institutions shape the narrative of possibility. Where rules are predictable and proportionate, imagination expands within a known horizon. Where rules are dense, volatile, and discretionary, imagination contracts. Agents adapt not by creating but by complying. Entrepreneurship becomes a juridical skill rather than a productive one.

Across all these domains, the decisive factor is not merely the technical content of policy but its capacity to be interpreted as meaningful by those who live under it. Institutions flourish when they are not merely obeyed but understood. They decay when they are complied with but no longer believed in.

This interpretative legitimacy cannot be produced by propaganda or enforced by coercion. It arises only when institutions resonate with lived experience. It is built slowly through credibility, consistency, and mutual recognition. It is destroyed quickly through arbitrariness, asymmetry, and contempt for the narratives through which individuals understand their own lives.

Here, the ethical dimension of entrepreneurship becomes fully visible. The entrepreneur does not act in a moral vacuum. He enters a social field thick with meaning. His success or failure transmits signals not only about efficiency but about the plausibility of certain life projects. When entrepreneurial initiative is systematically punished, the message transmitted is not merely economic but existential: that initiative is futile, that projection is dangerous, that dependence is safer than responsibility.

Conversely, when entrepreneurship is institutionally honoured, not through privilege but through fair openness, the message transmitted is that initiative matters, that the future is open, that responsibility is meaningful. A society that structurally affirms this message does not merely grow economically. It grows in moral confidence.

Human flourishing thus appears as the emergent outcome of a delicate interplay between freedom and form, between imagination and institution, between initiative and protection. It cannot be designed. It can only be cultivated. It cannot be commanded. It can only be made possible.

This is why every attempt to redefine flourishing in purely material or purely metric terms ultimately fails. Flourishing includes material sufficiency, but it is not exhausted by it. It includes security, but it is not reducible to protection. It includes recognition, but it is not identical with status. It includes growth, but it is not measurable as growth. It includes meaning, and meaning is not countable.

The technocratic state, however, increasingly attempts to govern flourishing through indicators. Well-being becomes a composite index. Happiness becomes a survey score. Opportunity becomes a percentile. Inclusion becomes a ratio. Each of these metrics may illuminate one fragment of human experience. None can encompass the drama of a life.

This substitution of measurement for meaning produces a distorted anthropology. Human beings are reimagined as carriers of attributes rather than as narrators of destinies. Policy intervenes not in lives but in distributions. Flourishing is no longer something that persons pursue through interpretation and responsibility. It becomes something that systems deliver through optimization.

This is the final consequence of the colonization of meaning by measurability: the transformation of human flourishing from a lived achievement into an administered outcome. And an administered flourishing is a contradiction in terms. What is administered cannot be freely owned. What is delivered cannot be responsibly achieved. What is optimized cannot be meaningfully chosen.

A hermeneutical political economy therefore restores the link between flourishing and interpretation. It insists that human beings flourish not when they are maximized but when they are recognized as agents capable of understanding, choosing, erring, learning, and beginning again. It understands the economy not as a machine for producing outputs but as a process through which society learns how to live with scarcity, time, and uncertainty.

Entrepreneurship, in this perspective, becomes not merely a driver of growth but a school of freedom. It educates individuals in risk, judgment, responsibility, and creativity. It confronts them with the stubbornness of reality and the fragility of plans. It weans them from the illusion that the world owes them success and invites them into the discipline of earning meaning through action.

Policy, when aligned with this vision, ceases to aspire to manage flourishing directly. It aims instead to defend the interpretative spaces within which flourishing may emerge. It limits itself not because it is indifferent to human welfare, but because it understands that welfare without freedom is impoverished, and freedom without interpretation is blind.

In such a society, the ultimate measure of economic success is not the height of aggregates but the depth of participation. Not how much is produced, but how meaningfully it is produced. Not how efficiently resources are allocated, but how responsibly they are imagined. Not how smoothly systems run, but how humanly they allow people to fail and begin again.

Human flourishing, then, is not a condition to be delivered by policy. It is a horizon to be protected by institutions and interpreted by free persons. It is the fragile, emergent achievement of a society that remembers that the economy exists for human beings, not the other way around.

1.10. The Pretence of Knowledge and the Future of Civilizational Governance

The long journey through meaning and mechanism, prudence and control, complexity and measurability, theory and policy, freedom and administration brings us inevitably to the decisive civilizational conflict of our time: the conflict between the *humility of understanding* and the *pretence of knowledge*. This conflict does not concern only economists or policy makers. It concerns the very way in which modern societies conceive of reason, power, responsibility, and the human person.

The pretence of knowledge does not begin as tyranny. It begins as impatience. It arises from the legitimate desire to alleviate suffering quickly, to fix what appears broken, to correct what seems unjust. But when this impatience divorces action from understanding, intervention from interpretation, and authority from fallibility, it mutates into something far more dangerous than error: it becomes epistemological hubris. It is the belief that reality is transparent to technique, that complexity is dissolvable into data, that uncertainty is reducible to risk, that coordination is programmable, and that meaning itself can be replaced by metrics.

This belief now structures the dominant imagination of governance. We are told that with enough information we can foresee crises; with enough computation we can eliminate uncertainty; with enough regulation we can optimize behaviour; with enough indicators we can manufacture wellbeing. Politics is reframed as system management. Society is reframed as a controllable artifact. Human beings are reframed as adjustable variables.

Against this vision, we have here articulated a radically different anthropology and epistemology. It has defended the reality of interpretation against the fantasy of control. It has reestablished economics as a science of understanding rather than a technology of domination. It has restored public policy to the ancient dignity of prudence rather than the modern illusion of engineering. It has reintroduced time as creative becoming rather than mechanical succession. It has defended plural causation against monocausal obsession. It has protected human flourishing against administrative appropriation.

What finally emerges is not a technical doctrine but a civilizational choice. On one side stands the civilization of control. It seeks security through supervision, predictability through surveillance, justice through administration, flourishing through optimization. It fears uncertainty because it fears freedom. It distrusts interpretation because it cannot measure it. It abolishes judgment because judgment is fallible. It replaces responsibility with procedure and then congratulates itself on its neutrality. It governs through numbers because numbers do not argue back.

On the other side stands the civilization of meaning. It accepts uncertainty as the price of freedom. It cultivates institutions as grammars of interpretation rather than machines of distribution. It treats entrepreneurship as a creative vocation rather than as a residual function. It sees policy not as outcome-design but as condition-protection. It knows that human beings flourish not when they are optimized, but when they are recognized as agents capable of understanding, choosing, failing, and beginning again.

Between these two civilizations lies not a technical disagreement, but a metaphysical divide. The pretence of knowledge is not merely an intellectual mistake. It becomes politically lethal when it denies its own limits. When theory claims to predict the future, policy claims to command it. When prediction fails—as it must—policy does not retreat. It escalates. Each failure is interpreted not as evidence of epistemic limits but as justification for further control. Thus, the tragic spiral of modern governance unfolds: intervention generates unintended consequences; unintended consequences justify more intervention; complexity increases; prediction fails again; control deepens.

At every stage of this spiral, the same pattern repeats: responsibility is displaced upward into systems and downward into populations, but never resides where power is exercised. No one commands, no one decides, no one is guilty—yet everything is decided.

Hermeneutical political economy breaks this spiral at its root. It insists that power must remain personally exposed. That judgment must remain morally burdened. That failure must remain a source of learning rather than a trigger for domination. That institutions must remain revisable rather than sacralized. That theory must remain critical rather than prophetic.

This is why humility is not an optional virtue in public life. It is a structural necessity. Without humility, interpretation collapses into domination. Without fallibility, knowledge collapses into ideology. Without openness, order collapses into administration. Without tragedy, responsibility collapses into procedure.

The future of governance will not be decided by whether states intervene more or less. It will be decided by *how* they understand intervention. Will they understand it as engineering or as judgment? As optimization or as interpretation? As control or as stewardship? These are not policy choices. They are metaphysical commitments enacted through institutions.

And the future of economics will be decided accordingly. Will economics continue its drift toward algorithmic abstraction and measurement fetishism? Or will it recover its vocation as an interpretative science of human coordination, entrepreneurship, time, uncertainty, and meaning? Will it become a servant of technocracy or a critical conscience of power?

The most dangerous confusion of modern times is not between socialism and capitalism, or between markets and states. It is between *management* and *governance*. Management optimizes systems. Governance interprets human orders. Management seeks performance. Governance seeks legitimacy. Management requires compliance. Governance requires consent. Management eliminates discretion. Governance presupposes judgment.

The substitution of management for governance is the hidden revolution

of our age. Its effects are already visible: in the hollowing out of politics
into administration, in the displacement of debate by benchmarking, in the
conversion of citizenship into performance, in the transformation of freedom
into monitored choice.

Against this silent revolution, hermeneutical political economy raises a
final claim: that a society can be efficiently administered and yet existentially
impoverished; that it can be perfectly managed and yet profoundly unjust;
that it can optimize everything except the meaning of living.

Human flourishing cannot be engineered because it is not a mechanical
product. It is an existential achievement. It arises where interpretation meets
responsibility, where freedom meets form, where time meets meaning, where
failure meets learning. It requires institutions, but it overflows every institutional design. It requires policy, but it cannot be delivered by policy. It requires
economics, but it is not produced by economics.

It requires, above all, the courage to live without guarantees.

The pretence of knowledge promises certainty without tragedy. But a
world without tragedy is not a world without suffering; it is a world without
meaning. We argued that the acceptance of uncertainty is not an intellectual
resignation but the deepest affirmation of human dignity. To admit that we
do not fully know is to admit that reality is not fully ours to command. To
admit that the future is open is to admit that human creativity still matters.

The civilizational task before us, then, is not to build a perfectly predictable
economy, nor to design a flawlessly optimized society, nor to administer a fully
measurable wellbeing. It is to sustain the fragile interpretative spaces in which
free persons can imagine futures, bear responsibility, learn from failure, and
create meaning together in time.

Economics, when faithful to itself, protects those spaces by reminding
power of its limits. Public policy, when faithful to its vocation, defends those
spaces by acting with prudence rather than presumption. Institutions, when
faithful to their purpose, stabilize those spaces without suffocating them.
Entrepreneurship, when faithful to its essence, continually reopens those spaces
by introducing the new.

In the end, the deepest function of political economy is not to manage
prosperity but to protect the conditions under which prosperity can still be
meaningfully pursued. Between measurability and meaning, between control and humility, between administration and flourishing, the destiny of
our civilization will be decided—not by superior technique, but by superior
understanding.

And understanding is always an interpretative act.

LESSON 2

Competing (Macro)Visions In Economic Policy: Measuring Versus Understanding And Policy-Led Growth Versus Entrepreneurship-Led Models

INTRODUCTION

Modern macroeconomic policy is born from a tension that is as old as political economy itself, yet has become sharper in our age: the tension between the desire to govern outcomes and the duty to respect processes; between the ambition to measure and the vocation to understand; between the promise that policy can *make* growth and the older intuition that growth is, in its essence, an emergent accomplishment of entrepreneurial discovery within an institutional order. The present chapter is organised around these two tensions. The first concerns the meaning of "economic growth" and the consequences of reducing it to a numerical target. The second concerns the determinants of growth and the persistent rivalry between two visions: one that sees policy as the primary lever of development and one that sees entrepreneurship—understood broadly as the creative and coordinating force of human action—as the true engine of dynamic prosperity.

This is not merely an academic dispute about models. It is a civilisational dispute about how societies understand themselves. When the economy is imagined as a machine that produces measurable output, macro policy naturally takes the form of engineering: stabilise fluctuations, optimise performance, hit targets. When the economy is recognised as a living process of interpretation unfolding through time, macro policy becomes something different: an art of prudence under uncertainty, tasked less with "delivering growth" than with preserving the conditions under which discovery, adaptation, and institutional learning can occur. The difference between these visions is not cosmetic. It shapes what governments attempt, what economists promise, what citizens expect, and—ultimately—what kinds of lives become possible.

A useful point of departure is to restore a distinction that has been progressively eroded: economics as a science of understanding and public policy as an art of action. When these domains are confused, economics is pressured to become a technology of control and policy is tempted to become the mechanical application of formulas. The result is the technocratic imagination: the belief that with sufficient data, sufficient modelling sophistication, and sufficient administrative reach, uncertainty can be abolished and the future rendered manageable. In such an epistemological climate, the growth problem becomes a dashboard problem: select indicators, set targets, calibrate instruments, evaluate performance. Yet the very drive to replace understanding with measurement often produces an inversion: the more precisely we measure, the less we understand; the more aggressively we intervene, the less we genuinely govern.

To see why, we must begin where macroeconomics usually ends: not with policy instruments, but with the ontology of economic life. Economic reality is not given as a set of neutral data points awaiting statistical treatment. It is given as a field of interpreted meanings, shaped by the intentions, expectations, fears, hopes, and imaginative projections of acting persons. The German term *verstehen* captures the point: to understand an action is not merely to correlate it with an outcome but to re-enter the horizon of meaning within which the action became intelligible to the actor. When economics forgets this, it does not become more scientific; it becomes less real.

The macro policy debate—Keynesian stimulus versus austerity, activist stabilisation versus rules, industrial policy versus market liberalisation—often appears as a contest between ideological camps. But beneath the surface lies a deeper divide: whether the object of governance is a set of measurable aggregates or a living order of social coordination. This chapter therefore does not treat "competing visions" as a list of schools. It treats them as rival metaphysics of the economy and rival ethics of governance. The goal is not to declare one side virtuous and the other wicked, but to clarify what each vision presupposes about knowledge, time, causality, institutions, and human agency, and to show how those presuppositions shape both growth measurement and growth policy.

2.1. GROWTH AS A NUMBER AND GROWTH AS A MEANING

The language of economic growth, in mainstream discourse, is overwhelmingly the language of measurement. Growth is the percentage change of real GDP. Development is the level of GDP per capita. Progress is the closing of a "gap" measured against a benchmark. Recessions are "negative growth" and recoveries are "return to trend". This language is not neutral. It encodes a conception of the economy as a machine whose performance can be summarised by a single output statistic. Once the economy is imagined this way, the political temptation is immediate: if output is the object, policy becomes the lever.

Yet GDP, though indispensable for national accounting, is an ex-post accounting construct. It records the value of final goods and services already exchanged. It captures results, not processes. It is therefore silent on the intertemporal structure of production: the changing combinations of capital goods, entrepreneurial plans, and expectations through which the economy actually moves.

The GDP number tells us that "more" was produced, but not *how* the structure of production was reconfigured, what kinds of knowledge were discovered, what kinds of errors were made and corrected, and what kinds of coordination problems were solved or created.

This limitation is not merely technical; it is conceptual. When GDP becomes the lens through which growth is seen, economic life is redefined as a sequence of measurable outputs rather than as a complex process of interpretation unfolding in historical time. The richness of the cyclical experience—the shifting expectations, learning processes, and capital reconfigurations that occur through time—risks being reduced to the oscillation of a single aggregate variable. Growth becomes the rate of change of a number; the drama of coordination becomes a graph.

The problems deepen when GDP is treated as a policy target. Because GDP is denominated in money terms and adjusted only imperfectly for price changes, it conflates monetary and real phenomena. Monetary expansions that distort the structure of production may increase measured GDP even as they sow the seeds of future contraction.

If policy is assessed by short-term GDP performance, interventions that boost nominal spending or temporarily increase measured activity can appear successful even when they intensify underlying discoordination. The indicator then becomes not a servant of understanding but a seductive idol: it rewards what can be counted, not what sustains coherence through time.

A further and more fundamental issue concerns value. GDP assumes that economic value is additive and homogeneous. But value, as the subjectivist tradition insists, arises from interpretation, not objective aggregation. Each act of valuation is context-bound, historically situated, and meaning-laden. The attempt to compress such qualitative phenomena into a single quantitative index therefore leads to a loss of meaning.

GDP can count transactions; it cannot tell us what those transactions meant for the actors involved, what hopes they embodied, what expectations they expressed, what kinds of institutional trust they presupposed, and what kinds of human flourishing they enabled or eroded.

This is why the obsession with measurability is not an innocent methodological preference but a cultural force that reshapes governance itself. When public value is defined through metrics, individuals begin to see themselves as units of performance. Students become test scores, workers become productivity indices, patients become cost profiles, and entrepreneurs become recipients of incentives. The plural richness of human identity is flattened into numerical output. As governance becomes increasingly organised around targets, indicators, and benchmarks, the vocabulary of prudence, judgment, and political responsibility is displaced by the vocabulary of optimisation, compliance, and output measurement.

In such a world, growth policy becomes a programme of indicator maximisation. But this is precisely where the paradox emerges: the more intensely performance is measured, the more its meaning erodes. When learning becomes instrumental to tests, when innovation becomes a subsidy category, when governance becomes metric compliance, the very qualities that sustain long-term growth—trust, creativity, entrepreneurial confidence, institutional memory—are endangered by the managerial logic that claims to foster them.

To challenge this is not to romanticise ignorance or to reject quantification. Measurement has its place. Numbers can illuminate, indicators can discipline illusions, and data can reveal patterns that otherwise remain hidden. The problem begins when measurement is treated as the supreme criterion of truth and legitimacy, so that what cannot be measured is treated as marginal or irrelevant. In that inversion, the unmeasurable does not disappear; it is simply silenced. Yet the unmeasurable often carries what matters most.

A hermeneutical approach to growth begins, therefore, by restoring the hierarchy: measurement must remain a servant of understanding, not its master. Indicators must remain signs, not idols.

The policy question then changes. It is no longer "How can we increase GDP?" as if the economy were a machine. It becomes "How can we sustain and deepen the processes of coordination, discovery, and learning through which societies expand their possibilities of flourishing?".

This reframing has immediate macroeconomic implications. Consider how business cycles are typically measured and discussed. The standard tradition, from early national income estimates to modern cycle dating, defines cycles as fluctuations in real GDP and related indicators. While this tradition brought statistical discipline, it also redefined the phenomenon itself. The cycle became a numerical pattern rather than a complex process of human interpretation.

It is then natural to describe recessions as deviations from trend and recoveries as returns to normality. The policy corollary is equally natural: use fiscal and monetary levers to smooth deviations, stabilise the path, and restore trend. Yet the GDP-based measurement of cycles reinforces the illusion of control. If fluctuations are deviations from a stable growth trend, policymakers can imagine that stability can be restored by adjusting levers.

The danger is not simply that the levers may fail. The deeper danger is that the attempt to govern a living process as if it were a mechanical system becomes itself a source of instability, generating new cycles through artificial signals, distorted expectations, and intertemporal discoordination.

A hermeneutical approach calls for rethinking what it means to measure a cycle. To measure hermeneutically is not to assign a single numerical value but to interpret evolving meanings that actors attach to circumstances—meanings manifested in expectations, investment plans, and intertemporal coordination.

The cycle is then understood not as a mechanical oscillation of output but as a sequence of interpretative phases through which entrepreneurial imagination, imitation, overextension, recognition, and learning unfold through time. The economist's task becomes the reconstruction of coordination and miscoordination, not merely the dating of peaks and troughs.

Once we accept this, "growth" itself cannot remain a mere number. Growth becomes a qualitative transformation of the productive structure, an expansion of the division of labour, an accumulation of institutional trust, and a deepening of entrepreneurial discovery. Measured output may accompany these processes, but it cannot substitute for their understanding. This is why, in the interpretative perspective, the economy is not a machine producing measurable output but a kaleidic process of interpretation unfolding in historical time.

2.2. COMPETING MACRO VISIONS AS COMPETING VIEWS OF KNOWLEDGE

If growth is not simply a number, then the macro policy debate cannot be merely a debate about how strongly to pull this or that lever. It becomes a debate about the limits of knowledge and the appropriate posture of governance under uncertainty. A central lesson from the complexity tradition is that the policy result depends on the fit between a model's assumptions and reality, not on the elegance of the theory itself.

Classical economists were acutely aware of this limitation. They did not derive definitive policy blueprints from simplified models; they derived a general posture of caution—often labelled laissez-faire, yet frequently misunderstood. Laissez-faire did not mean "do nothing"; it meant: think very carefully before entering into the complexities of the economy, because those complexities are likely to produce results quite different from what was intended.

In modern policy debate, however, laissez-faire is often caricatured as market fundamentalism, while interventionism is defended as scientific control. Complexity economics suggests that both caricatures miss the point. The crucial issue is not whether policy is active or passive, but whether it is humble or hubristic; whether it treats its own knowledge as provisional and context-dependent, or whether it treats its models as blueprints for social design.

The story of how macroeconomics "lost complexity" illustrates this. In the mid-twentieth century, the aspiration emerged that macroeconomics might have laws distinct from microeconomics, laws that could be used for control. Abba Lerner's "functional finance" became a canonical expression of this spirit: maintain demand, adjust taxes and spending, manage interest rates, and if sound finance principles conflict, so much the worse for sound finance.

The point here is not to litigate Lerner's rules line by line, but to notice the epistemic posture: the state is assumed capable of maintaining a "reasonable level of demand", of identifying the "optimum amount of investment", and of using fiscal and monetary tools to deliver these outcomes. The economy becomes an object of management; macro policy becomes a technology of optimisation.

This posture persists across many contemporary frameworks, even when their technical apparatus differs. Whether one speaks in Keynesian, New Keynesian, monetarist, or modern rules-based language, the shared ambition is often the same: define stable relationships among aggregates and design interventions to achieve targets. Where models differ is in which relationships are emphasised and which frictions are assumed. Yet the risk is common: policy is tempted to believe that the future can be rendered predictable and manageable, that sufficient measurement and sufficient computing power can dissolve uncertainty.

Against this stands a rival vision: macroeconomics as a study of social coordination under dispersed knowledge, and policy as an art that must respect the limits of what can be known. The mainline tradition—associated with Hayek, Buchanan, Coase, North, Ostrom, and others—emphasises the market as a process, shaped by institutions and culture, in which individuals respond to property, prices, profits, and losses. It rejects the textbook ideal of perfect rationality and perfect information and insists that the relevant unit of analysis is acting individuals, not abstract aggregates. This is not a rejection of macro questions; it is a reorientation of them. The macroeconomy is not an entity "above" individuals; it is the emergent pattern of their interactions within institutional rules. It is therefore profoundly sensitive to changes in rules, expectations, and interpretative frameworks. The Lucas's critique, highlighted in applied mainline economics, makes the point in a specific way: policy changes alter the structure of econometric models because individuals adjust their behaviour in response to policy regimes.

Once behaviour is understood as interpretative adaptation rather than mechanical response, the dream of stable policy multipliers and invariant macro laws becomes fragile. At this point, public policy theory reinforces the warning from another angle. In policy studies, the ideal of comprehensive rationality—clear goals, comprehensive analysis, ordered stages from formulation to implementation—has long been criticised as descriptively inaccurate and prescriptively inadequate. Policymakers do not and cannot optimise comprehensively; they operate under bounded rationality, using shortcuts, seeking satisfactory rather than optimal solutions, and building on past decisions through incremental adjustments.

Policy cycles can be useful as organising metaphors, but few serious analysts believe policymaking can be divided into stages unproblematically. Policymaking is a never-ending process in which evaluation becomes the first stage of the next policy and inherited commitments constrain future choices. This matters for macro policy because it undermines a common technocratic fantasy: the fantasy that "the government" can choose a macroeconomic optimum and then implement it as if executing a plan. In reality, macro policy is made by fragmented institutions, through negotiated settlements among interests, within path-dependent constraints created by previous policies, and through implementation layers that often translate radical intentions at the top into incremental changes at the bottom. The state is not a single mind; it is a complex ecology of agencies, incentives, routines, and interpretative frames.

If one combines this with the hermeneutical insight that policy interventions reshape not only incentives but meanings, the engineering ideal collapses further. A tax is never just a fiscal instrument; it is also a signal about what a society values. Regulation is never merely a constraint; it is also an interpretative frame imposed upon entrepreneurial imagination. Monetary regimes communicate trust or mistrust in the future.

Policy therefore intervenes in the hermeneutical fabric of society. It influences what agents understand as permitted, encouraged, rewarded, or discouraged. The policymaker becomes, indirectly, an author of social narratives. This is why public policy cannot be reduced to applied economics and cannot be routinised into a rulebook. Policy is an art—phronesis—practical wisdom under uncertainty. It requires the disciplined integration of theoretical insight, empirical observation, institutional memory, and ethical reflection. It deals with contingent circumstances whose full structure cannot be known in advance.

Once this is accepted, "competing macro visions" appear in a new light. They are not merely disagreements about parameter values or the slope of curves. They are disagreements about whether human affairs are governable by technique or only navigable by prudence; whether uncertainty is an external obstacle that better information will dissolve or an internal condition of social existence; whether economic growth is a deliverable to be engineered or an emergent achievement to be cultivated.

2.3. THE MEASUREMENT TEMPTATION AND THE POLITICS OF LEGITIMACY

The modern drive to measure is inseparable from the modern drive to legitimise governance through performance. When legitimacy is defined primarily through quarterly outcomes, annual targets, or compliance with benchmarks, responsibility contracts to the short term. Policy becomes reactive rather than reflective. It chases visible effects rather than cultivating invisible conditions.

This creates a dangerous substitution. In classical political thought, legitimacy arises from orientation to the common good through public deliberation. In technocratic governance, legitimacy is redefined as procedural correctness and metric compliance. Ends no longer need to be justified; it is enough to demonstrate that the algorithm was followed. Citizens become objects of administration rather than participants in collective judgment.

In macroeconomics, this substitution appears as the belief that good policy is policy that stabilises indicators: inflation within target, unemployment within a range, growth close to trend, debt ratios within thresholds. None of these indicators is irrelevant. The problem is the belief that, once selected, they can substitute for judgment about what matters, for whom, and at what cost. Yet every act of measurement is already an act of interpretation. Every indicator embodies a theory of what matters. Every benchmark encodes a hierarchy of values. The dream of value-free governance through numbers is a political myth.

Moreover, the ethical danger of technocracy is not only that it may be wrong; it is that it depersonalises responsibility. Decisions are executed by systems. Authority becomes anonymous. Harm becomes "unintended" and therefore morally neutralised. The more rigorously policy adheres to procedure, the less anyone appears responsible for its consequences.

In macro policy, this can be seen when failures are attributed to shocks, modelling error, data revisions, or unfortunate lags, rather than to the inherent limits of what can be known and controlled. The discourse becomes technical precisely where moral responsibility should become sharper.

A hermeneutical political economy insists on restoring the personal dimension of judgment to governance. It refuses to treat uncertainty as a technical defect to be eliminated and recognises it as an existential condition to be inhabited wisely. To govern is not to engineer but to interpret, not to optimise but to discern, not to program but to respond.

This is the first major conclusion of the "measuring versus understanding" theme: growth cannot be reduced to an indicator without being distorted, and macro policy cannot be legitimised by metrics without eroding the space of judgment and responsibility that humane governance requires. But we have not yet reached the core controversy. Even if we agree that measurement is limited, we might still insist that policy is the primary determinant of growth. We now turn, therefore, to the second theme: policy versus entrepreneurship.

2.4. What makes societies grow: the policy-centred vision

The policy-centred vision of growth begins from a plausible observation: institutions, incentives, and public goods matter. Roads, legal systems, education, public health, macro stability, and the rule of law do not fall from the sky. Many of these conditions are influenced by policy. Moreover, the macro environment—especially monetary and fiscal regimes—shapes the predictability of planning, the security of contracts, and the stability of expectations. It is therefore tempting to conclude that growth is primarily a function of policy design and state capacity.

In its strongest form, this vision becomes developmentalism: the state as architect of structural transformation. Industrial policy selects sectors, channels finance, subsidises innovation, coordinates investment, and protects infant industries. Fiscal policy mobilises resources for infrastructure and human capital. Monetary policy manages aggregate demand to avoid recessions that might destroy productive capacity. The state becomes the agent that "makes" growth happen.

This vision often gains credibility from crises. When markets appear unstable and social costs appear severe, the desire for stabilisation becomes morally urgent. The cycle is then interpreted as a pathology to be suppressed. Countercyclical policy becomes a duty. In a GDP-centric framework, this is natural: if the cycle is a deviation of output from trend, stabilisation is simply the restoration of normality through levers.

But even within the policy-centred vision, serious analysts recognise difficulties. Applied mainline economics, for example, stresses how hard it is to disentangle proximate and deep causes of growth. Trade may affect growth directly through exchange and indirectly by encouraging policy change. Geography may matter directly through disease environment and indirectly through trade opportunities. Natural resources may shape institutions which shape policy choices which shape growth. In such nested relationships, regression analysis can struggle, and "measurement without theory" cannot credibly answer the big question of why some nations are rich and others poor.

Public policy scholarship adds further realism. Even if a government knows what it wants, it may not be able to do it. Policymaking is constrained by bounded rationality, incrementalism, inherited commitments, policy communities, and implementation realities. Radical change is difficult, not only because of political resistance but because policy is embedded in path-dependent institutional structures that create increasing returns to existing arrangements. The state cannot simply "choose" a new growth model and implement it as if pressing reset.

Complexity economics goes still further. In systems with nonlinear dynamics, path dependence, nested structures, and sensitive dependence on initial conditions, policy interventions can have unintended consequences that standard models ignore. The classical humility about intervention is not ideology; it is a recognition that the economy's complexity makes direct control unreliable.

The policy-centred vision thus faces an epistemic problem and an institutional problem. The epistemic problem is that policymakers cannot know enough to engineer complex social outcomes reliably. The institutional problem is that even if they knew, the policymaking system is fragmented and path-dependent, making comprehensive rational control impossible.

But there is a third problem, deeper than the first two: the entrepreneurial problem. The policy-centred vision often treats entrepreneurship as an object to be stimulated by incentives rather than as the living source of novelty that makes growth possible. It imagines growth as the result of correctly structured payoffs. Yet growth, in dynamic reality, is not only a response to incentives; it is also the creation of new possibilities that did not previously exist and therefore could not have been incentivised in advance.

To grasp this, we need the alternative vision.

2.5. GROWTH AS DYNAMIC EFFICIENCY: ENTREPRENEURSHIP AS THE ENGINE

The entrepreneurial vision begins from a different conception of efficiency.

In standard welfare economics, efficiency is often defined statically: given resources, preferences, and technology, allocate optimally. But societies do not live in a world where these givens are stable. Preferences evolve, knowledge changes, technologies emerge, and institutions adapt. In such a world, the central economic problem is not allocating given resources efficiently; it is discovering what the resources are capable of, what consumers might value, and what combinations of knowledge might become possible.

This is why the theory of dynamic efficiency places entrepreneurship at the centre. Its chief criticism of "adaptive efficiency" approaches is that they can become reactive rather than proactive, focusing on societies' ability to adapt to shocks, while neglecting the entrepreneurial drive that is itself the source of endogenous change and the coordinating force that makes adaptation possible. Dynamic efficiency is fuelled by entrepreneurship and combines both the creative and coordinating dimensions of economic life—dimensions that are often studied separately and partially.

Here growth is not a policy output but a market process. Entrepreneurs imagine new products, discover new methods, reconfigure production, enter new markets, and revise industrial organisation. In doing so, they generate both novelty and coordination. They do not merely respond to an environment; they reshape it. Growth is therefore inseparable from uncertainty. To create is to venture into the unknown. A society that seeks to abolish uncertainty through control abolishes entrepreneurship in the process.

This entrepreneurial vision does not deny the importance of institutions; it relocates them. Institutions matter not as levers to deliver outcomes, but as conditions that enable or disable entrepreneurial discovery. The most significant institutional condition is property rights—broadly understood as secure rights of use, exclusion, and transfer within a framework of contract and law. Where property rights are undefined or insecure, the entrepreneurial incentive to discover and create is weakened, and coordination problems intensify. Where property rights are clear, entrepreneurs can internalise costs, appropriate gains within legal rules, and discover solutions to problems that otherwise appear as "market failures".

A striking implication follows: many "public good" and "externality" problems are not intrinsic market defects but results of institutional coercion that prevents the definition and defence of property rights. When the state does not intervene coercively, entrepreneurial creativity tends to discover technical, juridical, and institutional innovations that resolve apparent public good situations. The classic examples include barbed wire resolving commons conflicts and privately run lighthouses using institutional mechanisms to charge beneficiaries. The set of public goods tends, dynamically, to become empty as entrepreneurship discovers exclusion mechanisms and cooperative forms.

This is not an argument that the state is never needed. It is an argument that entrepreneurship is far more powerful—and far more institutionally creative—than static theory assumes. The state's primary macroeconomic role, in this vision, is not to replace entrepreneurial discovery but to avoid suppressing it through coercive distortions and to maintain the legal-institutional order within which discovery can proceed.

At this point, the entrepreneurial vision of growth becomes inseparable from the "measuring versus understanding" theme. Entrepreneurship is not easily measurable because it is the creation of what does not yet exist. Models can measure outcomes ex post; they cannot measure novelty ex ante. When policy evaluation relies on short-term measurable outputs, it systematically undervalues the invisible conditions of growth: trust, predictability, freedom of entry, institutional integrity, and the cultural legitimacy of entrepreneurial risk-taking.

In other words, the entrepreneurial vision implies a different ethics of policy. Technocracy seeks to govern outcomes; prudence seeks to govern conditions. Technocracy fixes targets; prudence cultivates contexts. Technocracy manages variables; prudence attends to meanings.

The macro question then is not "Which sectors should we subsidise?" but "What institutional environment will preserve the freedom and confidence necessary for entrepreneurs to discover solutions we cannot yet imagine?"

2.6. MONETARY AND FISCAL POLICY THROUGH THE LENS OF INTERPRETATION

The contrast becomes concrete when we apply it to the classic macro domains: monetary and fiscal policy. In a technocratic and GDP-centred framework, monetary and fiscal policy are stabilisation tools. If output is below potential, stimulate demand; if inflation rises, tighten; if unemployment increases, boost spending; if debt ratios rise, consolidate. These rules presuppose that macro relationships are sufficiently stable for instruments to deliver targets, and that the main macro problem is the deviation of aggregates from desired paths.

In an interpretative and entrepreneurial framework, the central macro issue is coordination through time. The interest rate is not simply a lever to manage investment; it is a price that coordinates intertemporal plans, linking saving, investment, and the structure of production. When monetary policy manipulates interest rates, it does not merely reprice time; it reshapes entrepreneurial imagination, household aspirations, and the symbolic meaning of saving and debt.

If the rate is pushed below the level consistent with underlying time preferences and real resource availability, it can generate a pattern of investment that is not sustainable, leading to later correction. In such a world, policy "stabilisation" can become a generator of cycles.

This perspective reframes the cycle itself. The theory of the natural cycle developed by the Author interprets crises as functional episodes of re-coordination—painful but necessary corrections that preserve vitality. Rather than suppressing instability, policy should avoid amplifying it through artificial credit expansion or excessive fiscal manipulation.

Stability is not the absence of fluctuation; it is the ability of the system to renew itself through fluctuations. When cycles are measured primarily through GDP, these structural and interpretative dimensions vanish. GDP captures results, not processes; it is silent on capital structure and plan compatibility. It also encourages the illusion of control: if the cycle is an output deviation, policy can imagine itself as a technician restoring the machine to trend. A hermeneutical approach instead calls for measurement that remains faithful to meaning: interpreting expectations, capital reconfiguration, monetary alignment with time preferences, and the coherence of plans—what one might call the economy's hermeneutical coherence.

Notice what changes in the policy stance. The goal is not to abolish downturns but to avoid producing systemic mis-signals that magnify discoordination. Policy must be judged not only by immediate indicator performance but by whether it preserves the institutional and monetary conditions under which entrepreneurial learning can correct errors without being overwhelmed by artificially induced distortions.

This does not yield a simplistic "always tighten" or "always spend" rule. It yields prudence. It also yields an ethical warning: when policy interventions are evaluated through short-term indicators, the horizon of responsibility contracts. Policy becomes reactive, chasing visible effects, optimising flows, neglecting structures.

Macro policy becomes a performance regime rather than an institutional guardianship.

2.7. INSTITUTIONS, INNOVATION, AND THE POLICY–ENTREPRENEURSHIP RELATIONSHIP

The policy-centred and entrepreneurship-centred visions are often presented as mutually exclusive. In reality, they describe different causal layers. Policy cannot "replace" entrepreneurship, but it can shape the institutional environment in which entrepreneurship either flourishes or suffocates. The question is how to conceptualise this relationship without slipping back into technocratic engineering.

A useful bridge is the recognition that policies can play a dual role in relation to innovation. Policies can be catalysts: they can hinder or facilitate innovation depending on design and implementation. Policies can also be innovations themselves: genuinely novel ways of addressing challenges, not merely by influencing actors but by embodying new institutional forms.

This framing preserves the centrality of entrepreneurship while recognising that institutional design—including policy—can expand or narrow the space of discovery. Yet even here, the hermeneutical warning remains. Innovative policies are not merely technical fixes; they are interventions into meanings. A reform can strengthen trust and predictability, or it can destabilise expectations and erode legitimacy. A policy introduced into a culture of civic trust does not mean the same thing as the same policy imposed into a culture of suspicion. Instruments gain meaning within institutional contexts.

The growth literature increasingly confirms that institutions correlate with innovation capacity. Strong protection of property rights, safeguarding of intellectual property, reduction of trade barriers, and expansion of economic freedom correlate with higher levels of innovation capacity. Policies cannot replace the market test; they can only facilitate innovation or embody innovation. Ultimately, investment must pass through the discipline of the market, where consumers determine which initiatives endure.

This is where the entrepreneurial vision becomes normatively demanding. It does not say "policy is irrelevant". It says: policy must respect the ontological priority of entrepreneurial discovery. In practical terms, this often implies that the most growth-relevant policies are not the most visible "growth programmes" but the most mundane institutional safeguards: rule of law, contract enforcement, property rights, regulatory predictability, openness to exchange, and monetary regimes that do not falsify intertemporal signals.

Applied mainline economics offers an empirical complement: indices of economic freedom tend to correlate positively with growth and other measures of well-being, though GDP does not capture all dimensions people value. Even where such correlations are debated, the interpretative point stands: growth is not merely the result of spending; it is the emergent consequence of exchange under rules.

The theory of dynamic efficiency strengthens this point by emphasising that the main obstacle to dynamic efficiency is not merely transaction costs but genuine entrepreneurial error: the failure to discover or create profit opportunities due to insufficient alertness. Even in a hypothetical world of zero transaction costs, the system would fail to achieve dynamic efficiency if opportunities remained undiscovered.

This reminds us that growth is not guaranteed by removing frictions alone. Growth requires entrepreneurial imagination, the capacity to perceive what others do not, and the institutional freedom to act upon those perceptions. This has direct implications for industrial policy and state-led innovation strategies. If innovation is fundamentally a process of discovery under uncertainty, then attempts to "plan innovation" face a logical limit: the planner cannot know in advance what will be discovered. Subsidies can accelerate imitation, but imitation is not the same as creative discovery. Targets can encourage compliance, but compliance is not entrepreneurship. In the worst case, policy can redirect entrepreneurial energies away from serving consumers and toward serving the subsidy regime, creating a form of rent-seeking dynamism that looks like activity in indicators while hollowing out real discovery.

A complexity perspective reinforces the caution. In nonlinear systems, interventions can reduce resilience even when they increase measured efficiency. A drive for optimality by one metric can produce fragility by another. The policy debate must therefore return "outside the ring" and put broader questions back on the table: institutional structure, norms, resilience, and the possibility of bottom-up social entrepreneurship.

2.8. Policy realism: bounded rationality, incrementalism, and the limits of macro design

Even if one grants that certain policy reforms could improve institutional conditions for entrepreneurship, a further problem remains: the state's ability to implement reforms is limited. This is not merely a political problem; it is an epistemic and organisational problem.

Policy theory stresses that comprehensive rationality is an ideal-type. In reality, bounded rationality dominates. Policymakers satisfice. They rely on shortcuts. They seek acceptable approximations rather than optimal solutions. Incrementalism emerges as both descriptive realism and sometimes normative counsel: decision-makers do not search widely; they build on past decisions; radical change can be inappropriate because it rides roughshod over negotiated settlements and institutionalised expectations.

Moreover, policy change is constrained by inheritance before choice. New governments inherit massive commitments. Much expenditure continues by routine. New policies are often revisions of old policies addressing past failures. Path dependence and increasing returns make it costly to choose a different path once resources have been devoted to an established policy.

From a hermeneutical angle, what technocratic models classify as irrational inertia can often be the trace of tacit wisdom accumulated through experience. Institutions stabilise meaning across time. Reform that ignores this interpretative function risks destroying what cannot easily be rebuilt. The critique of institutions must itself be prudent, distinguishing between what preserves meaning and what preserves power.

This does not imply conservatism as a principle. It implies prudence as a virtue. Public policy navigates between blind conservatism and reckless rationalism. It must preserve with intelligence and change with restraint. In macroeconomic policy, this means that grand designs—whether market-fundamentalist deregulation programmes or ambitious industrial policy masterplans—often fail not only because the economy is complex, but because the polity is complex. Implementation is filtered through agencies, bureaucratic routines, and street-level discretion. Radical policy at the top becomes incremental change at the bottom.

If one combines this with the Lucas's critique and the interpretative nature of human action, the ambition to "control the macroeconomy" begins to look less like science and more like a metaphysical longing to abolish uncertainty. But uncertainty is not a defect of social life; it is its condition. The price of freedom is uncertainty. The price of creativity is unpredictability.

The implication is not fatalism; it is a different kind of responsibility. Responsibility is not the promise to deliver precise outcomes. It is the commitment to preserve humane conditions for learning, correction, and discovery, while acknowledging that policy choices will have second- and third-order effects that cannot be measured in advance.

2.9. Reinterpreting "growth determinants": from levers to conditions

We can now restate the "policy versus entrepreneurship" theme more carefully. Growth determinants can be classified, not as a list, but as a hierarchy of causation. At the surface are proximate determinants: investment rates, labour participation, productivity measures, sectoral composition. These are often the objects of policy attention because they are measurable. But beneath them are deeper determinants: institutions, norms, legal predictability, openness to exchange, and the cultural legitimacy of entrepreneurship. These deeper determinants shape the space in which entrepreneurial discovery can occur. They are harder to measure, slower to change, and easier to destroy than to build.

Policy can influence these deeper determinants, but not in the way an engineer adjusts machine settings. Policy influences the interpretative architecture of institutions: what people come to expect from law, from money, from contracts, from the future. When macro policy becomes erratic, when rules become discretionary, when metrics replace judgment, entrepreneurial confidence erodes. When monetary regimes distort intertemporal signals, investment plans become systematically misaligned. When regulation becomes unpredictable or captured by privileged interests, creative destruction is replaced by defensive rent-seeking.

The role of policy, then, is primarily negative and enabling rather than positive and commanding. It should prevent coercive distortions that impede coordination and discovery, and it should sustain institutions that internalise costs and allow gains to be appropriated within legal rules. In this sense, the most pro-growth policy is often not a "growth programme" but institutional integrity: property rights, contract law, predictable taxation, openness to trade, and a monetary framework that does not falsify price signals.

This does not mean that all active policy is misguided. It means that active policy must be evaluated by whether it strengthens or weakens the conditions of entrepreneurial discovery. A policy may be interventionist yet prudential, if it cultivates contexts rather than fixates on targets. Conversely, a policy may be "market-oriented" yet technocratic, if it reduces social life to indicators and treats reform as blueprint redesign.

Complexity economics and hermeneutical political economy converge here: technocracy focuses on first-order measurable effects; prudence attends to second- and third-order consequences that appear later, indirectly, through channels no model anticipated. And because the most decisive goods—trust, legal predictability, entrepreneurial confidence—cannot be produced by decree, policy must understand itself as cultivating, not manufacturing.

2.10. A DISCIPLINED ALTERNATIVE TO "GROWTH FETISHISM"

If growth is not merely GDP, and if entrepreneurship is not merely an incentive response, what should a disciplined macro policy framework look like? It would begin by redefining the policy aim. The aim is not the maximisation of a single measurable aggregate. The aim is the preservation of a social order capable of sustained learning and creative adaptation. In such an order, growth emerges as a by-product of dynamic efficiency—of the continuous discovery of better ways to satisfy human needs and aspirations.

Second, it would adopt a different epistemic humility. It would recognise that the social world is a field of interacting interpretations whose future cannot be deduced from present conditions. What has not yet been imagined cannot be modelled. What has not yet been discovered cannot be optimised.

Third, it would restore the proper relationship between economics and policy. Economic theory provides a grammar of constraints, not a blueprint. Without theory, policy is reckless improvisation; but when theory is mistaken for a plan, it becomes ideology. The art of policy stands to economics as medicine stands to physiology: knowledge is indispensable, but treatment is always contextual, interpretative, and ethically charged.

Fourth, it would redesign measurement as interpretation. Instead of treating GDP as the sovereign indicator, it would use quantitative data as one source among others in an interpretative reconstruction of economic processes: capital structure, expectations, plan coherence, institutional trust, and the alignment between monetary signals and real preferences. This is not an invitation to abandon data, but to embed data within meaning.

Finally, it would treat entrepreneurship not as a sector or a programme but as a dimension of human agency that permeates the entire economy—including the institutional sphere. Entrepreneurial creativity can discover not only new products but also new institutional solutions. In the absence of coercive suppression, it can resolve coordination problems that static theory treats as permanent.

CONCLUSION: COMPETING VISIONS AND THE CHOICE OF A CIVILISATION

We can now summarise the rivalry between macro visions in a single contrast.

The technocratic vision sees growth as a measurable output to be engineered. It treats the economy as a machine, policy as a lever, and legitimacy as indicator performance. It seeks refuge in dashboards because what resists measurement resists control. Its promise is stability, predictability, and managerial competence. Its danger is the erosion of understanding, responsibility, and freedom: a world governed by systems in which decisions occur without authors and harm unfolds without villains.

The interpretative-entrepreneurial vision sees growth as an emergent achievement of discovery and coordination through time. It treats the economy as a living process of meanings, policy as prudence under uncertainty, and legitimacy as responsibility oriented toward the common good rather than mere metric compliance. It recognises that freedom is inseparable from uncertainty and that creativity cannot be planned because it consists precisely in the appearance of what was not predictable. Its promise is not control but flourishing: a society that preserves space for interpretation, error, revision, and learning.

The choice between these visions is not absolute; elements of each can be combined. But the hierarchy matters. When measurement rules understanding, policy becomes technocracy. When understanding rules measurement, policy can regain its ethical core as prudence.

In the end, macroeconomic policy is not only about growth rates. It is about the kind of human world a society chooses to inhabit. If the economy is a drama of meaning, then growth is not merely "more". It is the expansion of human possibilities through time—possibilities made real by entrepreneurship and sustained by institutions worthy of free persons.

LESSON 3

Competing (Micro)Visions In Economic Policy: Power, Taxation And Externalities

3.1. THE MICRO FOUNDATIONS OF POLITICAL POWER: FROM ACTION TO AUTHORITY

Modern political economy often begins at the wrong level of analysis. It starts from aggregates, institutions, systems, and outcomes, and only later—if at all—descends to the individual whose actions generate those very phenomena. This methodological inversion is not a merely technical error; it is a moral one. By beginning from abstractions rather than from acting persons, political economy silently transforms human beings into objects of policy rather than subjects of meaning. The micro foundations of political economy are therefore not simply analytical; they are ethical and hermeneutical. They concern how power emerges from individual action, how authority claims legitimacy over that action, and how coercion becomes morally disguised as coordination.

This chapter is devoted to what may be called *competing visions at the micro level*: not competing models or policy instruments, but competing anthropologies. At stake is the question of whether individuals are to be understood as responsible moral agents embedded in networks of meaning, or as variables to be adjusted in pursuit of externally defined objectives. The difference between these visions becomes particularly stark when one examines the most intimate point of contact between the individual and political power: taxation, regulation, and the moral claim to correct individual behaviour in the name of collective good.

In macroeconomics, competing visions often manifest themselves in debates over stabilization, growth, or redistribution. At the micro level, however, the conflict is more fundamental. It concerns the right to command, the right to correct, and ultimately the right to judge. Who has the authority to say that a given action is socially harmful? Who has the legitimacy to impose costs on individuals for behaviours that are deemed undesirable? And on what epistemic and moral grounds can such authority be exercised?

A hermeneutical political economy must begin from the insight that economic action is meaningful action. Individuals do not merely respond to incentives; they interpret their situation, form expectations, evaluate trade-offs, and act within a horizon of values that cannot be reduced to measurable outcomes. This insight, central to the Austrian tradition and to interpretative social science more broadly, radically alters how we should think about power and policy. If action is meaningful, then interference with action is never neutral. It is always an intervention into a web of meanings, intentions, and moral self-understandings.

This is why the micro level is the decisive battleground for political economy. It is here that power encounters personhood, that authority confronts agency, and that policy reveals its moral presuppositions. The rhetoric of public interest, efficiency, or social welfare often conceals a deeper claim: the claim that some actors—policymakers, regulators, experts—possess superior knowledge not only of consequences, but of what ought to be valued. This claim is rarely made explicit. Instead, it is embedded in technical language, statistical aggregates, and seemingly objective indicators. Yet once stripped of its technocratic veneer, it appears for what it is: a moral assertion backed by coercive power.

3.1.1 Power as a Relationship, Not a Resource

To understand the nature of political power at the micro level, one must abandon the naïve conception of power as a thing that can be possessed, accumulated, or benevolently exercised. Power is not a stock; it is a relationship. It emerges from interactions among individuals within institutional frameworks that structure expectations and constrain behaviour. In this sense, power is always relational, contextual, and historically situated.

Political economy often treats power as exogenous. Governments are assumed to "have" power, which they then use to correct market failures, internalize externalities, or redistribute resources. Such a view obscures the fact that governmental power itself is constituted through individual compliance, acceptance, and acquiescence. Even coercive power relies on a complex web of beliefs about legitimacy, obligation, and authority. The moment these beliefs erode, power becomes naked force—and even force has limits.

From a hermeneutical perspective, power is inseparable from interpretation. Individuals comply with rules not only because of sanctions, but because they interpret those rules as legitimate, reasonable, or unavoidable. Authority, therefore, is not merely imposed; it is recognized. This recognition is never automatic. It must be continuously reproduced through narratives, symbols, and institutional rituals that reaffirm the moral standing of those who command.

This insight has profound implications for political economy. If power depends on interpretation, then policy effectiveness cannot be reduced to measurable outcomes alone. A tax may raise revenue, but at the cost of eroding the perceived legitimacy of the state. A regulation may reduce a targeted behaviour, but in doing so it may undermine individual responsibility, foster resentment, or encourage evasion. These effects are not easily captured by standard metrics, yet they are central to the long-term sustainability of political authority.

3.1.2 Authority and the Moral Claim to Obedience

Authority differs from power in that it involves a normative claim. To exercise authority is not merely to coerce, but to claim the right to be obeyed. This right may be grounded in tradition, consent, expertise, or legality, but it always rests on a moral foundation. Even the most technocratic policy implicitly asserts that obedience is justified because it serves some higher good.

The crucial question, therefore, is not whether authority exists, but how it is justified. In modern political economy, authority is often justified procedurally. If a policy emerges from democratic processes, it is deemed legitimate. If it is implemented according to the rule of law, it is considered morally acceptable. Yet procedural legitimacy does not exhaust the moral dimension of authority. A law may be procedurally valid and yet substantively unjust. A tax may be legally imposed and yet morally questionable.

This distinction is particularly important when authority extends into the realm of personal choice. When the state taxes income, regulates consumption, or penalizes certain behaviours, it is not merely coordinating collective action. It is making a judgment about what individuals may do with their own resources and bodies. Such judgments require more than procedural justification; they require a moral rationale that can withstand scrutiny.

The danger of modern political economy lies precisely in its tendency to bypass this moral scrutiny. By framing policy issues in terms of efficiency, optimization, or social welfare, it presents moral judgments as technical necessities.

The question is no longer whether the state has the right to intervene, but how effectively it can do so. Means displace ends; technique replaces ethics.

A hermeneutical approach resists this displacement. It insists that questions of authority cannot be reduced to questions of effectiveness. A policy that "works" in terms of measurable outcomes may still be illegitimate if it violates the moral agency of individuals or arrogates to the state a role it cannot justifiably claim.

3.1.3   From Individual Action to Fiscal Power

Nowhere is the tension between power, authority, and moral legitimacy more evident than in taxation. Taxation represents the most direct and pervasive intrusion of political authority into individual economic life. It is the point at which abstract notions of public finance translate into concrete obligations imposed on specific persons. Every tax bill is a moral claim: a demand that an individual surrender a portion of the fruits of his or her action for purposes defined by others.

Traditional public finance theory often treats taxation as a neutral instrument. Taxes are necessary to fund public goods, correct externalities, or redistribute income. The legitimacy of taxation is assumed rather than examined. Yet from a micro perspective, taxation is never neutral. It alters incentives, reshapes behaviour, and, more fundamentally, redefines the boundary between what belongs to the individual and what belongs to the collective.

The constitutional political economy tradition, particularly as developed by Buchanan and his collaborators, has done much to uncover the dangers inherent in this power. By modelling the state not as a benevolent maximizer of social welfare but as a potential Leviathan, this tradition forces us to confront the reality that those who wield fiscal power are themselves guided by incentives and interests. The power to tax, as famously noted, is the power to destroy—not only economic activity, but also the moral foundations of a free society.

However, even this insight must be deepened through a hermeneutical lens. The danger of taxation is not merely that it may be excessive or inefficient, but that it may erode the individual's sense of authorship over his or her own life. When taxation becomes opaque, unpredictable, or morally justified by vague appeals to social good, individuals cease to perceive themselves as responsible agents and begin to see themselves as subjects of an impersonal system.

This erosion of agency has long-term consequences that cannot be captured by fiscal statistics. It affects trust, civic engagement, and the willingness to cooperate voluntarily. It encourages strategic behaviour, evasion, and rent-seeking.

Most importantly, it transforms the relationship between the individual and the state from one of conditional consent to one of resigned compliance.

3.1.4 Competing Micro Visions

At the heart of these issues lie two competing visions of the individual in political economy. The first vision sees individuals as moral agents whose actions are guided by subjective meanings and values. In this view, the role of political institutions is primarily negative: to protect property rights, enforce contracts, and provide a stable framework within which individuals can pursue their own ends. Authority is limited, and coercion is justified only in narrowly defined circumstances.

The second vision sees individuals as objects of policy, whose behaviour must be guided, corrected, or optimized to achieve collective goals. Here, authority is expansive, and coercion is justified by reference to outcomes rather than rights. The individual's own interpretation of his or her actions is subordinated to external evaluations of harm, efficiency, or welfare.

These visions are not merely theoretical. They shape how policymakers think about taxation, regulation, and social intervention. They influence whether externalities are seen as moral conflicts requiring negotiation or as technical problems requiring correction. They determine whether humility or hubris characterizes the exercise of power.

This chapter will argue that many contemporary policy debates—particularly those surrounding taxation of "sin goods", harm reduction, and behavioural regulation—are best understood as clashes between these competing micro visions. The language of social optimum and measurable harm often serves to mask a deeper moral claim: that the state knows better than individuals how they ought to live.

3.1.5 Toward a Hermeneutical Critique of Micro Policy

A hermeneutical political economy does not deny the existence of social problems, nor does it romanticize individual choice. It recognizes that actions have consequences, that conflicts arise, and that institutions are necessary. What it denies is the possibility of a morally neutral, technocratically justified authority to engineer outcomes without regard for meaning, interpretation, and responsibility.

Such an approach demands humility—not only epistemic humility about what can be known and measured, but moral humility about what can be legitimately commanded. It calls for a re-examination of the foundations of fiscal and regulatory power, beginning from the micro level where individuals experience policy not as an abstract system, but as a concrete demand on their lives.

In the sections that follow, this critique will be developed in detail. We will examine the moral authority to tax and the constitutional limits of fiscal power; we will interrogate the concept of externalities and the fiction of a social optimum; and we will return, once again, to the themes of measurability and humility that run through this book. Throughout, the aim will not be to offer policy prescriptions, but to illuminate the competing visions that underlie them.

Political economy, when reduced to technique, becomes an instrument of domination. When restored to its hermeneutical roots, it can once again become a discipline of understanding—one that respects the dignity of the acting person and the tragic limits of human knowledge.

3.2. POWER, AUTHORITY, AND THE RIGHT TO TAX: BETWEEN COERCION AND MORAL LEGITIMACY

Few acts of political power reveal the moral foundations of a society as clearly as taxation. Unlike regulation, which often operates indirectly through permissions and prohibitions, taxation confronts the individual in the most concrete and unavoidable manner. It is not an abstract adjustment of incentives; it is a direct claim over the fruits of individual action. Each tax obligation is an embodied encounter between authority and agency, between collective claims and personal responsibility. For this reason, taxation cannot be understood merely as a fiscal instrument. It is, at its core, a moral phenomenon.

Modern political economy has systematically attempted to neutralize this moral dimension. Taxation is presented as a technical necessity, a neutral means to fund public goods, correct market failures, or achieve distributive objectives. The language employed is deliberately antiseptic: efficiency, optimal taxation, revenue sufficiency, incidence, elasticity. Yet beneath this technical vocabulary lies a far more radical assertion—the assertion that some authority possesses the right to decide how much of an individual's labour, income, or consumption may be appropriated for purposes defined externally to that individual's own ends.

A hermeneutical political economy refuses to accept this assertion as self-evident. It demands that the moral authority to tax be explicitly examined rather than silently presupposed. To ask whether taxation is efficient is a secondary question. The primary question is whether, and under what conditions, taxation is legitimate.

3.2.1 Taxation as Coercion, Not Exchange

One of the most persistent confusions in public finance is the tendency to treat taxation as a form of exchange. Taxes are described as the price paid for public goods, as a contribution to collective services, or as a membership fee for social cooperation. This analogy is deeply misleading. Exchange, in its economic sense, is voluntary. It presupposes consent, the ability to refuse, and the mutual recognition of subjective value. Taxation, by contrast, is compulsory. It is enforced by the threat of sanctions, ultimately backed by physical coercion.

This observation is not ideological; it is definitional. To deny the coercive nature of taxation is to empty the concept of coercion of meaning. The fact that taxation is administered through legal procedures rather than arbitrary violence does not alter its fundamental character. Law structures coercion; it does not eliminate it.

The coercive nature of taxation does not automatically render it unjust. All legal systems rely on coercion to some degree. The enforcement of contracts, the protection of property rights, and the punishment of crime all involve the legitimate use of force. The crucial distinction lies in the purpose and scope of that coercion. Coercion aimed at preventing aggression differs fundamentally from coercion aimed at directing individual resources toward collectively defined ends.

From a micro perspective, this distinction is decisive. When the state taxes an individual, it does not merely prevent harm to others; it actively appropriates resources that the individual has acquired through purposeful action. The justification for such appropriation cannot be derived solely from outcomes. It requires a moral argument about authority, obligation, and the limits of individual sovereignty.

3.2.2 The Moral Presuppositions of Fiscal Power

The right to tax presupposes answers to a series of moral questions that modern public finance theory prefers to leave unasked. What, if anything, does the individual owe to society simply by virtue of existing within it? Who defines the content of that obligation? On what grounds can the state claim precedence over individual plans and priorities?

Traditional welfare economics attempts to bypass these questions by appealing to aggregate outcomes. If taxation increases social welfare, reduces inequality, or corrects inefficiencies, it is deemed justified. Yet this reasoning rests on a crucial sleight of hand: it substitutes collective metrics for individual moral standing. The individual's loss is justified not because it is consented to, but because it contributes to an aggregate improvement defined by others.

A hermeneutical approach exposes the fragility of this justification. Social welfare functions do not exist independently of interpretation. They are constructed artifacts that reflect specific value judgments about whose preferences count, how they are weighted, and what outcomes are desirable. To invoke social welfare as a moral trump card is to smuggle contested ethical assumptions into technical analysis.

The constitutional political economy tradition associated with Buchanan and Brennan represents a decisive break with this technocratic moralism. By treating the state as a potential revenue-maximizing Leviathan rather than a benevolent planner, it reintroduces realism into the analysis of fiscal power. Governments are not abstract embodiments of the common good; they are collections of individuals operating under incentives. The power to tax, once granted, will tend to be expanded, exploited, and defended by those who benefit from it.

Yet even this insight remains incomplete unless it is integrated into a deeper moral anthropology. The danger of Leviathan is not only that it extracts too much, but that it reshapes the moral relationship between the individual and political authority. When taxation is justified primarily by outcomes rather than consent, individuals are gradually transformed from authors of their own economic lives into instruments of policy objectives.

3.2.3 Consent, Constitution, and the Illusion of Moral Closure

Defenders of expansive fiscal authority often appeal to consent as the ultimate source of legitimacy. In democratic societies, taxation is said to be justified because it is enacted by representatives chosen by the people. The constitution, in this view, functions as a social contract that authorizes the state to tax within specified limits.

This argument contains an element of truth, but it is frequently overstated. Consent in modern democracies is at best indirect, fragmented, and temporally distant. Individuals do not consent to specific taxes in the way they consent to contracts. They inherit fiscal obligations through membership in a political community they did not choose. Moreover, democratic processes do not eliminate coercion; they merely determine who wields it.

Buchanan's emphasis on constitutional constraints arises precisely from this recognition. If taxation is inherently coercive, then its legitimacy cannot rest on presumed benevolence. It must be bounded by rules that protect individuals against the unchecked expansion of fiscal power. Constitutional limits on taxation are not technical devices; they are moral safeguards designed to preserve individual autonomy over time.

However, even constitutionalism can become an illusion of moral closure. Written rules cannot anticipate all future contingencies, nor can they prevent the gradual normalization of fiscal overreach. As Buchanan and Wagner showed in their analysis of democratic deficit bias, fiscal institutions evolve in ways that systematically favour higher spending, higher taxation, and deferred costs. What begins as an exceptional measure becomes routine; what is justified as temporary becomes permanent.

From a hermeneutical standpoint, the erosion of fiscal restraint is not merely institutional; it is interpretative. Citizens come to reinterpret taxation not as an extraordinary intrusion requiring justification, but as a natural and unquestionable feature of social life. This shift in interpretation is perhaps the most profound victory of Leviathan.

3.2.4 Taxation and the Dignity of the Acting Person

At the micro level, the moral problem of taxation concerns dignity. To act economically is to project oneself into the future, to form plans, to assume responsibility for one's choices. Income and wealth are not merely material quantities; they are crystallizations of past action and anticipations of future possibilities. To tax is therefore to intervene in the narrative structure of individual life.

This insight is almost entirely absent from standard public finance analysis. Taxes are treated as flows and stocks, detached from the lived experience of those who pay them. Yet individuals do not experience taxation as an abstract transfer; they experience it as a constraint on their ability to pursue self-chosen ends. The higher and more opaque the tax burden, the weaker the perceived link between effort and reward, responsibility and outcome.

The erosion of this link has moral consequences. When individuals no longer perceive themselves as primary authors of their economic success or failure, responsibility is externalized. Risk-taking declines, dependence increases, and resentment grows. These effects are not anomalies; they are predictable responses to a fiscal environment that weakens the moral feedback between action and consequence.

From this perspective, the legitimacy of taxation cannot be assessed solely by reference to what the state does with the revenue. Even benevolent spending does not automatically justify coercive extraction. The question is not only whether taxation finances good outcomes, but whether it respects the moral agency of those who are taxed.

3.2.5 The Slippery Boundary Between Protection and Direction

A minimal state that taxes to protect property rights and enforce contracts operates within a fundamentally different moral universe than a state that taxes to direct behaviour. The former uses coercion to prevent coercion; the latter uses coercion to shape choices. This distinction, often blurred in policy debates, is central to a hermeneutical critique of fiscal power.

Once taxation is justified as a tool for correcting individual behaviour—discouraging "bad" consumption, incentivizing "good" choices, or engineering social outcomes—the state implicitly claims moral authority over individual ends. The individual is no longer treated as a moral agent capable of learning from experience, but as a subject requiring guidance.

This shift is rarely acknowledged explicitly. Instead, it is presented as a response to market failures, externalities, or behavioural biases. Yet the moral claim remains the same: that policymakers possess superior knowledge not only of consequences, but of what individuals ought to value.

A hermeneutical political economy insists that this claim be confronted rather than disguised. To tax is not merely to raise revenue; it is to assert authority over meaning. It is to say that certain uses of one's resources are less legitimate than others, not because they violate rights, but because they conflict with externally defined objectives.

3.2.6 Taxation Beyond Outcomes

The ultimate weakness of outcome-based justifications for taxation lies in their indifference to process. If a tax produces desirable effects, it is deemed justified, regardless of how it reshapes individual agency, expectations, and moral responsibility. Yet from a micro perspective, process matters. How outcomes are achieved is inseparable from what those outcomes mean.

A society that relies heavily on coercive fiscal instruments to achieve social goals may succeed in altering behaviour, but at the cost of infantilizing its citizens.

Responsibility is transferred upward; moral judgment is centralized. Over time, this dynamic corrodes the very social fabric that policy claims to protect.

The right to tax, therefore, cannot be treated as morally neutral. It must be continuously justified, constrained, and interpreted in light of its impact on individual agency. To ignore this dimension is to reduce political economy to social engineering.

In the next part, this analysis will be extended to the concept of externalities and the notion of social optimum. We will see how the language of harm and correction often functions as a moral shortcut—one that allows policymakers to bypass the difficult question of legitimacy by appealing to ostensibly objective measures of social cost.

3.3. EXTERNALITIES, HARM, AND THE FICTION OF THE SOCIAL OPTIMUM

Few concepts have exercised as much influence over modern micro-policy as that of externalities. They occupy a privileged position in economic pedagogy, policy analysis, and regulatory rhetoric. Externalities are routinely invoked as the decisive justification for state intervention: when individual actions impose costs on others, markets are said to fail, and political authority is called upon to restore efficiency, fairness, or social optimality. In this narrative, externalities appear as an objective defect of decentralized action, a technical anomaly that requires correction by an enlightened authority.

From a hermeneutical political economy, this narrative is deeply problematic. Not because external effects do not exist, but because the way they are conceptualized, measured, and politicized conceals fundamental moral and epistemic assumptions. The theory of externalities, as commonly deployed, transforms conflicts of interpretation into technical problems, moral disagreement into quantitative imbalance, and political judgment into administrative necessity. It thereby becomes one of the most powerful vehicles through which authority claims legitimacy over individual action.

At the micro level, the concept of externalities marks a decisive shift in how we understand social interaction. It reframes relationships between persons not as encounters among moral agents, but as flows of costs and benefits that can be aggregated, priced, and optimized. This shift is not neutral. It carries with it an implicit anthropology and a specific vision of the role of political power.

3.3.1 From Interaction to Externality: A Conceptual Transformation

In ordinary human experience, what economists label as externalities are simply interactions. Individuals live in proximity to others; their actions affect one another in countless ways. Noise, smell, aesthetic displeasure, moral offense, admiration, emulation—these are all features of social life. They are not anomalies; they are constitutive of coexistence. To live among others is to be exposed to the consequences of their choices, just as one's own choices reverberate beyond oneself.

The economic concept of externalities abstracts from this lived reality. It isolates a subset of interactions, defines them as costs or benefits imposed on third parties, and evaluates them relative to a hypothetical benchmark of efficiency. In doing so, it implicitly assumes that there exists a determinate social optimum against which actual outcomes can be judged. Deviations from this optimum are labelled failures, and policy intervention is presented as the means of correction.

This abstraction is powerful, but it is also deeply reductive. It suppresses the interpretative dimension of social interaction. What counts as a cost or a benefit is not given by nature; it depends on preferences, values, expectations, and cultural context. One person's annoyance is another's indifference; one person's pleasure is another's offense. To treat these subjective experiences as commensurable units of social cost is already to impose a particular moral and epistemic framework.

A hermeneutical approach insists that externalities are not objective facts waiting to be corrected, but interpretations of social interaction. They arise when one person judges another's action as harmful relative to some normative standard. The crucial question, therefore, is not whether external effects exist, but who has the authority to define them, to measure them, and to decide how they should be addressed.

3.3.2 The Social Optimum as a Moral Fiction

The notion of a social optimum occupies a central place in the standard treatment of externalities. Policy intervention is justified by reference to the gap between private and social costs, and the aim of intervention is to align individual behaviour with socially optimal outcomes. This framework presupposes that such an optimum can be identified, measured, and pursued through policy instruments.

From a hermeneutical perspective, this presupposition is untenable. The social optimum is not an observable state of the world; it is a constructed ideal that reflects particular normative judgments about what ought to matter and how different interests should be weighted. There is no Archimedean point from which society can be optimized without remainder.

The attempt to define a social optimum inevitably privileges some interpretations over others. It elevates certain harms to policy-relevant status while ignoring others. It assigns numerical weights to experiences that are qualitatively heterogeneous. In doing so, it transforms moral disagreement into technical disagreement and political contestation into administrative calculation.

This transformation has profound consequences. Once a social optimum is posited, deviation from it becomes a problem to be solved rather than a disagreement to be negotiated. Policy intervention appears not as a moral choice among competing visions, but as a neutral act of correction. Authority is thus naturalized, and coercion is justified as efficiency.

The fiction of the social optimum is particularly seductive because it allows policymakers to bypass the question of legitimacy. If a policy moves society closer to the optimum, it is deemed justified, regardless of how it affects individual agency, responsibility, or dignity. Outcomes displace processes; results trump rights.

3.3.3 *Externalities and the Expansion of Moral Authority*

The political power of the externalities framework lies in its capacity to convert moral claims into technical necessities. When an action is labelled as generating negative externalities, it is no longer merely undesirable; it becomes illegitimate. The individual's own evaluation of his or her action is overridden by an external assessment of social cost.

This dynamic is especially evident in policies targeting so-called "sin goods" or "pleasure consumption". Consumption choices that involve risk, indulgence, or moral controversy are routinely justified targets of taxation and regulation on the grounds that they impose costs on society. Health expenditures, productivity losses, and social burdens are invoked as measurable externalities that warrant intervention.

Yet this reasoning rests on a crucial moral leap. It assumes that the state has the right to define which consequences count as socially relevant costs and to assign responsibility for them. It presumes that individual choices can be evaluated independently of the individual's own valuation and responsibility for risk. In effect, it treats individuals not as moral agents capable of bearing the consequences of their actions, but as sources of social cost to be managed.

The harm-reduction framework developed in some of the Author's works offers a powerful critique of this approach. Rather than denying the existence of harm, it challenges the moral absolutism embedded in prohibitionist and punitive policies. It recognizes that individuals engage in risky behaviours not out of ignorance or malice, but as part of their pursuit of meaning, pleasure, and identity. To respond to such behaviours with coercion is not to eliminate harm, but to displace it—often in more destructive forms.

3.3.4 Harm, Responsibility, and Moral Agency

At the micro level, the crucial issue is not harm as such, but responsibility for harm. In a free society, individuals are presumed to be responsible for their choices and for the foreseeable consequences of those choices. This presumption underpins moral agency and personal dignity. When responsibility is collectivized through the language of externalities, this presumption is undermined.

Consider the standard argument that certain consumption choices impose costs on public health systems and therefore justify taxation or regulation. This argument implicitly assumes that individuals are not responsible for their own health outcomes, or that their responsibility is overridden by collective concern. The state steps in not merely to prevent harm to others, but to correct individuals for harming themselves in ways that generate social costs.

From a hermeneutical standpoint, this move is deeply problematic. It collapses the distinction between self-regarding and other-regarding actions, and in doing so it vastly expands the scope of legitimate intervention. Once the state assumes responsibility for mitigating the consequences of individual choices, it acquires a corresponding authority to regulate those choices. Moral authority and fiscal power thus reinforce one another.

Harm reduction offers an alternative vision. It accepts that harm cannot be eliminated from human life and that attempts to do so through coercion often exacerbate the very problems they seek to solve. Instead of moralizing behaviour, it focuses on minimizing negative consequences while preserving individual agency. This approach does not deny social concern; it redefines it in a way that respects the interpretative nature of human action.

3.3.5 Measurement, Externalities, and the Illusion of Objectivity

One of the reasons the externalities framework has been so influential is its apparent measurability. Social costs can be estimated, quantified, and incorporated into policy analysis. Numbers convey authority; they suggest objectivity and inevitability. Yet this appearance is deceptive.

The measurement of externalities involves a long chain of assumptions: about causal relationships, about counterfactual scenarios, about the valuation of life, health, and well-being. Each step in this chain reflects interpretative choices that are rarely made explicit. By the time the final figure is presented—a cost per unit consumed, a tax rate per pack, a social burden per behaviour—the moral judgments embedded in it have disappeared behind a façade of precision.

A hermeneutical political economy insists on bringing these judgments back into view. It asks not only how externalities are measured, but why certain effects are counted and others ignored. It questions the authority of those who perform the measurement and the purposes to which the measurements are put.

Most importantly, it challenges the idea that measurability confers moral legitimacy. The fact that a harm can be quantified does not mean that it can be justly coerced away. Measurement is not justification. To conflate the two is to commit a category error with profound political consequences.

3.3.6 Externalities as Conflicts, Not Failures

At the micro level, what are called externalities are often better understood as conflicts of interest or value. Neighbours disagree about noise; citizens disagree about acceptable risk; communities disagree about moral norms. These conflicts are an inevitable feature of pluralistic societies. To treat them as market failures requiring centralized correction is to misunderstand their nature.

Conflicts require negotiation, adaptation, and institutional evolution. They do not admit of final optimization. Attempts to resolve them through top-down policy often freeze one interpretation into law, marginalizing others and foreclosing learning. In this sense, the externalities framework, when coupled with coercive authority, tends to suppress rather than manage social complexity.

A hermeneutical approach favours institutional arrangements that allow for decentralized adjustment and mutual accommodation. Property rights, liability rules, and voluntary agreements provide mechanisms through which conflicts can be addressed without presuming a single social optimum. These mechanisms respect the plurality of interpretations and preserve space for moral agency.

3.3.7 The Moral Shortcut of Externalities

The enduring appeal of the externalities concept lies in its function as a moral shortcut. By labelling an action as socially costly, policymakers can bypass the difficult work of moral persuasion and proceed directly to coercion. Taxes, bans, and regulations appear not as impositions, but as corrections demanded by reason.

Yet this shortcut comes at a high price. It erodes the distinction between harm prevention and moral governance. It transforms the state from an arbiter of rights into a manager of outcomes. Over time, it fosters a political culture in which individuals are expected to conform not because they are convinced, but because deviation is penalized.

A hermeneutical political economy resists this trajectory. It insists that the legitimacy of intervention cannot be derived solely from external effects. It must be grounded in respect for individual agency, in humility about what can be known and controlled, and in a recognition of the tragic limits of social engineering.

In the next part, these themes will be brought together in a broader reflection on measurability and humility. We will return to the epistemic foundations of micro-policy and examine why the obsession with measurement so often leads to moral overreach and institutional fragility.

3.4. Again on Measurability and Humility: The Ethics of Not Knowing

Every exercise of political power presupposes a claim to knowledge. To tax, to regulate, to prohibit, or to incentivize is never merely to act; it is to assert that one knows enough about reality, about consequences, and about human behaviour to justify intervention. In modern political economy, this epistemic claim is rarely articulated explicitly. Instead, it is embedded in numbers, models, indicators, and metrics that present themselves as neutral representations of reality. Measurability becomes the surrogate for understanding, and precision substitutes for wisdom.

The recurring insistence on measurability is not an innocent methodological preference. It is a moral stance disguised as technical rigor. It expresses a belief that what matters can be measured, that what cannot be measured does not matter, and that authority may legitimately act upon what is measured as if it exhausted reality. Against this belief, a hermeneutical political economy raises a fundamental objection: social reality is not given to us as a set of quantities, but as a field of meanings. To ignore this is not merely to commit an epistemic error, but to perpetrate a moral one.

This chapter has already shown how measurability underwrites the moral authority to tax and the policy use of externalities. Here, the argument is brought to its culmination. The problem is not that measurement is impossible, nor that quantitative analysis is useless. The problem is the *pretension* that measurement confers legitimacy, and the corresponding *absence of humility* in the exercise of micro-policy.

3.4.1 Measurement as Closure

Measurement is an act of closure. To measure is to select, to delimit, and to exclude. In the natural sciences, this closure is often justified because the objects of inquiry are relatively stable and the variables of interest can be isolated with reasonable confidence. In the social sciences, and especially in political economy, such conditions do not hold. Human action is intentional, contextual, and historically situated. It is guided by expectations that evolve over time and by interpretations that cannot be fully anticipated.

Yet modern policy analysis routinely treats social phenomena as if they were amenable to the same kind of closure as physical systems. Externalities are quantified, behavioural responses are modelled, and optimal interventions are calculated. This process creates the illusion that uncertainty has been tamed and that discretion has been replaced by necessity. What remains unseen is the vast residue of meaning that escapes measurement.

From a hermeneutical standpoint, this residue is not marginal; it is central. What individuals believe, fear, hope for, and interpret cannot be reduced to data points without distortion. The attempt to do so transforms lived experience into an abstraction that is more tractable for policymakers but less faithful to reality. The danger lies not in abstraction per se, but in forgetting that abstraction has occurred.

When measurement is mistaken for understanding, policy becomes blind to its own limits. It begins to act as if the map were the territory, as if the indicator captured the phenomenon, and as if what is visible to the analyst were all that exists. This blindness is the epistemic root of policy hubris.

3.4.2 The Pretence of Knowledge Revisited

The critique of the "pretence of knowledge" is often associated with macroeconomic planning, but its relevance at the micro level is no less profound. Micro-policy interventions—taxes on specific goods, regulations of particular behaviours, targeted incentives—are often justified precisely because they appear modest, precise, and evidence-based. Their limited scope creates a false sense of epistemic security.

Yet the micro level is where complexity is most intense. Individual choices are embedded in dense networks of meaning, habit, identity, and social interaction. Small interventions can have disproportionate effects, not because individuals behave irrationally, but because they reinterpret their environment in light of new constraints. These reinterpretations cannot be modelled ex ante; they emerge through experience.

A hermeneutical political economy insists that this emergent dimension is not a flaw to be corrected, but a feature to be respected. It calls for humility in the face of complexity—not the humility of inaction, but the humility of restraint. This humility recognizes that policy interventions alter not only incentives, but narratives. They change how individuals understand their own actions and responsibilities.

When policymakers act as if they possess sufficient knowledge to fine-tune behaviour, they implicitly deny this interpretative dimension. They treat individuals as predictable responders rather than meaning-creating agents. The result is not merely policy failure, but moral displacement: responsibility shifts from the individual to the system, and agency is diluted.

3.4.3 Measurability and the Moralization of Policy

One of the most insidious effects of measurability is its role in moralizing policy while claiming neutrality. Numbers appear objective, and policies justified by numbers appear morally incontestable. If a tax reduces consumption by a measurable percentage, if a regulation lowers a quantified risk, if an intervention improves an index, then opposition can be dismissed as irrational or ideological.

This dynamic is particularly evident in policies justified by health, safety, or social cost metrics. Once a behaviour is associated with a measurable harm, it becomes morally suspect. The individual's own evaluation of risk, pleasure, or meaning is overridden by an externally imposed calculus. Moral disagreement is reframed as resistance to evidence.

From a hermeneutical perspective, this is a profound category mistake. Evidence can inform judgment, but it cannot replace it. Numbers do not speak for themselves; they speak through the interpretative frameworks that give them meaning. To present policy as dictated by data is to obscure the normative choices embedded in data selection, measurement, and interpretation.

Humility requires acknowledging this obscurity rather than exploiting it. It requires policymakers to recognize that their interventions reflect particular values and priorities, not objective necessities. It requires them to engage in moral persuasion rather than relying on technical authority.

3.4.4 The Ethics of Not Knowing

At the heart of hermeneutical political economy lies an ethics of not knowing. This is not an invitation to relativism or paralysis, but a recognition of the limits inherent in governing a society of free and responsible individuals. Not knowing does not absolve policymakers of responsibility; it constrains the scope of legitimate action.

To admit not knowing is to accept that individuals may understand their own circumstances better than distant authorities, that they may learn from experience in ways that cannot be anticipated, and that diversity of behaviour is not necessarily a problem to be solved. It is to recognize that error correction in a free society occurs primarily through decentralized processes rather than centralized design.

This ethics stands in sharp contrast to the dominant policy mindset, which treats uncertainty as a justification for intervention rather than a reason for caution. Risks must be managed, harms must be reduced, and outcomes must be optimized—even if the means of doing so undermine the very agency that allows societies to adapt.

A hermeneutical approach reverses this logic. It holds that the greater the uncertainty, the stronger the case for humility; the more complex the phenomenon, the weaker the claim to centralized control. This does not imply the absence of institutions, but it does imply institutions that enable learning rather than impose solutions.

3.4.5 Humility as a Political Virtue

Humility is rarely celebrated as a political virtue. It does not lend itself to slogans, nor does it produce easily communicable successes. Yet without humility, political power becomes self-justifying and self-expanding. The belief that problems can be measured and solved encourages ever more ambitious interventions, each one justified by the apparent success of the previous.

In the micro domain, this expansion is particularly dangerous. It gradually erodes the space of individual choice under the guise of optimization. What begins as a corrective measure becomes a normative standard; what begins as an exception becomes a rule. Over time, individuals internalize policy judgments as moral judgments, and self-regulation gives way to external control.

Humility interrupts this trajectory. It reminds policymakers that authority is provisional, that knowledge is partial, and that moral legitimacy cannot be derived from statistical significance. It re-centres political economy on the acting person rather than the managed outcome.

Conclusion: Competing Visions Revisited

The competing visions that structure this chapter now come into full view. On one side stands a vision of political economy as a science of control, grounded in measurability and confident in its capacity to optimize behaviour. In this vision, authority flows naturally from expertise, and legitimacy is secured by outcomes.

On the other side stands a hermeneutical vision that understands political economy as a science of meaning. In this vision, authority is constrained by moral limits, legitimacy rests on respect for agency, and policy is guided by humility rather than ambition. Measurement informs judgment but does not replace it; intervention is cautious, reversible, and open to revision.

These visions are incommensurable not because they disagree about techniques, but because they rest on different understandings of the human person. One treats individuals as objects of policy; the other treats them as subjects of meaning. One seeks to perfect society; the other seeks to preserve the conditions under which imperfect individuals can learn, adapt, and flourish.

To govern is to act under uncertainty. The question is not whether uncertainty can be eliminated, but how it is acknowledged. Measurability offers the comfort of apparent control, but at the cost of moral blindness. Humility offers no such comfort, but it preserves the dignity of the acting person.

A hermeneutical political economy chooses humility not as a strategy, but as a principle. It recognizes that the most dangerous policies are often those that appear most reasonable, most scientific, and most well-intentioned. Against the seduction of precision, it affirms the irreducible openness of social life.

In doing so, it reclaims political economy as a discipline not of domination, but of understanding.

Lesson 4

Fiscal Policy: Definition, Objectives, Tools

4.1. What Fiscal Policy Is: Meaning, Scope, and Intellectual Origins

Fiscal policy, in the language of standard economic theory, designates the set of governmental decisions concerning public expenditure, taxation, and borrowing, undertaken with the explicit aim of influencing economic activity. It refers, in its most elementary definition, to the management of the public budget and of the state's balance sheet. In this sense, fiscal policy is inseparable from the existence of a political authority endowed with the power to tax, to spend, and to incur liabilities on behalf of the community. It presupposes a public sector capable of collecting resources from private agents and reallocating them across time, sectors, and social groups. As such, fiscal policy is not merely a technical apparatus but an institutional practice embedded in the historical evolution of the modern state.

In contemporary textbooks, fiscal policy is commonly introduced alongside monetary policy as one of the two principal instruments of macroeconomic stabilization. While monetary policy operates primarily through the control of money supply and interest rates, fiscal policy acts directly on aggregate demand via government spending and taxation. This distinction, which appears straightforward in analytical terms, is the product of a long intellectual sedimentation. It reflects the gradual differentiation, within economic thought, between public finance as a branch concerned with revenue and expenditure, and macroeconomics as a field concerned with aggregate outcomes such as output, employment, and inflation. Fiscal policy emerges precisely at the intersection of these two traditions.

Classical political economy, from Adam Smith to David Ricardo, certainly reflected on taxation, public debt, and government expenditure, yet it did not conceptualize "fiscal policy" as an active tool for macroeconomic management. Taxes were discussed primarily in terms of fairness, efficiency, and administrative feasibility; public spending was treated largely as a necessity of governance, defence, and justice; public debt was often regarded with suspicion, as a burden imposed on future generations. The state was present, but it was not imagined as an engineer of aggregate demand. Economic order was thought to arise predominantly from market processes, guided by prices, competition, and the division of labour. Public finance belonged to the sphere of governance rather than to that of economic steering.

The conceptual birth of fiscal policy, in the modern sense, is inseparable from the Keynesian revolution. The Great Depression shattered the confidence in the self-equilibrating properties of the market economy and opened the intellectual space for a rethinking of the role of the state. With John Maynard Keynes, government budgets ceased to be viewed merely as instruments of revenue extraction and expenditure allocation; they became levers through which aggregate demand could be stabilized. Deficits and surpluses were reinterpreted not as moral or accounting failures but as functional outcomes of countercyclical management. The public budget was transformed into a macroeconomic variable.

In this new framework, fiscal policy acquired a dual identity. On the one hand, it remained rooted in the traditional concerns of public finance: who pays taxes, who receives transfers, how public goods are funded, and how debt is serviced. On the other hand, it became a macroeconomic instrument aimed at smoothing business cycles, mitigating recessions, and supporting employment. This duality persists in modern treatments. Textbooks explicitly situate fiscal policy within the macroeconomic architecture, while continuously reminding the reader that fiscal actions are constrained by incentives, institutional arrangements, and political realities.

From a standard theoretical perspective, fiscal policy is defined by three core components: government spending, taxation, and public borrowing. Government spending includes purchases of goods and services, public investment, and transfer payments. Taxation encompasses all compulsory levies imposed on individuals and firms, whether on income, consumption, property, or transactions. Public borrowing allows the government to finance expenditures in excess of current revenues, thereby shifting the fiscal burden across time. These components are unified by the government budget constraint, which states that spending must ultimately be financed through taxes, borrowing, or money creation. Although this constraint is often treated as a technical identity, it carries profound analytical and normative implications, shaping debates about sustainability, intergenerational equity, and fiscal responsibility.

In standard macroeconomic analysis, fiscal policy is often formalized through simplified models that abstract from institutional complexity. Government spending is represented as an exogenous variable, taxes as either lump-sum or distortionary levies, and deficits as residuals. These abstractions serve a pedagogical purpose: they allow economists to isolate the effects of fiscal actions on output, employment, and prices. In this sense, fiscal policy becomes a parameter that can be adjusted to observe changes in equilibrium outcomes. The government appears as a unitary actor, capable of implementing coherent policies with predictable effects.

Yet even within orthodox theory, fiscal policy is not conceived as an omnipotent instrument. Its effectiveness is conditional on context. The same increase in government spending may have radically different effects depending on whether the economy is operating below potential, whether resources are idle or fully employed, and whether private agents anticipate future tax liabilities. Modern textbook treatments emphasize that fiscal policy works best under specific circumstances, particularly during severe downturns characterized by insufficient aggregate demand. In such contexts, public spending can mobilize unused resources without displacing private activity, thereby generating a net increase in output.

This contextual understanding is central to the contemporary mainstream view. Fiscal policy is not a permanent substitute for market coordination but a contingent response to extraordinary conditions. In normal times, excessive fiscal activism may crowd out private investment, distort incentives, and accumulate unsustainable debt. In emergencies—wars, depressions, financial crises—it may represent the least costly option among imperfect alternatives. This pragmatic stance distinguishes modern textbook Keynesianism from its earlier, more ambitious formulations.

The scope of fiscal policy, as defined in standard theory, extends beyond short-term stabilization. It also encompasses long-term considerations related to growth, infrastructure, human capital, and social insurance. Public investment in education, health, and infrastructure is often justified on the grounds of positive externalities and market failures. Redistribution through taxation and transfers is defended as a means of reducing inequality and providing social insurance against risks that markets cannot efficiently insure. In this broader sense, fiscal policy overlaps with social policy, development policy, and institutional design.

However, even when fiscal policy is assigned multiple roles, mainstream economics tends to preserve a clear analytical separation between means and ends. Objectives such as growth, stability, and equity are taken as given, while fiscal instruments are evaluated in terms of their efficiency in achieving these goals. The government is implicitly assumed to possess the legitimacy to define social objectives and the technical competence to pursue them. Fiscal policy thus appears as an exercise in applied optimization, constrained by trade-offs but guided by measurable targets.

This understanding reflects the deeper epistemological orientation of modern economics, which privileges quantification, aggregation, and model-based reasoning. Fiscal policy is framed as a set of measurable interventions producing quantifiable outcomes. Deficits can be expressed as percentages of GDP; multipliers can be estimated econometrically; debt sustainability can be assessed through ratios and projections. The complexity of social reality is translated into indicators and parameters. This translation is not perceived as problematic within the standard approach; on the contrary, it is regarded as the very condition of scientific rigor.

Historically, the consolidation of fiscal policy as a central domain of economic analysis coincided with the expansion of the modern welfare state. As governments assumed responsibility for social security, unemployment insurance, healthcare, and pensions, public budgets grew in size and complexity. Fiscal decisions began to affect not only macroeconomic aggregates but also the life trajectories of individuals. Taxes and transfers shaped incentives, expectations, and social norms. The fiscal state became a pervasive presence in economic life.

Standard theory responds to this expansion by refining its analytical tools. Concepts such as automatic stabilizers, fiscal multipliers, and structural deficits are introduced to capture the dynamic interaction between the economy and the budget. Automatic stabilizers, such as progressive taxes and unemployment benefits, are praised for dampening fluctuations without discretionary intervention. Structural deficits are distinguished from cyclical deficits to assess the underlying stance of fiscal policy. These refinements illustrate the adaptability of the mainstream framework and its capacity to incorporate institutional details without abandoning its core assumptions.

At the same time, the modern treatment of fiscal policy remains deeply shaped by the macroeconomic paradigm within which it operates. Aggregate demand and aggregate supply serve as the primary lenses through which fiscal actions are evaluated. Government spending increases aggregate demand; taxes reduce disposable income; deficits stimulate output when private demand is insufficient. The economy is portrayed as a system that can be nudged toward equilibrium through calibrated interventions. Fiscal policy is one of the hands on the control panel.

This image of control, however moderated by caveats and qualifications, is constitutive of the standard definition of fiscal policy. To speak of fiscal policy is already to presuppose a certain vision of the economy: one in which aggregate variables are meaningful, causal relationships are stable enough to be exploited, and policy instruments can be designed to achieve predefined outcomes. These presuppositions are rarely made explicit at the introductory level. They form the tacit background against which fiscal policy is taught and discussed.

This section has deliberately remained within this orthodox horizon. Its purpose has been to reconstruct, sympathetically and faithfully, the standard understanding of fiscal policy as it emerges from mainstream economic theory and modern textbooks. Fiscal policy appears here as a legitimate, if imperfect, tool of macroeconomic management; as an institutional practice grounded in the fiscal powers of the state; and as a domain in which economic analysis seeks to inform political decision-making. The deeper questions raised by this vision—about knowledge, legitimacy, and the meaning of policy itself—will be approached only later. For now, it is sufficient to have clarified what fiscal policy is understood to be, before asking whether it can be what it claims to be.

4.2. The Objectives of Fiscal Policy in Orthodox Theory

Within standard economic theory, fiscal policy is not defined merely by its instruments but, more fundamentally, by the objectives it is presumed to serve. These objectives provide the normative and analytical justification for public intervention through taxation, spending, and borrowing. They supply the reasons why fiscal policy exists as a distinct domain of economic analysis and why it is taught, discussed, and evaluated as a legitimate component of macroeconomic governance. In orthodox treatments, objectives precede tools: one must first identify what fiscal policy is meant to accomplish before assessing how effectively it does so.

The conventional framework identifies three broad objectives of fiscal policy: macroeconomic stabilization, allocative efficiency, and distributive justice. This tripartite structure, while often presented as a tidy taxonomy, reflects a long intellectual process through which economists have attempted to reconcile positive analysis with normative concerns. It also mirrors the evolution of the modern state, whose fiscal activity has progressively expanded from the provision of core public goods to the management of economic fluctuations and the pursuit of social objectives.

The stabilization objective occupies a central place in modern macroeconomics. Fiscal policy is expected to mitigate the amplitude of business cycles by counteracting fluctuations in aggregate demand. When private spending collapses during a recession, expansionary fiscal policy—higher government spending or lower taxes—is intended to sustain demand, limit unemployment, and prevent deflationary spirals. Conversely, when the economy overheats, contractionary fiscal policy may be used to restrain demand and curb inflationary pressures. This vision of fiscal policy as a countercyclical stabilizer is one of the most enduring legacies of Keynesian economics.

In contemporary textbook treatments stabilization is presented not as a permanent mode of intervention but as a conditional response to specific macroeconomic circumstances. The emphasis is placed on context: fiscal policy is most justified when monetary policy is constrained, when interest rates approach the zero lower bound, or when shocks primarily affect aggregate demand rather than productive capacity. The objective is not to fine-tune the economy continuously but to act decisively in moments of acute disequilibrium.

Stabilization is typically framed in terms of measurable macroeconomic variables. Output gaps, unemployment rates, inflation, and growth trajectories serve as indicators of whether the economy is operating above or below potential. Fiscal policy is evaluated according to its ability to close output gaps, reduce involuntary unemployment, and restore growth. In this analytical setting, success and failure are defined quantitatively. The effectiveness of fiscal policy becomes a matter of estimating multipliers, timing interventions appropriately, and minimizing leakages through imports or savings.

Alongside stabilization, orthodox theory assigns fiscal policy an allocative role. This objective derives from welfare economics and the recognition that markets, while powerful coordination mechanisms, may fail to allocate resources efficiently under certain conditions. Public goods, externalities, and natural monopolies constitute the canonical cases in which private markets are unable to deliver socially optimal outcomes. Fiscal policy, through targeted spending and taxation, is expected to correct these failures.

Public goods, defined by non-rivalry and non-excludability, cannot be efficiently provided through voluntary market transactions. National defence, basic infrastructure, and certain forms of knowledge production exemplify this category. Fiscal policy enables their provision by pooling resources through taxation and allocating them collectively. The allocative objective here is not redistribution in the narrow sense but the facilitation of activities that enhance overall welfare and would otherwise be undersupplied.

Externalities further expand the allocative justification for fiscal intervention. When private actions impose costs or benefits on others that are not reflected in market prices, the resulting allocation deviates from the social optimum. Taxes, subsidies, and public spending are proposed as instruments to internalize these externalities. Pollution taxes, subsidies for education, and public health expenditures are routinely cited examples. Fiscal policy thus appears as a corrective mechanism, aligning private incentives with social costs and benefits.

In this allocative dimension, objectives are framed in efficiency terms. The benchmark is Pareto optimality or, more realistically, improvements in social surplus. Fiscal policy is justified insofar as it moves the economy closer to an efficient allocation of resources. The language is technocratic: distortions are identified, corrective measures are designed, and outcomes are assessed relative to an abstract social optimum. The legitimacy of fiscal intervention is grounded in the presumed existence of such an optimum and in the capacity of policymakers to approximate it.

The third major objective of fiscal policy in orthodox theory is redistribution. Markets generate income distributions that reflect differences in endowments, skills, luck, and bargaining power. While these distributions may be efficient in a narrow economic sense, they are not necessarily regarded as socially acceptable. Fiscal policy is therefore assigned the task of redistributing income and wealth to achieve greater equity, reduce poverty, and provide social insurance.

Redistribution is typically justified on both ethical and pragmatic grounds. Ethical arguments appeal to notions of fairness, social justice, or equal opportunity. Pragmatic arguments emphasize the role of redistribution in maintaining social cohesion, political stability, and aggregate demand. Progressive taxation and transfer programs are portrayed as mechanisms through which society expresses collective preferences regarding inequality and risk-sharing.

Within standard theory, redistribution is treated as a distinct objective, analytically separable from stabilization and allocation. Taxes and transfers are evaluated according to their distributive impact, often using measures such as the Gini coefficient or poverty rates. The trade-off between equity and efficiency is acknowledged but not regarded as insurmountable. Well-designed fiscal systems are said to achieve redistribution with minimal distortion to incentives, particularly when redistribution targets income rather than productive activity.

These three objectives—stabilization, allocation, and redistribution—are often presented as complementary, yet orthodox theory recognizes that tensions may arise among them. Expansionary fiscal policy aimed at stabilization may increase public debt, potentially constraining future redistribution or investment. Taxes designed to redistribute income may distort labour supply or investment decisions, affecting allocative efficiency. Public spending programs may serve redistributive goals while failing to enhance productivity or growth. The art of fiscal policy, within the standard paradigm, consists in managing these trade-offs.

To navigate these tensions, orthodox theory increasingly emphasizes rules, frameworks, and institutional constraints. Fiscal rules, such as deficit ceilings or debt limits, are justified as means of anchoring expectations and preventing excessive discretion. Independent fiscal councils are proposed to enhance transparency and discipline. Medium-term budget frameworks seek to align short-term stabilization with long-term sustainability. These institutional innovations are presented as refinements that allow fiscal policy to pursue its objectives without succumbing to political opportunism.

Underlying this entire framework is a specific conception of policy rationality. Objectives are assumed to be identifiable, coherent, and aggregable. Society is presumed to possess preferences regarding stability, efficiency, and equity, which can be translated into policy goals. Policymakers are viewed as agents tasked with selecting the appropriate mix of fiscal instruments to achieve these goals, subject to constraints. Economic analysis provides guidance by clarifying causal relationships and quantifying expected outcomes.

In this sense, the objectives of fiscal policy are inseparable from the broader epistemology of mainstream economics. They presuppose that economic reality can be sufficiently understood through aggregate indicators and that normative judgments can be operationalized through policy targets. The distinction between ends and means is maintained: economics advises on means, while society—or its political representatives—chooses ends. Fiscal policy occupies the space where these two domains intersect.

It is important to note that orthodox theory does not deny the complexity of fiscal objectives. Textbook discussions increasingly acknowledge uncertainty, political frictions, and implementation problems. Yet these complications are treated as constraints on optimization rather than as challenges to the very formulation of objectives. Stabilization, allocation, and redistribution remain the guiding stars of fiscal policy, even when their precise realization is acknowledged to be imperfect.

This section has therefore reconstructed the objectives of fiscal policy as they are conventionally understood within mainstream economics. Fiscal policy is expected to stabilize the macroeconomy, correct market failures, and redistribute income in accordance with societal preferences. These objectives provide the justificatory backbone of fiscal intervention and shape the evaluation of fiscal actions. Only once these objectives are clearly articulated can one turn to the instruments through which they are pursued, and to the conditions under which they succeed or fail.

4.3. THE INSTRUMENTS OF FISCAL POLICY: TAXES, SPENDING, DEFICITS, AND DEBT

Having clarified the objectives assigned to fiscal policy within orthodox economic theory, it is now possible to turn to the instruments through which those objectives are pursued. In standard treatments, fiscal policy is not an abstract aspiration but a concrete set of actions implemented through the public budget. These actions are conventionally grouped into four interrelated domains: government spending, taxation, budget balances, and public debt. Together, they constitute the operational core of fiscal policy and define the channels through which the state intervenes in economic life.

Government spending is the most visible and, in many respects, the most intuitive fiscal instrument. It encompasses the direct purchase of goods and services by the public sector, public investment in infrastructure and capital formation, and transfer payments to households and firms. In macroeconomic analysis, government spending enters aggregate demand directly. An increase in public expenditure raises total demand for goods and services, thereby stimulating production and employment, at least in the short run. This directness explains why spending is often portrayed as the most powerful fiscal lever, particularly in times of economic distress.

Orthodox theory distinguishes carefully among different categories of public spending. Purchases of goods and services, such as infrastructure projects or public-sector wages, are treated as direct injections into aggregate demand. Transfer payments, by contrast, affect demand indirectly by altering disposable income. Their impact depends on the marginal propensity to consume of recipients. Public investment occupies a special position, as it is expected not only to stimulate short-term demand but also to enhance long-term productive capacity. Textbook discussions emphasize that the composition of spending matters as much as its level.

Within this framework, the effectiveness of government spending is commonly analyzed through the concept of the fiscal multiplier. The multiplier measures the total change in output resulting from an initial change in public expenditure. A multiplier greater than one implies that government spending generates additional rounds of private spending, amplifying its initial impact. Orthodox theory recognizes that the size of the multiplier is not fixed. It depends on structural features of the economy, such as openness to trade, the responsiveness of monetary policy, the degree of slack in labour and capital markets, and the expectations of private agents.

Taxation constitutes the second major instrument of fiscal policy. Taxes finance public spending, shape incentives, and influence the distribution of income. In macroeconomic models, taxes affect aggregate demand by altering disposable income and consumption. A reduction in taxes increases house-holds' after-tax income, potentially boosting consumption and investment. An increase in taxes has the opposite effect, restraining demand. From this perspective, tax policy operates symmetrically to spending, though often with a weaker and more uncertain impact.

Standard theory distinguishes among different types of taxes according to their bases and behavioural effects. Income taxes, consumption taxes, payroll taxes, and property taxes each have distinct implications for labour supply, saving, and investment. Orthodox analysis places considerable emphasis on the distortionary effects of taxation. Taxes are said to create wedges between private and social returns, potentially discouraging productive activity. The challenge of tax policy, within this paradigm, is to raise sufficient revenue while minimizing efficiency losses.

This concern with distortion gives rise to the ideal of broad tax bases and low marginal rates. Lump-sum taxes, which do not alter behaviour, are often used as analytical benchmarks, even though they are acknowledged to be unrealistic and politically infeasible. In practice, fiscal systems rely on a mix of taxes that balance revenue needs, equity considerations, and administrative constraints. Orthodox theory evaluates these systems by comparing their efficiency costs and distributive effects, seeking designs that approximate optimal taxation.

Taxes also play a crucial role in automatic stabilization. Progressive income taxes reduce disposable income more than proportionally during expansions and less than proportionally during recessions, thereby dampening fluctuations in aggregate demand. This stabilizing property is often praised for operating without discretionary intervention. Automatic stabilizers are seen as a way of reconciling stabilization objectives with concerns about policy lags and political delays.

Government spending and taxation together determine the budget balance. When expenditures exceed revenues, the government runs a deficit; when revenues exceed expenditures, it runs a surplus. In orthodox macroeconomics, deficits and surpluses are not judged intrinsically but contextually. A deficit may be appropriate during a recession, while a surplus may be desirable during an expansion. The budget balance thus becomes a policy variable, adjusted over the business cycle to achieve stabilization objectives.

To assess fiscal stance more accurately, mainstream analysis distinguishes between cyclical and structural components of the budget balance. The cyclical component reflects automatic responses of revenues and expenditures to economic conditions, while the structural component represents the underlying fiscal position at a given level of output. This distinction allows economists to evaluate whether a deficit reflects deliberate expansionary policy or merely the effect of a downturn. Structural balances are often used as indicators of fiscal sustainability and discipline.

Public debt is the cumulative result of past deficits. It represents the stock of outstanding government liabilities and serves as the intertemporal dimension of fiscal policy. Orthodox theory treats public debt as a means of smoothing taxes over time and financing expenditures whose benefits extend to future generations. Borrowing allows the government to avoid sharp tax increases or spending cuts in response to temporary shocks. In this sense, debt is portrayed as a rational instrument of intertemporal allocation.

At the same time, public debt introduces constraints and risks. Interest payments absorb fiscal resources, potentially crowding out other expenditures. High debt levels may raise concerns about sustainability, leading to higher borrowing costs or loss of market confidence. Orthodox analysis emphasizes that debt must be evaluated relative to the economy's capacity to service it, often measured by the debt-to-GDP ratio. Sustainability is framed as a matter of ensuring that debt grows no faster than the economy in the long run.

The interaction between deficits, debt, and private behaviour occupies a prominent place in orthodox discussions. The concept of crowding out captures the idea that government borrowing may displace private investment by raising interest rates. When the economy operates near full capacity, expansionary fiscal policy may simply reallocate resources rather than increase total output. In such cases, deficits are seen as ineffective or even counterproductive. This concern reinforces the view that fiscal policy should be reserved for periods of slack.

Another influential idea in this domain is Ricardian equivalence. According to this proposition, forward-looking households may anticipate that government deficits imply future taxes and therefore increase saving in response to fiscal expansion, neutralizing its effect on demand. While orthodox theory recognizes that the strict conditions required for Ricardian equivalence are rarely met in practice, the concept serves as a caution against assuming automatic effectiveness of fiscal policy. Expectations matter, and fiscal instruments operate within an intertemporal framework shaped by beliefs about future policy.

The orthodox toolkit also includes fiscal rules and constraints designed to discipline the use of these instruments. Balanced-budget rules, debt ceilings, and expenditure limits are justified as mechanisms to prevent excessive deficits and debt accumulation. Such rules are said to enhance credibility, reduce uncertainty, and align fiscal policy with long-term objectives. Within this view, rules do not negate the role of fiscal policy but structure it, constraining discretion in normal times while allowing flexibility in exceptional circumstances.

Across all these instruments, a common analytical logic prevails. Fiscal policy is understood as a set of levers that affect aggregate variables through identifiable channels. Government spending injects demand; taxes withdraw demand; deficits shift resources across time; debt embodies intertemporal choices. Each instrument has predictable effects, conditional on assumptions about behaviour, institutions, and expectations. The task of economic analysis is to clarify these effects and guide policymakers in selecting the appropriate mix.

Yet even within this orthodox framework, the use of fiscal instruments is accompanied by an awareness of limits. Implementation lags, political constraints, and uncertainty about multipliers are acknowledged as practical challenges. The timing of spending projects, the legislative process of tax changes, and the responsiveness of private agents introduce frictions that complicate policy execution. These issues, however, are generally treated as technical problems to be mitigated rather than as fundamental challenges to the concept of fiscal policy itself.

This section has presented the instruments of fiscal policy as they are conventionally understood in mainstream economics. Taxes, spending, deficits, and debt form an integrated system through which the state seeks to influence economic outcomes. They are analyzed with precision, embedded in formal models, and evaluated against clearly defined objectives. This instrumental vision of fiscal policy sets the stage for examining how these tools are deployed over the business cycle and how they interact with broader macroeconomic dynamics.

4.4. FISCAL POLICY AND THE BUSINESS CYCLE: ORTHODOX THEORY AND PRACTICE

Within the standard macroeconomic framework, fiscal policy finds its most explicit and most widely discussed application in relation to the business cycle. Economic fluctuations—periodic expansions and contractions in output, employment, and income—constitute the empirical phenomenon that most forcefully motivates the use of fiscal instruments. Orthodox theory does not deny the cyclical nature of capitalist economies; rather, it seeks to explain fluctuations and to determine whether, when, and how public intervention can mitigate their social and economic costs. Fiscal policy is thus presented as a response to instability rather than as a permanent substitute for market coordination.

The modern treatment of business cycles distinguishes sharply between normal fluctuations and extraordinary disruptions. In ordinary times, cyclical movements are often interpreted as the outcome of changing preferences, technological shocks, or sectoral reallocations. In such circumstances, the role of fiscal policy is typically regarded as limited. Markets are presumed capable of adjusting, albeit imperfectly, through price changes, investment responses, and labour mobility. Fiscal intervention, if excessive, risks distorting these adjustment processes and generating inefficiencies. This cautious stance reflects the influence of both classical and neoclassical traditions within contemporary macroeconomics.

The justification for active fiscal policy becomes more compelling in the presence of severe downturns. Recessions characterized by widespread unemployment, idle capacity, and collapsing demand challenge the assumption that market forces alone will restore equilibrium in a timely manner. It is in this context that orthodox theory assigns fiscal policy a central stabilizing role. Expansionary fiscal measures are expected to counteract deficiencies in aggregate demand, arrest downward spirals, and shorten the duration of economic slumps.

Keynesian economics provides the intellectual foundation for this view. When private consumption and investment fall simultaneously, total demand may decline below the level required to sustain full employment. Prices and wages may not adjust quickly enough to restore balance, particularly in the presence of nominal rigidities, debt contracts, and pessimistic expectations. Fiscal policy, by injecting demand directly into the economy, can compensate for the collapse of private spending. Government becomes the spender of last resort.

Contemporary orthodox treatments refine this argument by specifying the conditions under which fiscal intervention is most effective. Fiscal policy is said to work best when the economy operates significantly below potential output and when monetary policy is constrained. The zero lower bound on nominal interest rates, for example, limits the capacity of central banks to stimulate demand through conventional means. In such circumstances, fiscal expansion is presented as a necessary complement—or even a temporary substitute—for monetary policy. This reasoning features prominently in modern textbook discussions.

In these analyses, the concept of slack is crucial. When labour and capital are underutilized, government spending does not merely reallocate resources; it activates resources that would otherwise remain idle. The risk of crowding out private activity is therefore reduced. Expansionary fiscal policy can raise output and employment without generating significant inflationary pressures. This argument underpins the orthodox defence of fiscal stimulus during deep recessions and financial crises.

The experience of the Great Depression occupies a privileged place in this narrative. It is frequently cited as the paradigmatic case in which expansionary fiscal policy was both justified and necessary. Orthodox interpretations emphasize that the Depression was primarily a demand-driven phenomenon and that the scale of unemployment was such that crowding out was minimal. Although historians and economists continue to debate the relative importance of fiscal and monetary factors, mainstream textbooks tend to regard the expansion of government spending during the 1930s as a crucial step toward recovery.

More recent crises, including the global financial crisis of 2008–2009, have reinforced this perspective. The collapse of financial intermediation and the sudden contraction of private demand revived concerns about deflationary spirals and prolonged stagnation. Fiscal stimulus packages were widely implemented, justified by the extraordinary nature of the shock and the limits of monetary policy. Orthodox theory interprets these interventions as consistent with its core principles: exceptional measures for exceptional times.

At the same time, standard analysis stresses that fiscal policy is subject to significant timing issues. Recognition lags, decision lags, and implementation lags complicate the use of discretionary fiscal measures. By the time a recession is identified, legislation enacted, and spending deployed, economic conditions may have changed. These lags raise the risk that fiscal policy will be procyclical rather than countercyclical, exacerbating fluctuations instead of smoothing them. This concern motivates the emphasis on automatic stabilizers as a preferable first line of defence.

Automatic stabilizers operate through existing fiscal structures rather than discretionary decisions. Progressive taxes reduce disposable income more during expansions and less during contractions, while unemployment benefits and social transfers increase automatically when employment falls. These mechanisms are praised for responding quickly to economic changes without requiring political intervention. In orthodox theory, they embody a form of built-in fiscal responsiveness that mitigates cycles while avoiding the pitfalls of discretionary action.

Discretionary fiscal policy nevertheless retains a role in severe downturns. Orthodox treatments emphasize that the scale of some shocks exceeds the capacity of automatic stabilizers. In such cases, deliberate increases in spending or targeted tax cuts may be necessary to restore confidence and demand. The challenge lies in designing interventions that are timely, temporary, and targeted. Timeliness ensures that stimulus arrives when it is needed; temporariness reduces concerns about long-term debt accumulation; targeting aims to maximize multipliers by directing resources toward agents with high propensities to spend.

Fiscal policy over the business cycle is also analyzed in relation to expectations. Private agents form beliefs about future taxes, spending, and economic conditions. These beliefs influence consumption and investment decisions in the present. Orthodox theory acknowledges that poorly communicated or inconsistent fiscal actions may undermine confidence and reduce effectiveness. Conversely, credible commitments to countercyclical policy may stabilize expectations and amplify the impact of fiscal measures. Credibility thus becomes an integral component of effective fiscal management.

The interaction between fiscal and monetary policy is another central theme. Orthodox macroeconomics increasingly emphasizes policy coordination. Monetary policy is typically regarded as the primary stabilization tool in normal times, due to its speed and flexibility. Fiscal policy is seen as a secondary instrument, activated when monetary policy is insufficient or constrained. Coordination problems may arise when fiscal expansion conflicts with monetary tightening or when policy signals send mixed messages to markets. Effective stabilization requires coherence between fiscal and monetary authorities.

In expansionary phases of the business cycle, orthodox theory adopts a more restrained view of fiscal policy. As output approaches potential and unemployment declines, the risks associated with expansionary fiscal measures increase. Inflationary pressures may emerge, and crowding out becomes more likely. In such contexts, contractionary fiscal policy—reducing deficits or running surpluses—is often recommended. The objective shifts from stimulating demand to preserving stability and rebuilding fiscal space for future downturns.

This countercyclical ideal, however, is recognized as difficult to implement politically. Governments may find it easier to expand spending or cut taxes during recessions than to reverse these measures during booms. Orthodox analysis therefore emphasizes institutional mechanisms designed to enforce discipline, such as fiscal rules and medium-term frameworks. These mechanisms aim to align actual fiscal behavior with the theoretical ideal of countercyclical policy.

Across these discussions, the business cycle functions as the temporal structure within which fiscal policy is evaluated. Fiscal actions are judged not in isolation but in relation to the phase of the cycle and the nature of the underlying shock. Recessions call for expansion; booms call for restraint. This temporal logic is central to the orthodox conception of fiscal policy as a stabilizing force rather than a source of persistent distortion.

This section has thus reconstructed the mainstream understanding of fiscal policy as a cyclical instrument. Fiscal intervention is justified primarily as a response to macroeconomic instability, particularly in severe downturns. Its effectiveness depends on context, timing, expectations, and coordination with monetary policy. While orthodox theory acknowledges limitations and risks, it retains confidence in the capacity of fiscal policy to mitigate the social costs of economic fluctuations under appropriate conditions.

4.5. FISCAL POLICY, INCENTIVES, INSTITUTIONS, AND POLITICAL ECONOMY IN ORTHODOX THEORY

As orthodox economic theory matured in its treatment of fiscal policy, it became increasingly clear that the effectiveness of fiscal instruments could not be assessed solely through mechanical models of aggregate demand and supply. Taxes, spending, deficits, and debt operate within a social and institutional environment shaped by incentives, political constraints, and historical arrangements. Modern mainstream analysis therefore integrates fiscal policy into a broader framework that acknowledges the role of institutions and political economy, while still maintaining the analytical core of the standard paradigm.

At the heart of this integration lies the recognition that fiscal policy alters incentives. Taxes influence decisions regarding work, saving, investment, and risk-taking. Public spending shapes expectations about income security, social mobility, and the role of the state. Transfers affect labour market participation and household behaviour. Orthodox theory does not deny these effects; on the contrary, it treats them as central to the evaluation of fiscal measures. Fiscal policy is not neutral with respect to behaviour, and its success depends on how individuals and firms respond to the incentives it creates.

This incentive-based perspective reflects the broader methodological commitment of mainstream economics to rational choice. Individuals are assumed to respond systematically to changes in relative prices, including the implicit prices created by taxes and subsidies. Higher marginal tax rates on labour income may reduce labour supply; generous unemployment benefits may lengthen job search; investment tax credits may stimulate capital formation. Fiscal policy is thus analyzed as a set of signals that modify the opportunity sets facing economic agents.

Within orthodox theory, this focus on incentives generates a persistent concern with efficiency. Redistribution and stabilization are legitimate objectives, but they must be pursued in ways that minimize unintended behavioural distortions. The challenge is not whether fiscal policy should influence behaviour—it inevitably does—but whether it does so in a manner consistent with broader economic goals. This concern animates debates over optimal taxation, welfare design, and the structure of social insurance.

The incentive perspective also informs orthodox critiques of certain fiscal practices. Permanent increases in government spending financed by distortionary taxation may discourage private investment and innovation. Poorly designed subsidies may entrench inefficiencies or create dependency. Tax systems riddled with exemptions and loopholes may generate rent-seeking behaviour. These critiques do not reject fiscal policy as such; they seek to improve its design by aligning incentives more closely with stated objectives.

As the analysis of incentives deepened, orthodox theory increasingly incorporated insights from public choice and political economy. Fiscal policy is not implemented by a benevolent social planner but by political actors operating within democratic or quasi-democratic institutions. Voters, politicians, bureaucrats, and interest groups all have incentives that shape fiscal outcomes. Budgetary decisions reflect not only economic considerations but also electoral pressures, lobbying, and institutional constraints.

Public choice theory challenges the assumption that fiscal objectives are pursued impartially. Politicians may favour visible spending projects that yield electoral benefits, while postponing the costs through borrowing. Tax preferences may be granted to organized interests rather than designed according to efficiency principles. Deficits may persist not because they are optimal but because the political costs of consolidation exceed the perceived benefits. Orthodox economics incorporates these insights to explain deviations from the ideal of countercyclical and disciplined fiscal policy.

This political dimension does not invalidate the orthodox framework; rather, it complicates it. Fiscal policy is still evaluated in terms of stabilization, allocation, and redistribution, but the gap between theoretical prescriptions and observed outcomes is attributed to institutional and political frictions. The task of economic analysis becomes one of institutional design: how to create rules and frameworks that align political incentives with economic objectives.

Fiscal institutions play a central role in this endeavour. Budgetary procedures, fiscal rules, and oversight mechanisms are treated as determinants of fiscal performance. Balanced-budget requirements, debt ceilings, and expenditure rules are justified as devices to constrain opportunistic behaviour and enhance credibility. Independent fiscal councils are proposed to provide unbiased analysis and inform public debate. Medium-term expenditure frameworks aim to shift the focus from short-term electoral cycles to long-term sustainability.

Orthodox theory emphasizes that institutions matter because they shape expectations. Predictable fiscal frameworks reduce uncertainty for households and firms, facilitating planning and investment. Credible commitments to fiscal discipline lower borrowing costs and stabilize financial markets. In this sense, institutions are not merely administrative details but integral components of effective fiscal policy.

The concept of time inconsistency further illustrates the importance of institutions. Governments may promise fiscal restraint in the future while succumbing to expansionary pressures in the present. Rational agents anticipate this behaviour and adjust their expectations accordingly, reducing the effectiveness of policy announcements. Institutional constraints are proposed as solutions to this problem, binding future policymakers and enhancing credibility. Once again, the orthodox response is not to abandon fiscal policy but to embed it within robust institutional arrangements.

Another dimension of the orthodox treatment concerns intergenerational considerations. Public debt shifts fiscal burdens across time, raising questions about fairness between current and future taxpayers. Orthodox analysis frames this issue in terms of intertemporal optimization. Borrowing is justified when it finances investments that benefit future generations or smooths temporary shocks. Persistent deficits financing current consumption, by contrast, are criticized as imposing unjustified costs on the future. Fiscal institutions are therefore expected to safeguard intergenerational equity.

Despite this growing attention to incentives and institutions, orthodox theory retains a distinctive separation between economics and politics. Political economy is introduced to explain why fiscal outcomes may diverge from optimal prescriptions, not to question the legitimacy of those prescriptions themselves. The objectives of fiscal policy remain defined in economic terms, and the role of institutions is to facilitate their achievement. Politics is treated as a constraint, not as a constitutive element of policy meaning.

This separation is reflected in the normative posture of mainstream analysis. Economists provide guidance on how fiscal policy should be designed to achieve given objectives under given constraints. Whether those objectives are chosen appropriately, or whether the authority to choose them is legitimate, lies outside the scope of orthodox economics. Fiscal policy is thus framed as a technical response to economic problems, tempered by an awareness of political realities but not fundamentally altered by them.

This section has therefore completed the orthodox account of fiscal policy by situating its instruments within a landscape of incentives, institutions, and political constraints. Fiscal policy is no longer portrayed as a simple lever but as a complex process mediated by behaviour and governance. Yet the underlying vision remains intact: fiscal policy is a legitimate and potentially effective tool for achieving macroeconomic and social objectives, provided it is designed intelligently and embedded within appropriate institutional frameworks.

With this, the traditional exposition reaches its natural conclusion. The objectives, instruments, cyclical logic, and institutional context of fiscal policy have been presented as they are understood within standard economic theory. Only now, after this reconstruction, does it become possible to step back and raise more fundamental questions—not about the technical execution of fiscal policy, but about its epistemological foundations, its moral assumptions, and its claim to legitimacy.

4.6. A Preliminary Hermeneutical Critique of Fiscal Policy

Having reconstructed the orthodox understanding of fiscal policy—its definition, objectives, instruments, cyclical logic, and institutional embedding—it becomes possible to step back and ask a different kind of question. The question is no longer whether fiscal policy works under given assumptions, or how it might be improved through better design, but what kind of knowledge, authority, and vision of human action are presupposed by the very idea of fiscal policy as conventionally understood. This shift in perspective does not aim to refute the mainstream framework in its own terms. Rather, it seeks to illuminate the horizon within which that framework operates, and to identify the limits that arise from its underlying epistemology.

Orthodox fiscal policy rests on a conception of the economy as an object that can be acted upon from the outside. Aggregate demand, output gaps, multipliers, and debt ratios are treated as variables whose movements can be

influenced through calibrated interventions. This image of the economy as
a system responsive to policy inputs is not accidental; it reflects the broader
ambition of modern economics to emulate the natural sciences. Fiscal policy
becomes meaningful insofar as economic reality is assumed to be sufficiently
stable, measurable, and predictable to permit purposeful control. The economy,
in this view, is not merely interpreted but managed.

From a hermeneutical standpoint, this presupposition immediately raises a
tension. Economic reality is constituted by human action, and human action
is meaningful before it is measurable. Individuals do not respond mechanically
to fiscal stimuli; they interpret them. Taxes, transfers, and public spending
are not neutral signals but messages whose meaning depends on expectations,
narratives, and historical experience. Orthodox theory acknowledges expectations, yet it treats them as variables to be incorporated into models rather
than as expressions of situated understanding. The interpretative dimension
of economic life is thus reduced to a parameter.

The objectives of fiscal policy reveal a similar reduction. Stabilization, allocation, and redistribution are presented as technical goals, defined in terms of
measurable outcomes. Yet these objectives presuppose prior judgments about
what counts as stability, efficiency, or fairness. Orthodox theory assumes that
such judgments can be aggregated into social preferences and translated into
policy targets. The authority to define these objectives is taken for granted,
assigned implicitly to the political process, while economics concerns itself
with the means. From a hermeneutical perspective, however, the separation
between ends and means is far less clear. The choice of objectives already
embodies a particular interpretation of social order and human flourishing.

Consider stabilization. To stabilize output around a trend is to privilege
a certain conception of normality and deviation. Business cycles are framed
as disturbances to be corrected rather than as expressions of entrepreneurial discovery, structural change, and temporal coordination. Fiscal policy, in
seeking to smooth fluctuations, implicitly endorses a vision of economic life
in which volatility is primarily a cost rather than a source of learning. This
vision is not self-evident; it reflects a particular interpretation of economic
time and uncertainty.

Similarly, the allocative role of fiscal policy relies on the notion of a social
optimum against which market outcomes can be judged. Externalities and
public goods are defined relative to this benchmark, and fiscal instruments
are deployed to move the economy closer to it. Yet the social optimum is a
construct, not an observable fact. It emerges from a model that abstracts from
the interpretative processes through which individuals discover opportunities,

redefine preferences, and create new forms of coordination. The hermeneutical critique does not deny the existence of coordination problems; it questions the assumption that these problems can be diagnosed and corrected from a standpoint external to the process itself.

Redistribution, finally, brings the normative dimension into sharp relief. Orthodox theory treats redistribution as a legitimate objective chosen by society and implemented through fiscal means. Inequality is measured, targets are set, and transfers are designed accordingly. What remains largely unexamined is the moral authority implicit in this process: the authority to define what level of inequality is acceptable, what outcomes are unjust, and what forms of life deserve support. Fiscal policy here becomes an instrument not merely of economic adjustment but of moral classification. From a hermeneutical perspective, this raises questions about legitimacy that cannot be resolved by reference to efficiency or consent alone.

The instruments of fiscal policy further illustrate the limits of the orthodox vision. Taxes and spending are modelled as levers affecting behaviour through incentives. This modelling presupposes that individuals respond to fiscal signals in predictable ways. Yet incentives are interpreted, not merely received. A tax may be perceived as fair or arbitrary, temporary or permanent, supportive or punitive. These perceptions influence behaviour in ways that escape formal modelling. The same fiscal measure may generate compliance in one context and resistance in another, depending on trust, cultural norms, and historical memory.

Public debt exemplifies the temporal dimension of this problem. Orthodox analysis treats debt as an intertemporal allocation mechanism, justified by smoothing shocks or financing long-term investments. Debt sustainability is assessed through ratios and projections. What is less visible in this analysis is the narrative dimension of debt: how societies interpret obligations to the future, how trust in public institutions is formed or eroded, and how expectations about future taxation shape present behaviour. Debt is not merely a stock of liabilities; it is a promise whose credibility depends on shared meanings.

Institutions, in the orthodox account, are introduced to discipline fiscal policy and align incentives. Rules, councils, and frameworks are designed to constrain discretion and enhance credibility. From a hermeneutical standpoint, institutions are more than constraint devices; they are carriers of meaning. Fiscal rules signal what a society values—prudence, solidarity, growth, or stability. They shape expectations not only through enforcement but through interpretation. An institution that is perceived as externally imposed or technocratically opaque may undermine the very credibility it seeks to establish.

The political economy dimension of orthodox fiscal theory recognizes that policymakers are not neutral optimizers. Yet it continues to treat political behaviour as a deviation from an underlying economic rationality. Rent-seeking, opportunism, and electoral cycles explain why fiscal outcomes diverge from optimal prescriptions. The hermeneutical critique suggests a deeper issue: fiscal policy is inherently political because it involves authoritative interpretations of social needs and priorities. Politics is not a distortion of fiscal policy; it is constitutive of it.

This does not imply that fiscal policy is meaningless or illegitimate. It implies that its meaning cannot be exhausted by technical analysis. Fiscal policy is a practice embedded in a web of interpretations, expectations, and moral judgments. To treat it as a purely instrumental tool is to overlook the interpretative processes through which it acquires legitimacy and effectiveness. The orthodox framework, for all its sophistication, tends to obscure this dimension by translating meaning into measurement.

The purpose of this preliminary critique is not to reject the traditional approach to fiscal policy but to situate it. Orthodox theory provides valuable insights into the mechanisms through which fiscal actions influence economic outcomes. It clarifies trade-offs, highlights constraints, and offers guidance for policy design. Yet it operates within a specific epistemological horizon—one that privileges measurability, aggregation, and control. The hermeneutical perspective invites a broader view, one that acknowledges the limits of this horizon without dismissing its achievements.

Later chapters will return to fiscal policy from this interpretative standpoint, exploring in greater depth the questions of moral authority, legitimacy, and knowledge that have only been sketched here. For now, it is sufficient to recognize that fiscal policy, as traditionally conceived, is not merely a set of tools applied to an objectified economy. It is an interpretative act, grounded in assumptions about what the economy is, what society values, and what policymakers can know. To understand fiscal policy fully, one must therefore move beyond technique and toward meaning.

Appendix: A Technical Summary of Fiscal Policy according to Contemporary Textbooks

4.A. FISCAL POLICY AS AN INTERTEMPORAL POLICY PROBLEM

In modern macroeconomics, fiscal policy refers to the set of government decisions concerning public spending, taxation, and transfers, together with the resulting budget balance and the accumulation of public debt. Unlike purely descriptive treatments, contemporary macroeconomic textbooks analyse fiscal policy as an intertemporal choice problem subject to accounting constraints, behavioural responses, and institutional interactions—most notably with monetary policy. Fiscal policy is therefore not simply a question of "how much the government spends" or "how high taxes are", but of how these instruments operate over different time horizons and under different macroeconomic conditions.

A central feature of the mainstream approach is the explicit distinction between the short run, in which prices are sticky and output can deviate from its natural level, and the medium to long run, in which prices adjust and output is determined by supply-side factors. Fiscal policy tools have different effects across these horizons, and understanding this temporal dimension is essential for evaluating both the potential and the limits of government intervention.

4.B. THE GOVERNMENT BUDGET CONSTRAINT: ACCOUNTING AND SUSTAINABILITY

Any analysis of fiscal policy begins with the government budget constraint. In nominal terms, government expenditures—including purchases of goods and services and transfers to households—must be financed through tax revenues, the issuance of public debt, or money creation. Abstracting from seigniorage and consolidating interest payments, the change in government debt equals the primary deficit, defined as spending net of revenues excluding interest.

When expressed relative to GDP, the evolution of the debt-to-GDP ratio depends on three key variables: the primary balance, the real interest rate on government debt, and the growth rate of the economy. If the real interest rate exceeds the growth rate, stabilising the debt ratio requires persistent primary surpluses. If growth exceeds the interest rate, the debt ratio can remain stable even with moderate primary deficits. This relationship underlies the textbook discussion of debt sustainability and serves as the background constraint for all fiscal policy tools.

Crucially, the government budget constraint does not imply that budgets must be balanced every year. Mainstream political economy emphasizes that deficits can be appropriate and even desirable, particularly during recessions. What matters is not the absence of deficits per se, but whether fiscal policy is consistent with a sustainable intertemporal path for debt.

In nominal terms, the government's flow budget constraint can be written as

$$B_t = (1 + i_t)B_{t-1} + G_t + TR_t - T_t$$

where B_t denotes nominal government debt at the end of period t, i_t, is the nominal interest rate, G_t is government purchases of goods and services, TR_t represents transfers, and T_t denotes tax revenues.

Defining the primary deficit as $PD_t = G_t + TR_t - T_t$, the change in debt equals interest payments on existing debt plus the primary deficit. Dividing through by nominal GDP and expressing the relationship in real terms yields the standard debt dynamics equation used throughout modern macroeconomics:

$$\Delta b_t = (r_t - g_t)b_{t-1} + pd_t$$

where b_t is the debt-to-GDP ratio, r_t is the real interest rate, g_t is the real growth rate of the economy, and pd_t is the primary deficit as a share of GDP.

This equation plays a central role in textbook analysis because it shows that debt sustainability depends not only on fiscal choices but also on macroeconomic conditions. A government can run primary deficits without exploding debt if economic growth exceeds the interest rate, whereas even small deficits can become problematic when interest rates are persistently higher than growth.

4.C. FISCAL POLICY IN THE AD–AS FRAMEWORK

Mankiw introduces fiscal policy primarily through the Aggregate Demand–Aggregate Supply (AD–AS) model, which provides a clear and intuitive framework for understanding short-run fluctuations and long-run equilibrium. Aggregate demand represents the total demand for goods and services in the economy and is derived from equilibrium in the goods market. It depends positively on government spending and negatively on taxes, interest rates, and the price level.

Government purchases of goods and services are the most direct fiscal instrument in the AD–AS framework. An increase in government spending raises aggregate demand at any given price level, shifting the AD curve to the right. In the short run, when prices are sticky, this increase in demand leads to higher output and employment. The magnitude of the output response depends on the government spending multiplier, which captures the cumulative effect of higher spending on income and consumption.

The multiplier is larger when households have a high marginal propensity to consume and smaller when leakages through saving, taxation, and imports are significant. In an open economy, part of the increase in demand falls on imports, reducing the impact on domestic output. These considerations lead students to understand why fiscal policy may be more effective in some economies or circumstances than in others.

Taxes affect aggregate demand indirectly through disposable income. A reduction in taxes raises households' after-tax income, increasing consumption and shifting aggregate demand to the right. Because consumption responds only partially to income changes, the tax multiplier is typically smaller in absolute value than the spending multiplier. Transfers operate similarly, increasing demand by raising disposable income, with their effectiveness depending on the consumption behaviour of recipients.

In the long run, prices adjust, and the economy returns to its natural level of output. In the AD–AS framework, this corresponds to the vertical long-run aggregate supply curve. Fiscal policy cannot permanently raise output beyond this level. Instead, higher government spending or lower taxes lead to higher prices, crowding out private spending. This long-run neutrality result is a cornerstone of modern macroeconomic analysis and highlights the importance of distinguishing between stabilisation policy and structural policy.

4.C.1 Aggregate demand and fiscal instruments

In Mankiw's AD–AS framework, aggregate demand is derived from equilibrium in the goods and money markets. In a simplified closed economy, aggregate demand can be written as

$$Y = C(Y - T) + I(r) + G$$

where output Y equals consumption C, investment I, and government spending G. Consumption depends positively on disposable income $Y - T$, while investment depends negatively on the real interest rate r.

Government spending enters aggregate demand directly. An increase in raises demand one-for-one at any given price level. Taxes enter indirectly, by affecting disposable income and therefore consumption.

Solving for equilibrium output yields the familiar Keynesian multiplier result. If consumption takes the linear form $C = c_0 + c_1(Y-T)$, with $0 < c_1 < 1$, the government spending multiplier in a closed economy without taxes is

$$\frac{1}{1 - c_1}$$

When proportional taxes are introduced, the multiplier becomes smaller:

$$\frac{1}{1 - c_1(1 - t)}$$

where t is the tax rate.

4.C.2 Taxes, transfers, and the tax multiplier

A reduction in taxes raises disposable income and consumption, shifting aggregate demand to the right. The tax multiplier is given by

$$-\frac{c_1}{1 - c_1}$$

in the simplest model, and is smaller in absolute value than the spending multiplier. This result highlights an important asymmetry between fiscal tools: spending directly increases demand, while tax cuts operate indirectly through consumption behaviour.

Transfers function similarly to negative taxes. Their effectiveness depends crucially on who receives them. If recipients have a high marginal propensity to consume, transfers can have substantial short-run effects on aggregate demand.

4.C.3 Short run versus long run in the AD–AS model

In the short run, prices are sticky, and an increase in aggregate demand raises output and employment. In the long run, prices adjust, and output returns to its natural level, determined by labour supply, capital, and technology. In the AD–AS diagram, this corresponds to a vertical long-run aggregate supply curve.

Fiscal policy therefore affects output only temporarily. Permanent increases in government spending lead to higher prices, crowding out private demand rather than raising long-run output.

4.D. FISCAL POLICY IN THE IS–MP–PHILLIPS CURVE FRAMEWORK

Blanchard's IS–MP–Phillips Curve framework builds on the insights of the AD–AS model while providing a more explicit treatment of monetary policy and inflation dynamics. In this framework, the IS curve represents equilibrium in the goods market, the MP curve describes the central bank's interest rate rule, and the Phillips Curve captures the relationship between economic activity and inflation.

Fiscal policy enters the IS–MP–PC model primarily through the IS curve. An increase in government spending or a reduction in taxes raises autonomous demand, shifting the IS curve to the right. At a given real interest rate, output increases. The extent of the increase depends on how monetary policy reacts. If the central bank raises interest rates in response to higher output or inflationary pressure, part of the fiscal expansion is offset. If monetary policy accommodates the fiscal expansion, the increase in output is larger.

This framework makes the crowding-out mechanism explicit. Crowding out occurs when fiscal expansion leads to higher interest rates, reducing private investment and consumption. Importantly, crowding out is not a mechanical inevitability; it depends on the monetary policy rule and the state of the economy. This insight allows students to see why fiscal multipliers differ across regimes and historical periods.

The Phillips Curve introduces dynamics absent from the static AD–AS model. When fiscal policy pushes output above its natural level, inflation tends to rise. Over time, higher inflation feeds into wage-setting and price-setting behaviour, shifting the Phillips Curve and prompting a monetary tightening. As a result, output gradually returns to its natural level. Fiscal policy thus affects the path of output and inflation over time but not the long-run level of output.

4.D.1 The IS curve and fiscal expansion

Blanchard's IS–MP–PC framework replaces the AD–AS model with a system that explicitly incorporates monetary policy and inflation dynamics. The IS curve represents equilibrium in the goods market and can be written as

$$Y = C(Y - T) + I(Y, r) + G$$

An increase in government spending or a decrease in taxes shifts the IS curve to the right, raising output for any given real interest rate.

4.D.2 Monetary policy reaction and crowding out

The MP curve represents the central bank's interest rate rule, often written as

$$r = r^* + \phi_\pi \left(\pi - \pi^* \right) + \phi_y \left(Y - Y^n \right)$$

where r^* is the natural real interest rate, π inflation, and π^* the inflation target.

If fiscal expansion raises output above its natural level, the central bank may raise interest rates, reducing private investment. This is the crowding-out mechanism.

4.D.3 Inflation dynamics and the Phillips Curve

The Phillips Curve links inflation to economic activity:

$$\pi_t - \pi_{t-1} = \alpha\left(Y_t - Y^n\right)$$

Fiscal expansions that push output above potential generate inflationary pressure. Over time, higher inflation induces monetary tightening, bringing output back to its natural level.

4.E. Automatic stabilisers and discretionary fiscal policy

Both frameworks emphasise the role of automatic stabilisers, such as progressive income taxes and unemployment benefits. These mechanisms cause government revenues to fall and transfers to rise automatically during recessions, supporting disposable income and aggregate demand without new policy decisions. In expansions, the opposite occurs. Automatic stabilisers reduce output volatility and help smooth the business cycle.

Discretionary fiscal policy refers to deliberate changes in spending, taxes, or transfers enacted in response to economic conditions. While potentially powerful, discretionary policy is subject to significant lags. Recognition lags arise from uncertainty about the state of the economy, decision lags from the political process, and implementation lags from administrative constraints. For this reason, textbooks caution against relying on discretionary fiscal policy for short-run fine-tuning, while recognising its importance in responding to large shocks.

4.F. Fiscal policy at the zero lower bound

A key area where the IS–MP–PC framework adds insight is the analysis of fiscal policy at the zero lower bound on nominal interest rates. When interest rates are at or near zero, the central bank may be unable to provide sufficient stimulus through conventional monetary policy. In this case, the MP curve becomes flat, and fiscal expansions shift output without being offset by higher interest rates.

Under these conditions, fiscal multipliers are larger, and government spending becomes a particularly effective stabilisation tool. Fiscal expansion can also raise inflation expectations, lowering real interest rates and further stimulating private demand. This analysis has become central in modern macroeconomics and illustrates the importance of regime-dependent policy evaluation.

4.G. Long-run fiscal policy: incentives, public investment, and debt

In the long run, fiscal policy affects the economy primarily through supply-side channels. Taxes distort labour supply, saving, and investment decisions, while government spending reallocates resources between the public and private sectors. Public investment in infrastructure, education, and research can raise potential output by increasing productivity, but its effectiveness depends on efficiency and governance.

Public debt links short-run stabilisation to long-run sustainability. Running deficits during recessions can be optimal as part of a strategy of tax smoothing, avoiding sharp increases in distortionary taxes. However, persistent deficits without credible plans for stabilisation can raise debt to unsustainable levels, increasing interest rates and limiting future policy options.

4.H. Integrating AD–AS and IS–MP–PC: a unified view

Taken together, the AD–AS and IS–MP–Phillips Curve frameworks provide a comprehensive and internally consistent account of fiscal policy tools. The AD–AS model offers clarity and intuition regarding short-run demand effects and long-run neutrality, while the IS–MP–PC framework embeds fiscal policy in a dynamic setting with explicit monetary policy interaction and inflation dynamics.

For undergraduate students, the integration of these models highlights a central lesson of modern macroeconomics: fiscal policy is powerful but conditional. Its effects depend on economic slack, expectations, institutional arrangements, and the interaction with monetary policy. Government spending, taxes, and transfers are not isolated levers but components of an intertemporal policy strategy constrained by debt dynamics and shaped by behavioural responses.

Lesson 5

Monetary Policy: Definition, Objectives, Tools

5.1. What Monetary Policy Is: Definition, Scope, and Institutional Location

Monetary policy occupies a peculiar and privileged position within the architecture of modern political economy. It is at once presented as a highly technical field, entrusted to specialized institutions and professional expertise, and as a profoundly consequential domain of public action, shaping macroeconomic conditions that affect the entirety of social and economic life. In standard textbooks and policy discourse, monetary policy is commonly defined as the set of actions undertaken by a central bank to influence monetary and financial conditions in the economy, with the ultimate aim of achieving macroeconomic stability. This stability is typically articulated through objectives such as price stability, full employment, and sustainable economic growth, though the relative emphasis placed on each of these goals varies across time, countries, and institutional frameworks.

In its most conventional formulation, monetary policy refers to the management of the money supply and of short-term interest rates by a central monetary authority. The central bank, operating either as an independent or semi-independent institution, is endowed with the legal monopoly over the issuance of base money and with regulatory authority over the banking system. Through its policy instruments, it seeks to influence credit conditions, aggregate demand, inflation dynamics, and financial stability. In this sense, monetary policy is understood not as a direct allocation of resources, but as a framework-setting activity: it alters the general conditions under which decentralized economic decisions are made.

Mainstream macroeconomic theory presents monetary policy as one of the two principal branches of macroeconomic stabilization policy, alongside fiscal policy. While fiscal policy operates through government spending and taxation, monetary policy works through financial variables—most notably interest rates, liquidity conditions, and expectations. This distinction is central to the standard narrative, as it underpins the widespread belief that monetary policy can be implemented in a more flexible, timely, and politically insulated manner than fiscal interventions. The comparative advantage of monetary policy is thus often located in its speed, reversibility, and technical character, qualities that are thought to make it particularly suitable for short- to medium-term stabilization tasks.

The institutional location of monetary policy is equally central to its standard definition. In contemporary economies, monetary policy is almost universally entrusted to a central bank, whether explicitly independent or operating under a mandate defined by legislation. Independence is typically justified on the grounds that monetary policy is vulnerable to short-term political pressures, especially those associated with electoral cycles and fiscal dominance. By insulating monetary authorities from direct political control, societies are said to reduce the risk of inflationary bias and to enhance policy credibility. This argument, which has become a cornerstone of modern monetary institutional design, reflects a broader transformation in political economy: the delegation of key macroeconomic functions to rule-based or technocratically guided institutions.

The standard view thus conceives monetary policy as a specialized form of public governance, operating through abstract instruments rather than concrete commands, and relying on indirect mechanisms rather than direct controls. Money is treated as a policy variable, interest rates as controllable levers, and expectations as objects of strategic management. The economy, in turn, is modelled as a system responsive to these signals, adjusting its behaviour in accordance with changes in monetary conditions.

At this level of abstraction, monetary policy appears as a neutral and largely benevolent practice. It is portrayed as a stabilizing force, correcting market imperfections, smoothing business cycles, and anchoring expectations. The language used in textbooks reinforces this image: central banks "steer" the economy, "fine-tune" demand, and "anchor" inflation expectations. Monetary disturbances are framed as technical problems, solvable through appropriate calibration of policy instruments. The underlying assumption is that, although the economy may be complex, its key macroeconomic aggregates respond in sufficiently regular ways to systematic monetary interventions.

This conception of monetary policy rests on a particular understanding of money itself. In mainstream analysis, money is primarily a medium of exchange, a unit of account, and a store of value, whose quantity and price can be adjusted to influence economic outcomes. The institutional and historical dimensions of money, while acknowledged, tend to recede into the background. Money becomes an object of control rather than a social institution emerging from market processes. This abstraction is not accidental: it allows monetary policy to be framed as a technical activity, amenable to formal modelling and empirical measurement.

Yet even within this standard framework, monetary policy is recognized as a demanding task. Central bankers are assumed to operate under uncertainty, facing imperfect information and complex transmission mechanisms. As Cowen and Tabarrok repeatedly emphasize, "central banking is a hard job", precisely because the effects of monetary actions unfold with lags, interact with expectations, and depend on the structure of financial markets. Nonetheless, the prevailing view maintains that, despite these difficulties, systematic monetary policy can improve macroeconomic outcomes relative to laissez-faire or purely discretionary arrangements.

This standard definition, institutional framing, and justificatory narrative form the baseline from which any further discussion must proceed. Before examining objectives and tools, it is essential to understand that monetary policy, as conventionally conceived, is not merely a set of technical procedures. It is embedded in a broader vision of economic order, one that assigns a central coordinating role to monetary authorities and treats money as an instrument of policy rather than as a spontaneous outcome of social interaction.

5.2. The Objectives of Monetary Policy in the Standard Paradigm

Once monetary policy is defined as the deliberate management of monetary conditions by a central authority, the question of objectives becomes unavoidable. What, precisely, is monetary policy supposed to achieve? In mainstream macroeconomics, the objectives of monetary policy are typically articulated in terms of macroeconomic stabilization, with particular emphasis on price stability, output stabilization, and employment. Over time, these objectives have been codified in central bank mandates, formalized in policy rules, and embedded in the rhetoric of monetary authorities.

Price stability has emerged as the primary objective of monetary policy in most advanced economies. Inflation, understood as a sustained increase in the general price level, is widely regarded as economically harmful. Standard theory associates high and volatile inflation with distortions in relative prices, erosion of purchasing power, arbitrary redistributions of wealth, and increased uncertainty. By maintaining low and stable inflation, monetary policy is said to preserve the informational role of prices, facilitate long-term planning, and protect the real value of money balances.

The elevation of price stability to a central objective reflects both historical experience and theoretical developments. Episodes of hyperinflation and chronic inflation in the twentieth century left a deep imprint on economic thought and institutional design. These experiences reinforced the belief that unchecked monetary expansion can undermine economic and social order. As a result, modern central banking has increasingly converged on explicit or implicit inflation targets, often defined numerically and communicated transparently to the public.

In addition to price stability, monetary policy is commonly tasked with supporting high levels of employment and stable economic growth. In some institutional frameworks, such as that of the United States Federal Reserve, these objectives are explicitly stated as part of a "dual mandate". In others, employment and growth are treated as secondary goals, pursued insofar as they are compatible with price stability. The underlying assumption is that, in the long run, stable prices provide the best monetary environment for sustainable growth and employment, while short-run trade-offs may justify temporary deviations.

The standard macroeconomic framework conceptualizes these objectives through the lens of aggregate demand and supply. Monetary policy influences aggregate demand by affecting interest rates, credit conditions, and asset prices. Lower interest rates stimulate consumption and investment, raising output and employment; higher rates dampen demand, containing inflationary pressures. In this view, the central bank acts as a stabilizer, counteracting demand shocks and moderating business cycle fluctuations.

A further objective that has gained prominence in recent decades is financial stability. While traditionally treated as a separate concern, often assigned to regulatory authorities, financial stability has increasingly been integrated into the discourse of monetary policy. Financial crises have highlighted the deep interconnections between monetary conditions, credit expansion, asset prices, and systemic risk. As a result, central banks now frequently justify their actions in terms of preventing financial instability, maintaining orderly markets, and ensuring the smooth functioning of the payment system.

It is important to note that, within the standard paradigm, these objectives are often framed as complementary rather than conflicting. Price stability is seen as a precondition for sustainable growth; financial stability is viewed as necessary for effective monetary transmission; employment outcomes are expected to improve in a stable macroeconomic environment. Where trade-offs arise, they are typically analyzed within formal models, such as the Phillips curve framework, which describes a short-run relationship between inflation and unemployment.

Underlying this objectives-based framework is a particular conception of social welfare. Monetary policy is justified insofar as it improves aggregate outcomes relative to a counterfactual of unmanaged monetary conditions. The central bank is implicitly cast as a guardian of macroeconomic order, tasked with minimizing deviations from desirable paths of inflation and output. This welfare-theoretic foundation, though often implicit, informs both academic modelling and policy practice.

At the same time, mainstream theory acknowledges that monetary policy cannot achieve all objectives simultaneously or with precision. Long-run growth is ultimately determined by real factors such as technology, institutions, and human capital. Employment depends on labour market structures and incentives. Monetary policy, in this view, is powerful but not omnipotent. Its role is to provide a stable nominal framework within which real economic processes can unfold.

This recognition has led to a narrowing of monetary policy objectives in many institutional settings. The focus on price stability, often operationalized through inflation targeting, reflects an attempt to define a clear, measurable, and communicable goal. By anchoring expectations around a stable inflation rate, central banks aim to enhance credibility and reduce uncertainty. Monetary policy thus becomes not only an instrument of stabilization but also a device for expectation management.

Yet even in its most restrained form, the standard objectives of monetary policy presuppose a capacity to identify macroeconomic conditions, to diagnose deviations from desired outcomes, and to implement corrective measures. These presuppositions, while taken for granted in much of the literature, will later become the object of critical scrutiny. For now, it suffices to note that the standard paradigm presents monetary policy objectives as coherent, attainable, and broadly aligned with social welfare.

In the next part of the chapter, we will examine the standard tools of monetary policy, beginning with conventional instruments such as open market operations, policy interest rates, and reserve requirements, before moving to the evolution of unconventional tools. Only after the full architecture of standard monetary policy has been laid out will we open, in the final section of the chapter, a deliberately limited and preparatory critical reflection.

5.3. THE TRADITIONAL TOOLS OF MONETARY POLICY AND THEIR TRANSMISSION MECHANISMS

Once the objectives of monetary policy have been defined, the question naturally arises as to how a central bank is expected to pursue them in practice. In the standard framework, monetary policy is not exercised through direct commands to economic agents, nor through the allocation of resources by administrative fiat. Instead, it operates through a set of instruments designed to influence monetary and financial conditions indirectly, relying on the responsiveness of markets, institutions, and expectations. These instruments constitute what is commonly referred to as the toolkit of monetary policy.

At the core of this toolkit lies the central bank's control over the monetary base and over the short-term interest rate. Traditional monetary policy theory holds that, by managing the supply of base money and by steering short-term market interest rates, the central bank can influence broader financial conditions, including longer-term interest rates, credit availability, asset prices, and ultimately aggregate demand. The effectiveness of monetary policy thus depends not only on the tools themselves, but also on the transmission mechanisms through which policy actions propagate throughout the economy.

Historically, the most important and emblematic instrument of monetary policy has been the use of open market operations. Open market operations consist in the buying and selling of government securities by the central bank in the open market. When the central bank purchases securities, it injects reserves into the banking system, increasing the supply of base money and exerting downward pressure on short-term interest rates. Conversely, when it sells securities, it withdraws reserves, reducing liquidity and putting upward pressure on rates.

In the standard narrative, open market operations are valued for their flexibility, precision, and reversibility. Unlike more blunt instruments, they can be conducted on a daily basis and adjusted in response to evolving conditions. They also allow the central bank to target specific interest rates rather than fixed quantities of money, a shift that has become increasingly pronounced over the past decades. As Cowen and Tabarrok emphasize in their textbook, modern central banks typically operate by targeting an overnight interbank rate, using open market operations to keep market rates close to the desired policy level.

The centrality of the policy interest rate reflects a broader transformation in monetary policy practice. While earlier frameworks often emphasized control over monetary aggregates, contemporary monetary policy is predominantly interest-rate oriented. The policy rate, set or guided by the central bank, serves as a benchmark for the entire structure of interest rates in the economy. Through arbitrage and expectations, changes in the short-term policy rate are expected to influence longer-term rates, affecting borrowing costs for households and firms.

Alongside open market operations, traditional monetary policy includes standing facilities such as the discount window. Through the discount window, commercial banks can borrow reserves directly from the central bank, typically at a rate above the target policy rate. The discount rate thus acts as a ceiling for short-term market rates, while also serving as a lender-of-last-resort mechanism. In standard theory, the availability of central bank credit through the discount window helps to stabilize the banking system by providing liquidity in times of stress, thereby preventing temporary liquidity shortages from escalating into systemic crises.

Reserve requirements constitute another classical instrument of monetary policy, though their role has diminished in many advanced economies. By requiring banks to hold a fraction of their deposits as reserves at the central bank, monetary authorities can influence the amount of credit that banks are able to create. Higher reserve requirements constrain lending, while lower requirements expand banks' capacity to extend credit. In traditional textbook presentations, reserve requirements are often linked to the money multiplier framework, which describes how changes in base money translate into changes in broader monetary aggregates.

Although reserve requirements are conceptually powerful, in practice they are used sparingly. Frequent changes in reserve ratios are considered disruptive to banking operations, and many central banks have moved toward systems with minimal or even zero required reserves. Nevertheless, the theoretical importance of reserve requirements remains significant, as they illustrate the institutional linkage between central bank policy and the balance sheets of commercial banks.

Beyond these primary instruments, traditional monetary policy also relies on communication and signalling. While often treated as a supplementary aspect, communication has become an increasingly explicit component of the policy toolkit. Central banks issue statements, publish forecasts, and provide guidance about the future path of policy rates. This practice, commonly referred to as forward guidance, is grounded in the recognition that expectations play a crucial role in the transmission of monetary policy. By shaping expectations about future policy, the central bank seeks to influence current economic behaviour.

The emphasis on expectations reflects the evolution of macroeconomic theory toward forward-looking models. Economic agents are assumed to form expectations about future inflation, interest rates, and income, and to base their decisions on those expectations. Monetary policy, therefore, does not operate solely through current actions, but also through anticipated future actions. A credible commitment to a particular policy stance can influence long-term interest rates and investment decisions even before any concrete policy change occurs.

Underlying all these instruments is the notion of the monetary transmission mechanism. In standard macroeconomics, the transmission mechanism describes the channels through which monetary policy affects the real economy. The interest rate channel is typically presented as the primary mechanism: changes in policy rates influence borrowing costs, which in turn affect consumption and investment. Other channels include the credit channel, through which monetary policy affects the availability of loans; the asset price channel, through which policy influences equity and real estate prices; and the exchange rate channel, particularly relevant in open economies.

The transmission mechanism is central to the standard justification of monetary policy. It provides the causal link between central bank actions and macroeconomic outcomes. However, mainstream theory also acknowledges that these channels operate with variable lags and uncertain strength. The effects of monetary policy are not immediate, nor are they uniform across sectors and agents. This recognition has led to the development of increasingly sophisticated models and empirical techniques aimed at improving policy calibration.

In sum, the traditional tools of monetary policy form a coherent and well-articulated framework within mainstream macroeconomics. Open market operations, policy interest rates, standing facilities, reserve requirements, and communication strategies are all designed to influence monetary and financial conditions indirectly, relying on market mechanisms and expectations. The central bank, in this framework, is portrayed as a manager of aggregate conditions, adjusting its instruments in response to deviations from desired macroeconomic objectives.

5.4. A Preparatory Reflection: Tensions and Limits within the Standard Framework

Having reconstructed the standard definition, objectives, and tools of monetary policy as they are commonly presented in contemporary macroeconomics and institutional practice, it is now possible—and indeed necessary—to pause and reflect on the internal coherence and implicit presuppositions of this framework. This reflection does not yet amount to a full critique. Rather, it aims to identify a set of conceptual tensions that emerge from within the orthodox paradigm itself, tensions that call for deeper interpretative engagement.

The standard framework portrays monetary policy as a rational, purposive activity carried out by a specialized institution endowed with technical expertise and insulated from political pressures. Central banks are depicted as capable of identifying macroeconomic conditions, diagnosing deviations from desired outcomes, and implementing corrective measures through a well-defined set of instruments. Inflation, output gaps, and financial stress are treated as observable or at least estimable variables, susceptible to measurement and policy response. Yet even within mainstream analysis, this image is accompanied by repeated acknowledgments of difficulty and uncertainty. Monetary policy is widely described as operating with long and variable lags, through complex and imperfect transmission mechanisms, and under conditions of incomplete information. Central bankers are said to face fundamental uncertainty regarding both the current state of the economy and the future consequences of their actions. The familiar assertion that "central banking is a hard job" is not a rhetorical flourish but a recognition of these constraints.

This acknowledgment, however, raises a first tension. If the economy is complex, forward-looking, and shaped by heterogeneous expectations, on what basis can monetary authorities claim the epistemic capacity required to stabilize it? The standard response appeals to models, data, and institutional learning. Over time, central banks refine their analytical frameworks, improve their forecasts, and adjust their strategies. Policy errors are treated as deviations from an otherwise sound methodology, correctable through better information and improved techniques.

At this stage, the framework remains fundamentally technocratic. The limitations of knowledge are framed as practical obstacles, not as structural features of economic life. Uncertainty is something to be reduced, managed, or probabilistically modelled, rather than an irreducible condition of human action unfolding in real time. The economy continues to be treated as an object that can be observed from the outside, even if imperfectly.

A second tension concerns the relationship between monetary policy objectives and the means employed to achieve them. Price stability, output stabilization, and financial stability are presented as coherent and mutually reinforcing goals. Yet the tools of monetary policy operate primarily through monetary and financial variables—interest rates, liquidity conditions, asset prices—that have heterogeneous and uneven effects across agents, sectors, and time horizons. While the aggregate outcomes are emphasized, the distributional and structural consequences of monetary interventions remain largely implicit.

Within the standard paradigm, these distributional effects are often treated as secondary or unavoidable side effects. Monetary policy is justified by its aggregate benefits, and its legitimacy rests on the presumption that improving macroeconomic stability enhances overall welfare. Nonetheless, the reliance on aggregate indicators such as inflation rates or output gaps raises questions about what exactly is being stabilized, and for whom. These questions are not foreign to mainstream debate, but they are typically bracketed or deferred to other policy domains.

A further tension emerges from the evolving role of monetary policy tools themselves. As discussed in the previous part, traditional monetary policy has increasingly shifted from quantity-based control to interest-rate targeting and expectation management. This shift reflects a recognition of the limits of direct monetary control and the importance of credibility. Monetary policy becomes as much about communication as about concrete operations. The central bank seeks to shape expectations, anchor beliefs, and guide anticipations of future policy.

This evolution implicitly acknowledges that economic outcomes are not mechanically determined by policy instruments, but are mediated by interpretation and belief. Expectations are not passive responses to policy signals; they are active constructions formed by agents interpreting institutional behaviour. At this point, the standard framework begins to gesture—often unintentionally—toward an interpretative dimension of economic life. However, this dimension is still treated instrumentally, as something to be managed rather than understood in its own right.

The literature on rules versus discretion provides another entry point for reflection. While modern central banking frequently combines discretionary judgment with rule-like commitments, the underlying debate reveals a persistent unease with unconstrained policy authority. The appeal of rules lies in their predictability and their capacity to limit arbitrary intervention. Yet even rule-based regimes require interpretation, adjustment, and judgment in application. The tension between general rules and case-specific discretion remains unresolved, and it points to deeper questions about the nature of monetary authority itself.

These tensions are explored more explicitly in works that emphasize the institutional and constitutional dimensions of monetary policy. In particular, arguments stressing the importance of generality, predictability, and rule-like behaviour highlight the fragility of discretionary frameworks, even when exercised by competent and well-intentioned authorities. Without yet endorsing or rejecting these arguments, it is important to recognize that they arise from within the logic of monetary governance itself, not from an external ideological critique.

Finally, there is a tension between the temporal structure of monetary policy and the temporal nature of economic processes. Monetary policy operates through interventions that are inherently present-oriented—adjusting rates today in response to current indicators—while their effects unfold over extended and uncertain time horizons. Investment decisions, capital formation, and structural change are processes embedded in real time, shaped by expectations about an unknowable future. The standard framework acknowledges lags but tends to compress time into manageable segments, often distinguishing mechanically between short run and long run.

This abstraction allows policy analysis to proceed, but it risks obscuring the lived temporality of economic action. Money, credit, and interest rates are not merely variables in an equation; they are signals embedded in plans, projects, and expectations that extend into the future. To the extent that monetary policy reshapes these signals, it participates in the coordination—or miscoordination—of intertemporal plans. This insight, while not absent from mainstream theory, remains underdeveloped in standard presentations.

At this point, the limits of the orthodox framework become visible. Not as fatal flaws, but as conceptual boundaries. The standard definition of monetary policy presupposes measurability, controllability, and predictability. Its objectives assume that macroeconomic stability can be defined independently of deeper questions about meaning, coordination, and institutional context. Its tools rely on transmission mechanisms that are probabilistic, mediated by expectations, and historically contingent.

This chapter has deliberately refrained from pushing these observations to their logical conclusion. Its purpose has been to reconstruct the standard view faithfully, while allowing its internal tensions to surface. In the next chapters, we will engage these tensions explicitly, moving beyond technical analysis toward a hermeneutical interpretation of monetary policy—one that treats money not merely as a policy instrument, but as a social institution embedded in time, meaning, and human action.

Appendix: A Technical Summary of Monetary Policy
according to Contemporary Textbooks

5.A. MONETARY POLICY: DEFINITION, SCOPE, AND ANALYTICAL FRAMEWORK

In modern macroeconomics, monetary policy is defined as the set of actions
through which a central bank influences financial conditions in order to
achieve macroeconomic objectives such as price stability, output stabilization, and, in many institutional mandates, maximum sustainable employment.
Following the framework adopted in the textbooks by Olivier Blanchard and
N. Gregory Mankiw, monetary policy is best understood not as the direct
control of economic outcomes, but as the systematic management of nominal
variables, primarily short-term interest rates, that affect aggregate demand
and expectations.

A fundamental analytical distinction is made between final objectives,
intermediate targets, operational targets, and policy instruments. Final objectives—such as inflation and output—are influenced only indirectly and with
lags. Intermediate targets, such as longer-term interest rates or credit conditions,
are closer to real activity but still not directly controllable. Operational targets,
typically an overnight interbank rate, are the variables the central bank can
control with high precision on a day-to-day basis. Policy instruments are the
concrete tools—open market operations, standing facilities, reserve requirements, and communication strategies—used to achieve these targets.

This hierarchical structure reflects a core insight of modern macroeconomics: monetary policy operates through financial markets, not through direct
allocation of resources.

5.B. CENTRAL BANK MONEY, RESERVES, AND THE BALANCE-SHEET VIEW

A rigorous understanding of monetary policy tools begins with the central
bank balance sheet. In simplified form, the balance sheet of a central bank can
be written as:

Assets = Government securities + Loans to banks + Other assets

Liabilities = Currency in circulation + Bank reserves

The sum of currency in circulation and bank reserves constitutes base money
(or high-powered money), usually denoted by H or MB. While households

and firms primarily use bank deposits for transactions, banks require reserves to settle payments and meet regulatory or operational needs.

The central bank has monopoly control over base money, but it does not directly control broader monetary aggregates such as *M1* or *M2*, which depend on banks' lending decisions and the public's portfolio choices. This distinction underpins the modern shift away from monetary aggregate targeting toward interest-rate targeting.

5.C. THE MARKET FOR RESERVES AND THE OVERNIGHT INTEREST RATE

Modern monetary policy is implemented through the market for reserves, in which commercial banks lend and borrow reserves overnight. The equilibrium interest rate in this market, often denoted i, is determined by the interaction of reserve supply and reserve demand.

The demand for reserves R^d is typically downward-sloping in the interest rate, reflecting the opportunity cost of holding non-interest-bearing or low-interest reserves. It may also include institutional features such as reserve requirements or precautionary motives related to payment uncertainty.

The supply of reserves R^s is determined by the central bank. In the simplest textbook representation, the central bank fixes R^s and allows the interest rate to adjust. In practice, modern central banks instead fix the interest rate and adjust the supply of reserves endogenously to maintain that rate.

The operational target of monetary policy is thus the overnight interbank rate i_t, which the central bank seeks to align with its announced policy rate i_t^*.

5.D. OPEN MARKET OPERATIONS: MECHANICS AND ANALYTICAL ROLE

Open market operations are the core traditional instrument of monetary policy. They consist of purchases or sales of government securities by the central bank.

When the central bank purchases bonds worth $\Delta B > 0$, it credits banks' reserve accounts by the same amount:

$$\Delta R = \Delta B$$

This operation increases the supply of reserves, shifting the reserve supply curve to the right and exerting downward pressure on the overnight interest rate. Conversely, bond sales reduce reserves and increase the overnight rate.

In equilibrium, the central bank conducts open market operations such that:

$$i_t = i_t^*$$

In practice, these operations are often executed as repurchase agreements (repos) or reverse repos, allowing the central bank to fine-tune liquidity conditions on a temporary basis. Repos provide reserves against collateral with an agreement to reverse the transaction at a specified date, while reverse repos absorb reserves temporarily.

Blanchard emphasizes that open market operations are defensive as well as active. They are used not only to change the stance of policy, but also to offset autonomous fluctuations in reserve demand due to payment flows, government transactions, or financial market stress.

5.E. Standing facilities and the interest-rate corridor system

In modern operational frameworks, open market operations are complemented by standing facilities, which establish upper and lower bounds for the overnight rate.

The marginal lending facility (or discount window) allows banks to borrow reserves from the central bank at a rate i^L, typically above the policy rate. This rate forms a ceiling for the interbank rate:

$$i_t \leq i^L$$

The deposit facility allows banks to deposit excess reserves at a rate , forming a floor:

$$i_t \geq i^D$$

The policy rate lies between these two rates:

$$i^D \leq i^* \leq i^L$$

This interest-rate corridor ensures stability in the interbank market and reduces volatility. Within the corridor, open market operations are used to keep the market rate close to the policy rate. This system has become standard in advanced economies and is extensively discussed in modern textbooks.

5.F. Reserve requirements and averaging provisions

Reserve requirements mandate that banks hold a fraction of certain deposits as reserves:

$$R \geq \theta D$$

Historically, reserve requirements were viewed as a key tool for controlling the money supply through the money multiplier:

$$M = m \cdot H$$

where *m* is the money multiplier. However, modern textbooks stress that this framework is empirically weak, as banks do not passively lend out reserves but instead respond to credit demand and capital constraints.

Nevertheless, reserve requirements still influence the demand for reserves and thus the central bank's liquidity management. Averaging provisions—allowing banks to meet reserve requirements on average over a maintenance period—help stabilize short-term interest rates by smoothing reserve demand.

5.G. THE POLICY RATE AS THE CENTRAL INSTRUMENT

In modern monetary policy, the policy rate is the primary instrument and communication device. The central bank announces a target value for the short-term nominal interest rate and commits to using its operational tools to achieve it.

In macroeconomic models, this rate affects the economy through several channels. In the IS-LM framework, the policy rate influences investment and consumption by affecting the cost of borrowing. In New Keynesian models, it enters the Euler equation for consumption:

$$C_t = E_t C_{t+1} - \frac{1}{\sigma}\left(i_t - E_t \pi_{t+1} - r_t^n \right)$$

where i_t is the nominal interest rate, π_{t+1} expected inflation, and r_t^n the natural real interest rate.

By adjusting the policy rate, the central bank influences real interest rates in the short run and, through expectations, longer-term rates as well.

5.H. EXPECTATIONS, CREDIBILITY, AND FORWARD GUIDANCE

Modern macroeconomics places strong emphasis on expectations. Monetary policy affects not only current financial conditions but also beliefs about future policy actions.

Forward guidance is the explicit communication of the expected future path of the policy rate. In New Keynesian models, expectations of future interest rates enter directly into the determination of long-term rates:

$$i_t^{(n)} = \frac{1}{n} \sum_{k=0}^{n-1} E_t i_{t+k} + \text{term premium}$$

By committing to keep future short-term rates low, the central bank can reduce
long-term rates even when the current policy rate is constrained.

5.I. Unconventional monetary policy tools

When the policy rate reaches its effective lower bound, central banks may
deploy unconventional tools.

Large-scale asset purchases (quantitative easing) involve purchases of
long-term government bonds or private securities to reduce term premia and
long-term yields. These operations expand the central bank balance sheet but
differ from standard open market operations in their objective and scale.

Targeted lending operations provide funding to banks conditional on lending behaviour, aiming to stimulate credit supply directly.

These tools are integrated into the same analytical framework but operate
through different segments of financial markets.

5.J. Policy rules, discretion, and systematic behaviour

Modern textbooks describe monetary policy behaviour using policy rules, the
most famous being the Taylor rule:

$$i_t = r^* + \pi_t + \phi_\pi \left(\pi_t - \pi^* \right) + \phi_y \left(y_t - y_t^* \right)$$

This rule captures the systematic response of the policy rate to deviations of
inflation and output from their targets. While not mechanically followed, such
rules provide a benchmark for evaluating policy consistency and credibility.

Concluding synthesis

In the mainstream framework, monetary policy tools form an integrated
operational system centred on interest-rate control, liquidity management,
and expectation shaping. Open market operations, standing facilities, reserve
management, and communication strategies work together to implement the
policy rate, which serves as the central lever through which monetary policy
influences the economy.

This framework reflects a mature view of monetary policy as a market-based, expectation-driven, and institutionally constrained process, rather than a simple exercise in money creation or control.

Lesson 6

Policy Mix And Macroeconomic Stability

6.1. Macroeconomic Stability and the Birth of the Policy Mix

The notion of macroeconomic stability occupies a central position in the modern language of economic policy. It functions as both a descriptive benchmark and a normative aspiration, shaping how governments, central banks, and international institutions conceive their role in the economy. Stability, in this context, does not mean stasis. It does not imply the absence of change, nor the elimination of economic fluctuations altogether. Rather, macroeconomic stability is conventionally understood as a condition in which the fundamental aggregates of the economy—output, employment, prices, and public finances—evolve without disruptive volatility, persistent disequilibria, or cumulative imbalances that threaten social and political order.

In standard macroeconomic theory, stability is framed as a prerequisite for growth rather than as an alternative to it. An economy subject to chronic inflation, recurring fiscal crises, or violent business cycles is believed to undermine long-term investment, distort relative prices, and erode the informational function of markets. For this reason, the stabilization function of policy has become a defining feature of the modern state, particularly after the consolidation of macroeconomics as a distinct field in the twentieth century. The contemporary vocabulary of stabilization—output gaps, inflation targets, fiscal multipliers, automatic stabilizers—emerges from this intellectual lineage and reflects a shared conviction that macroeconomic outcomes can and should be managed through deliberate policy intervention.

The concept of a *policy mix* arises precisely from this stabilization ambition. It reflects the recognition that no single instrument is sufficient to secure macroeconomic stability across different states of the business cycle and under

137

varying structural conditions. Monetary policy and fiscal policy are therefore conceived as complementary tools, each operating through distinct transmission mechanisms, each affecting different margins of economic behaviour, and each subject to its own institutional constraints. The policy mix refers to the particular combination, timing, and orientation of these instruments in pursuit of shared macroeconomic objectives.

In its standard formulation, the policy mix is not an abstract theoretical construct but a practical framework for action. It presupposes a division of labour between monetary and fiscal authorities, typically embodied in the institutional separation between central banks and governments. Monetary policy is primarily assigned responsibility for price stability and, in some formulations, for smoothing short-term fluctuations in output and employment. Fiscal policy, by contrast, is tasked with demand management, redistribution, and the provision of public goods, while also contributing to stabilization through countercyclical spending and taxation. The policy mix thus becomes the arena in which these responsibilities intersect, sometimes reinforcing one another, sometimes pulling in opposite directions.

The emergence of the policy mix as a central category in macroeconomic analysis is inseparable from the historical experience of the Great Depression and its aftermath. The collapse of output and employment in the 1930s brought under trials the supporters of earlier laissez-faire doctrines and gave rise to a new confidence in active macroeconomic management. Keynesian economics, in particular, emphasized the role of aggregate demand in determining short-run economic performance and provided an intellectual justification for fiscal activism. Monetary policy, which had previously been viewed with skepticism due to its perceived ineffectiveness during the Depression, was gradually rehabilitated and reintegrated into the stabilization toolkit, especially with the development of new instruments and operating procedures.

By the postwar period, the idea that macroeconomic stability required coordinated policy action had become widely accepted. Governments experimented with various combinations of expansionary and contractionary measures, seeking to fine-tune economic performance and to smooth the business cycle. This period also witnessed the institutionalization of macroeconomic policy, with the creation of independent central banks, formal budgetary procedures, and international monetary arrangements designed to constrain destabilizing behaviour. The policy mix thus evolved not only as a theoretical concept but as a set of institutional practices embedded in constitutional, legal, and political frameworks.

Standard macroeconomic textbooks present the policy mix as a problem of optimization under constraints. Policymakers are assumed to pursue a limited set of well-defined objectives, typically including low and stable inflation, high employment, sustainable public finances, and steady economic growth. These objectives are treated as partially conflicting, requiring trade-offs and prioritization. Monetary and fiscal instruments are evaluated according to their effectiveness, speed, predictability, and side effects, and the appropriate mix is said to depend on the nature of the shock affecting the economy. Demand shocks, supply shocks, financial disturbances, and external imbalances are each associated with different recommended policy responses.

Within this framework, macroeconomic stability appears as a technical challenge amenable to analytical reasoning and empirical calibration. Models of aggregate demand and supply, Phillips curves, and intertemporal budget constraints provide the conceptual scaffolding for policy design. At the same time, institutional economics and public choice theory have emphasized that the effectiveness of the policy mix cannot be understood independently of political incentives, time inconsistency problems, and credibility constraints. Fiscal deficits, public debt accumulation, and inflationary bias are not treated merely as technical failures but as predictable outcomes of democratic decision-making under weak constitutional constraints.

This tension between technical aspiration and institutional reality runs throughout the standard discussion of policy mix and macroeconomic stability. On the one hand, macroeconomic policy is presented as a rational endeavour aimed at correcting market failures and stabilizing aggregate outcomes. On the other hand, the persistent recurrence of instability, crises, and policy failures raises questions about the limits of control and the unintended consequences of intervention. The policy mix thus occupies an ambiguous position: it is simultaneously the cornerstone of modern macroeconomic governance and a source of ongoing controversy.

Before turning to the specific instruments of monetary and fiscal policy and their interaction, it is therefore essential to clarify what mainstream economics means by stability itself. Stability does not imply equilibrium in a static sense, nor does it presuppose a frictionless economy smoothly converging to a natural state. Rather, stability is defined operationally as the avoidance of extremes: runaway inflation, deep and prolonged recessions, explosive debt dynamics, and systemic financial breakdowns. It is a pragmatic concept, grounded in historical experience and policy practice rather than in theoretical purity.

This pragmatic orientation explains why the policy mix has remained a flexible and evolving framework rather than a fixed rulebook. Different historical periods have favoured different combinations of policies, reflecting

changing economic conditions, intellectual fashions, and institutional arrangements. The inflationary crises of the 1970s shifted emphasis toward monetary
restraint and central bank independence. The global financial crisis of 2008
revived interest in fiscal stimulus and unconventional monetary measures. In
each case, the language of stability was invoked, but its operational meaning
adapted to new circumstances.

Understanding the policy mix, therefore, requires not only a grasp of the
technical tools at policymakers' disposal but also an appreciation of the broader
intellectual and institutional context in which those tools are deployed. It is
to this interaction between monetary and fiscal policy, and to their standard
objectives and mechanisms, that the next part of the chapter now turns.

6.2. MONETARY POLICY, FISCAL POLICY, AND THE STANDARD OBJECTIVES OF THE POLICY MIX

Within the conventional framework of macroeconomic analysis, the policy
mix is constructed around two primary instruments: monetary policy and
fiscal policy. Each is assigned a distinct functional role, justified by differences
in transmission mechanisms, institutional arrangements, and perceived effectiveness across time horizons. Although their interaction is often complex and
occasionally contentious, standard macroeconomics presents them as complementary components of a unified stabilization strategy, oriented toward a
common set of macroeconomic objectives.

At the centre of this framework lies the assumption that macroeconomic
outcomes can be influenced, though not perfectly controlled, through deliberate policy intervention. The economy is not viewed as a self-equilibrating
mechanism that reliably converges to full employment and price stability
on its own. Instead, it is understood as a system subject to recurrent disturbances—demand shocks, supply shocks, financial disruptions, and external
imbalances—that can generate persistent deviations from desired aggregate
outcomes. Monetary and fiscal policy are therefore conceived as corrective
devices, designed to counteract these disturbances and to stabilize the path of
economic activity.

6.2.1 Monetary Policy and the Pursuit of Price Stability

In standard presentations, monetary policy is primarily entrusted with the
objective of price stability. This assignment reflects both theoretical reasoning and historical experience. Inflation is regarded as a uniquely harmful

macroeconomic phenomenon because it distorts relative prices, erodes the purchasing power of money, redistributes wealth arbitrarily, and undermines the informational function of the price system. Persistent or volatile inflation is also believed to discourage long-term investment and to weaken social trust in economic institutions.

Modern macroeconomic theory links inflation fundamentally to the supply of money and credit relative to real economic activity. While short-run fluctuations in inflation may arise from supply shocks or changes in expectations, sustained inflation is typically attributed to accommodative monetary conditions. This diagnosis underpins the central role assigned to central banks in managing the money supply and steering short-term interest rates.

Over time, monetary policy has evolved from direct control of monetary aggregates to the indirect management of financial conditions through policy interest rates and, more recently, through balance-sheet operations. Central banks no longer attempt to fine-tune the quantity of money directly. Instead, they influence the cost and availability of credit by setting a short-term policy rate, which then propagates through the financial system, affecting borrowing, spending, and investment decisions. This interest-rate channel is complemented by expectations effects, as credible policy commitments shape private-sector behaviour in anticipation of future monetary conditions.

In standard macroeconomic models, the central bank faces a trade-off between stabilizing inflation and stabilizing real economic activity. While price stability is often presented as the primary or even exclusive objective, especially in inflation-targeting regimes, monetary policy is also expected to smooth cyclical fluctuations in output and employment. This dual concern is reflected in reaction functions that respond not only to deviations of inflation from target but also to measures of economic slack, such as the output gap or unemployment rate.

The institutional design of monetary policy is considered crucial for its effectiveness. Independence from short-term political pressures is widely viewed as a necessary condition for credibility and discipline. Historical episodes of high inflation have reinforced the belief that politically controlled monetary policy tends to accommodate fiscal deficits and electoral incentives, leading to inflationary bias. Granting operational independence to central banks is therefore seen as a way to anchor expectations, constrain opportunistic behaviour, and enhance the long-run stability of the monetary system.

Within the policy mix, monetary policy is often characterized as a flexible, fast-acting instrument, capable of responding quickly to changing economic conditions. Interest rates can be adjusted frequently, and financial markets tend to react almost instantaneously to policy signals. This responsiveness makes monetary policy particularly well suited to addressing short-term fluctuations in aggregate demand. At the same time, its effects are recognized as uncertain and subject to variable lags, complicating precise calibration.

6.2.2 Fiscal Policy and Aggregate Demand Management

Fiscal policy, by contrast, operates through government spending, taxation, and borrowing. In standard macroeconomic theory, it plays a central role in influencing aggregate demand directly. Changes in public expenditure inject purchasing power into the economy, while changes in taxation affect disposable income and consumption decisions. Unlike monetary policy, which works primarily through financial variables, fiscal policy has an immediate impact on real resource allocation.

The stabilization role of fiscal policy is rooted in the Keynesian insight that private demand may be insufficient to sustain full employment, particularly during recessions. In such circumstances, expansionary fiscal policy—higher government spending or lower taxes—is expected to raise aggregate demand and to mobilize underutilized resources. Conversely, during periods of over-heating or inflationary pressure, contractionary fiscal policy can help restrain demand and prevent excessive price increases.

Standard macroeconomics distinguishes between discretionary fiscal policy and automatic stabilizers. Discretionary measures involve deliberate policy changes, such as stimulus packages or tax reforms, enacted in response to economic conditions. Automatic stabilizers, by contrast, are built into the fiscal system and operate without new legislation. Progressive taxation, unemployment benefits, and income-linked transfers automatically dampen fluctuations in disposable income, cushioning the economy against shocks.

Fiscal policy is also assigned broader objectives beyond stabilization. Governments use fiscal instruments to provide public goods, redistribute income, and influence long-term growth through investment in infrastructure, education, and research. Within the policy mix, these structural and distributive functions coexist with the stabilization function, sometimes reinforcing it and sometimes complicating it. For instance, fiscal consolidation aimed at debt sustainability may conflict with short-term stabilization goals during a recession.

Public debt occupies a central place in the standard analysis of fiscal policy. Borrowing allows governments to smooth spending over time and to finance countercyclical interventions without immediate tax increases. However, persistent deficits and rising debt are viewed as potential threats to macro-economic stability. High debt levels may crowd out private investment, raise interest rates, and constrain future policy options. Concerns about fiscal sustainability therefore impose limits on the scope and duration of expansionary fiscal policy.

Public choice theory has added an important dimension to the analysis of fiscal policy by emphasizing political incentives. While standard models often assume benevolent policymakers optimizing social welfare, public choice scholars argue that democratic processes tend to generate systematic biases toward deficit spending. Voters favor public benefits without corresponding tax increases, and politicians face incentives to postpone fiscal adjustment. These dynamics can lead to chronic deficits and debt accumulation, undermining long-term stability.

6.2.3 Objectives of the Policy Mix

The policy mix is designed to reconcile the objectives pursued by monetary and fiscal policy within a coherent macroeconomic strategy. In standard formulations, these objectives include price stability, high and stable employment, sustainable public finances, and steady economic growth. None of these goals can be pursued in isolation without affecting the others. The policy mix therefore becomes a problem of coordination under constraints.

Price stability remains the cornerstone of macroeconomic stability, both because of its intrinsic importance and because of its role in anchoring expectations. High employment and output stability are closely related objectives, reflecting the desire to minimize the social costs of recessions and booms. Fiscal sustainability ensures that stabilization efforts today do not generate crises tomorrow. Economic growth, while influenced by structural factors beyond the scope of short-term policy, is facilitated by a stable macroeconomic environment.

In the standard view, monetary and fiscal policy contribute differently to these objectives. Monetary policy provides a nominal anchor and responds to cyclical fluctuations, while fiscal policy supports demand and addresses distributional and structural concerns. The effectiveness of the policy mix depends on the alignment of these instruments and on the credibility of the institutions implementing them.

Conflicts within the policy mix arise when monetary and fiscal policies pull in opposite directions. An expansionary fiscal stance combined with a restrictive monetary policy, for example, may neutralize stabilization efforts and generate policy uncertainty. Conversely, coordinated expansion or contraction can amplify policy effects. Standard macroeconomics therefore emphasizes the importance of consistency and communication between policy authorities, even when institutional independence is preserved.

At this stage of analysis, the policy mix appears as a technically manageable framework for achieving macroeconomic stability. Its instruments are clearly defined, its objectives widely shared, and its institutional foundations well established. Yet this apparent coherence conceals deeper tensions related to knowledge limitations, political incentives, and systemic complexity. These tensions become more visible when considering coordination problems, policy rules, and non-standard interventions such as price controls—issues to which the next parts of the chapter will turn.

6.3. COORDINATION, TRADE-OFFS, AND THE INTERNAL LOGIC OF THE POLICY MIX

Once monetary and fiscal policy are recognized as distinct yet interdependent instruments, the question of coordination becomes unavoidable. The policy mix is not simply the sum of two independent interventions; it is the outcome of their interaction over time, mediated by institutional arrangements, expectations, and behavioural responses. Standard macroeconomics therefore treats coordination as a central challenge of stabilization policy, even when both monetary and fiscal authorities are assumed to pursue broadly aligned objectives.

The need for coordination arises from the fact that monetary and fiscal policies affect the same macroeconomic variables through different channels and with different temporal profiles. Fiscal policy influences aggregate demand directly by altering government spending and taxation, while monetary policy affects demand indirectly by shaping financial conditions, interest rates, and credit availability. Because these channels operate simultaneously, their effects can either reinforce or offset one another, depending on the stance adopted by each authority.

In the simplest analytical representations, such as the IS–LM framework, coordination is depicted as the alignment of shifts in the goods market and the money market. An expansionary fiscal policy increases demand and raises output, but it may also put upward pressure on interest rates, potentially crowding out private investment. An accommodative monetary policy can offset this effect by supplying additional liquidity and stabilizing interest rates. Conversely, a restrictive monetary stance can neutralize fiscal expansion by tightening financial conditions, limiting the impact of government spending on real activity.

Although such models are highly stylized, they capture a key intuition that persists in more sophisticated frameworks: macroeconomic policy is an interactive system, not a set of isolated levers. The effectiveness of each instrument depends on the stance of the other, as well as on private-sector expectations about future policy actions. Coordination is therefore not merely a matter of simultaneous action but of mutual consistency over time.

6.3.1 Trade-offs and Policy Conflicts

Standard macroeconomic theory acknowledges that the objectives pursued through the policy mix are not always mutually compatible. Trade-offs arise both in the short run and in the long run, forcing policymakers to prioritize among competing goals. One of the most familiar trade-offs concerns inflation and unemployment. Although the long-run Phillips curve is widely regarded as vertical, implying no permanent trade-off, short-run dynamics can still confront policymakers with difficult choices. Expansionary policies may reduce unemployment at the cost of higher inflation, while contractionary policies may stabilize prices at the cost of lost output.

Fiscal policy introduces additional trade-offs related to public debt and intertemporal allocation. Expansionary fiscal measures may support short-term stabilization but worsen long-term debt dynamics, particularly if they become politically entrenched. Conversely, fiscal consolidation may enhance credibility and sustainability but exacerbate cyclical downturns. The policy mix must therefore navigate between the immediate demands of stabilization and the longer-term constraints of fiscal solvency.

These trade-offs are not purely technical. They are embedded in political and institutional contexts that shape how costs and benefits are perceived and distributed. Public choice theory emphasizes that policymakers may face asymmetric incentives, favouring visible short-term gains over diffuse long-term costs. This asymmetry complicates coordination, as monetary and fiscal authorities may respond differently to political pressures and electoral cycles.

Monetary policy, particularly when conducted by an independent central bank, is often insulated from such pressures. Its commitment to price stability may conflict with expansionary fiscal policies pursued by elected governments seeking to stimulate growth or finance public programs. In such cases, coordination breaks down not because of analytical disagreement but because of institutional separation and divergent accountability structures.

6.3.2 Policy Rules versus Discretion

A central theme in the standard discussion of coordination concerns the choice between policy rules and discretionary action. Rules are pre-announced guidelines that constrain policy behaviour, such as inflation targets, fiscal deficit limits, or balanced-budget requirements. Discretion allows policymakers to respond flexibly to unforeseen circumstances, adjusting instruments as conditions evolve.

Advocates of rules argue that they enhance credibility, reduce uncertainty, and mitigate time-inconsistency problems. When private agents believe that policymakers will adhere to stable rules, their expectations adjust accordingly, reinforcing policy effectiveness. Rules also limit the scope for opportunistic behaviour driven by short-term political incentives, a concern emphasized in public choice analyses of fiscal and monetary policy.

Discretion, however, is defended on the grounds that economic shocks are unpredictable and heterogeneous. Rigid rules may prevent timely and appropriate responses to crises, forcing policymakers to adhere to prescriptions that are ill-suited to current conditions. The global financial crisis, for example, prompted widespread deviations from established rules, as central banks engaged in unconventional monetary policies and governments implemented large fiscal interventions.

The policy mix is shaped by this tension between commitment and flexibility. Monetary policy has increasingly gravitated toward rule-like behaviour, exemplified by inflation targeting and systematic reaction functions. Fiscal policy, by contrast, remains more discretionary, reflecting the political nature of budgetary decisions and the diversity of fiscal objectives. Coordination becomes more challenging when one instrument is rule-bound and the other is not.

6.3.3 Institutional Design and the Coordination Problem

Standard macroeconomics recognizes that coordination is ultimately an institutional problem. The separation of monetary and fiscal authority, while intended to enhance discipline and credibility, also creates potential conflicts. Independent central banks may prioritize price stability even when fiscal authorities seek expansion, leading to policy standoffs or mixed signals to markets.

Various institutional mechanisms have been proposed to mitigate these conflicts. Formal consultation procedures, shared macroeconomic frameworks, and explicit mandates can facilitate information exchange and align expectations. At the international level, coordination becomes even more complex, as national policies interact through trade and financial flows. Monetary unions and fiscal compacts represent attempts to institutionalize coordination across borders, with varying degrees of success.

Complexity economics has further highlighted the limits of coordination in highly interconnected systems. Economic outcomes emerge from decentralized interactions among heterogeneous agents, and policy interventions can generate nonlinear and unintended effects. From this perspective, the policy mix cannot be engineered with precision, and coordination efforts must contend with deep uncertainty and incomplete knowledge.

While standard macroeconomics acknowledges these challenges, it often treats them as complications rather than as fundamental constraints.

6.3.4   Preparing the Ground for Non-Standard Instruments

The coordination problem of the policy mix creates fertile ground for the introduction of non-standard policy instruments. When monetary and fiscal policies are perceived as insufficient or ineffective, governments may resort to direct interventions aimed at stabilizing specific prices or markets. Price controls, subsidies, and administrative regulations are often justified as temporary measures to contain inflation, protect vulnerable groups, or prevent social unrest.

Within the standard framework, such measures are typically treated as auxiliary or exceptional tools rather than as core components of the policy mix. They are introduced when conventional instruments face political or technical limits, and they are expected to be removed once stability is restored. However, their interaction with monetary and fiscal policy raises additional coordination challenges, as they can distort price signals and interfere with the transmission mechanisms of standard instruments.

At this point, the policy mix begins to reveal its internal tensions. The more complex the coordination problem becomes, the stronger the temptation to bypass market mechanisms and to impose direct controls. Understanding the rationale for these interventions, as well as their limitations, requires a careful examination of price controls as a stabilization device—a task to which the next part of the chapter is devoted.

6.4.   Policy Rules, Institutional Constraints, and the Architecture of Macroeconomic Stability

As the coordination problem of the policy mix becomes more apparent, standard macroeconomic theory increasingly shifts attention from the choice of instruments to the design of institutions. The question is no longer merely how monetary and fiscal policy should be set at a given moment, but how the rules, constraints, and governance structures within which these policies operate can foster macroeconomic stability over time. In this sense, stability is reinterpreted as an institutional achievement rather than as the mechanical outcome of discretionary intervention.

This shift reflects a growing awareness that macroeconomic policy unfolds in a world of expectations. Private agents do not respond only to current policy actions; they form beliefs about future behaviour, institutional commitments, and the credibility of authorities. These expectations shape investment, consumption, wage bargaining, and price-setting decisions, thereby influencing macroeconomic outcomes in ways that can reinforce or undermine policy intentions. The institutional framework of the policy mix thus becomes a central determinant of its effectiveness.

6.4.1   The Logic of Rules in Macroeconomic Policy

Policy rules emerge in standard macroeconomics as a response to two interrelated problems: time inconsistency and credibility. Time inconsistency arises when policies that appear optimal in the short run become suboptimal once private agents adjust their expectations. A government may promise low inflation to anchor expectations, but later find it tempting to pursue expansionary policies to reduce unemployment. If such behaviour is anticipated, the initial promise loses credibility, and inflation expectations rise even before policy actions are taken.

Rules are designed to address this problem by constraining future policy choices in a predictable manner. By committing to a rule—such as an inflation target, a monetary growth guideline, or a fiscal deficit ceiling—authorities signal their intention to resist short-term temptations. If the commitment is credible, private agents incorporate it into their expectations, reducing the inflationary or destabilizing effects of discretionary intervention.

In monetary policy, this logic has led to the widespread adoption of rule-like frameworks. Inflation targeting, central bank independence, and transparent communication strategies are all institutional devices intended to bind policy behaviour over time. Even when central banks retain some discretion, their actions are expected to follow systematic patterns that can be anticipated and evaluated by markets.

Fiscal policy has proven more resistant to rule-based governance, largely because of its inherently political character. Budgetary decisions involve distributional choices, public goods provision, and social priorities that are difficult to encode in simple rules. Nevertheless, standard macroeconomics recognizes the value of fiscal rules in constraining deficit bias and promoting sustainability. Balanced-budget requirements, debt brakes, and expenditure ceilings are presented as mechanisms to align short-term stabilization efforts with long-term fiscal discipline.

6.4.2 Institutional Separation and Complementarity

The modern architecture of macroeconomic stability rests on a deliberate separation of monetary and fiscal authority. This separation is not accidental; it reflects a normative judgment about the sources of instability. Monetary instability is associated with political interference, deficit monetization, and inflationary finance. Fiscal instability is linked to electoral incentives, interest-group pressures, and the tendency to postpone adjustment.

By delegating monetary policy to independent central banks, standard macroeconomics seeks to insulate price stability from political pressures. Fiscal policy, by contrast, remains under democratic control, subject to constitutional and procedural constraints rather than technocratic delegation. The policy mix thus operates within a dual institutional structure, balancing independence and accountability.

This separation, however, does not eliminate the need for coordination. Independent monetary policy can only function effectively if fiscal policy remains broadly consistent with price stability. Excessive deficits and debt accumulation can undermine monetary control by increasing pressure for accommodative policies. Conversely, overly restrictive monetary policy can complicate fiscal adjustment by raising borrowing costs and suppressing growth. Institutional design therefore aims to create complementary incentives rather than rigid autonomy.

Standard macroeconomic analysis often frames this complementarity in terms of mutual constraints. Monetary policy provides a nominal anchor that disciplines fiscal behaviour, while fiscal rules support monetary credibility by limiting the temptation to inflate away debt. Stability emerges not from the omnipotence of either authority, but from the interaction of constrained decision-makers operating within a shared framework.

6.4.3 Stability as an Institutional Equilibrium

Within this perspective, macroeconomic stability is no longer understood as a continuous process of fine-tuning. Instead, it is conceived as an institutional equilibrium, sustained by credible commitments, predictable behaviour, and adaptive expectations. The role of policy is to maintain this equilibrium by responding to shocks without undermining the rules that anchor expectations.

This understanding marks a significant evolution from earlier visions of macroeconomic management. The ambition to smooth the business cycle through active intervention gives way to a more modest goal: preventing cumulative instability while allowing normal economic fluctuations to occur. Policy does not aim to eliminate cycles, but to prevent them from becoming destabilizing spirals of inflation, unemployment, or debt.

Complexity-oriented approaches within mainstream economics reinforce this shift. They emphasize that economies are adaptive systems characterized by nonlinear interactions, feedback loops, and emergent behaviour. In such systems, attempts at precise control are likely to fail. Rules and institutions are therefore valued not because they guarantee optimal outcomes, but because they provide a stable framework within which decentralized adaptation can take place.

6.4.4 The Limits of Institutional Governance

Despite its appeal, the rule-based institutional approach does not resolve all tensions within the policy mix. Rules must be interpreted, enforced, and occasionally revised. Exceptional circumstances—financial crises, pandemics, wars—often prompt temporary suspensions of established constraints. Each suspension, however justified in the short run, raises questions about credibility and precedent.

Moreover, rules themselves are products of political processes. Their design reflects compromises, power relations, and prevailing economic doctrines. Fiscal rules may be loosened or reinterpreted under pressure, and monetary mandates may be expanded to include additional objectives such as financial stability or climate considerations. Institutional stability is therefore dynamic rather than static, subject to gradual evolution and episodic disruption.

It is precisely in these moments of strain that the policy mix tends to expand beyond its conventional boundaries. When monetary and fiscal tools appear constrained by rules or institutional limits, policymakers may turn to alternative instruments that promise immediate and visible effects. Among

these, price controls occupy a prominent place. They offer the appearance
of direct action against inflation and social hardship, bypassing the complex
transmission mechanisms of standard policy tools.

The next section examines this turn toward price controls within the standard policy discourse, focusing on their rationale, mechanics, and limitations
as instruments of macroeconomic stabilization.

6.5. Price Controls as a Stabilization Instrument: Rationale, Mechanisms, and Limits

When conventional monetary and fiscal instruments appear insufficient, slow,
or politically costly, governments often turn to more direct forms of intervention in the price system. Among these, price controls—ceilings, freezes,
administered prices, and regulated margins—have historically played a recurrent role in attempts to preserve macroeconomic stability. Within the standard
policy discourse, price controls are typically justified as exceptional measures,
adopted in moments of acute inflationary pressure, social unrest, or perceived
market failure. They are presented not as substitutes for monetary and fiscal
policy, but as temporary complements designed to bridge a transitional phase
or to contain specific symptoms of instability.

The appeal of price controls is immediately intuitive. Inflation manifests
itself through rising prices, eroding purchasing power and generating visible
hardship. Unlike monetary tightening or fiscal consolidation, which operate indirectly and with uncertain lags, price controls promise immediate and
tangible relief. By capping prices on essential goods, rents, energy, or wages,
policymakers seek to shield households from sudden cost increases, stabilize
expectations, and prevent inflationary spirals driven by adaptive behaviour.
In this sense, price controls are framed as instruments of social protection as
much as of macroeconomic management.

Standard macroeconomic analysis acknowledges this political and social
rationale while remaining deeply skeptical about the effectiveness of price
controls as a stabilization tool. The skepticism does not stem from ideological
opposition to intervention per se, but from a theoretical understanding of
how prices function in a market economy. Prices are not merely accounting numbers; they are signals that coordinate decentralized decisions about
production, consumption, and investment. Interfering with these signals
alters behaviour in ways that often undermine the very objectives controls
are meant to achieve.

In conventional supply-and-demand analysis, a price ceiling set below the market-clearing level creates excess demand. Consumers demand more at the artificially low price, while producers supply less, given reduced profitability. The result is not stability but shortage. Goods may disappear from official markets, queues may form, and non-price rationing mechanisms emerge. Black markets, quality deterioration, and favouritism replace transparent price allocation. These effects are not incidental; they follow directly from the logic of constrained price adjustment.

The standard literature emphasizes that price controls do not eliminate inflationary pressures; they merely suppress their visible expression. Underlying imbalances between aggregate demand and aggregate supply persist. If inflation is driven by expansionary monetary or fiscal conditions, price controls can delay price increases temporarily but cannot resolve the root cause. Once controls are lifted, suppressed inflation often reemerges abruptly, sometimes with greater intensity. Historical experiences with wage and price freezes illustrate this pattern repeatedly.

From a macroeconomic perspective, price controls also interfere with the transmission mechanisms of monetary and fiscal policy. Monetary tightening, for example, is intended to slow demand by raising borrowing costs and moderating spending. If prices are administratively fixed, the adjustment may instead take place through quantities—reduced output, rationing, or unemployment—rather than through relative prices. Similarly, fiscal measures designed to reallocate resources may fail to achieve their intended effects if prices are prevented from reflecting scarcity and opportunity cost.

The literature on price controls highlights an additional, often underappreciated, dimension: the informational role of prices. Prices aggregate dispersed knowledge about preferences, technologies, and constraints. When prices are fixed or capped, this information is distorted or lost, making it more difficult for producers and consumers to adjust efficiently. In this sense, price controls impair not only allocative efficiency but also the economy's capacity to adapt to changing conditions. The damage extends beyond the controlled markets, as distorted signals propagate through supply chains and related sectors.

Standard policy analysis therefore treats price controls as inherently blunt instruments. They lack the precision of monetary tools and the targeting capacity of fiscal measures. While they may temporarily dampen measured inflation, they do so at the cost of creating hidden distortions that accumulate over time. The longer controls remain in place, the more severe these distortions tend to become, as incentives to evade regulation intensify and productive capacity erodes.

Despite these limitations, the persistence of price controls in policy practice demands explanation. One reason lies in the political economy of stabilization. Inflation imposes immediate and highly visible costs on voters, whereas the costs of price controls—shortages, quality decline, misallocation—are often less visible or can be attributed to external factors such as speculation or supply disruptions. Price controls thus offer policymakers a way to demonstrate action and concern, even when the underlying causes of instability remain unaddressed.

Another reason is the compartmentalized nature of policy governance. When monetary policy is constrained by institutional commitments and fiscal policy is limited by debt concerns or political deadlock, price controls may appear as a residual option. They can be implemented quickly, targeted selectively, and framed as temporary emergency measures. In this sense, price controls often emerge not from confidence in their effectiveness but from frustration with the limits of the standard policy mix.

The standard literature, however, consistently warns that such measures should be used, if at all, with extreme caution and for strictly limited durations. Effective stabilization, it argues, cannot be achieved by overriding the price system. Durable macroeconomic stability requires alignment between nominal policy instruments and real economic conditions. When price controls are used to mask rather than correct imbalances, they tend to postpone adjustment and amplify eventual disruption.

At the same time, mainstream analysis concedes that price controls may have short-term political or social benefits in exceptional circumstances, such as wartime economies or acute supply shocks. Even in these cases, their effectiveness depends on careful design, credible exit strategies, and complementary policies that address underlying pressures. Without such safeguards, price controls risk becoming entrenched, transforming from emergency tools into permanent features of economic governance.

This ambivalent assessment reflects the broader tension within the policy mix. The desire for stability encourages intervention, yet the mechanisms of intervention can undermine the very coordination and information processes upon which stability depends. Price controls thus occupy a liminal position in macroeconomic policy: neither fully embraced nor entirely rejected, they are repeatedly rediscovered in moments of crisis and repeatedly judged inadequate in retrospect.

It is precisely this tension—between the aspiration to control outcomes and the limits imposed by knowledge, incentives, and systemic complexity—that prepares the ground for a deeper critical assessment of macroeconomic stabilization.

6.6. MACROECONOMIC STABILITY AND THE LIMITS OF CONTROL: TOWARD A CRITICAL RECONSIDERATION

Having surveyed the standard architecture of the policy mix and its role in the pursuit of macroeconomic stability, it becomes possible to identify the internal tensions that remain unresolved within the conventional framework. Monetary policy, fiscal policy, institutional rules, and auxiliary instruments such as price controls are presented as components of a coherent stabilization strategy, yet their effectiveness ultimately rests on assumptions about knowledge, coordination, and controllability that are far from innocuous. Even before advancing a full critique, the standard discourse itself reveals points of strain that invite reconsideration.

At its core, the modern conception of macroeconomic stability presupposes that aggregate economic outcomes can be meaningfully defined, measured, and steered. Stability is articulated in terms of inflation rates, output gaps, employment levels, debt ratios, and fiscal balances. These aggregates serve both as diagnostic indicators and as policy targets. They allow policymakers to describe the state of the economy in a common language and to justify intervention as a response to observable deviations from desired benchmarks. Yet this reliance on aggregates already introduces a subtle abstraction. Economic life is reduced to a set of macro-variables whose movements are treated as proxies for social well-being, coordination, and order.

Within the standard framework, this abstraction is not regarded as problematic. It is considered a necessary simplification, justified by the complexity of economic systems and the practical demands of governance. Policy does not aim at perfect control but at reasonable approximation. Stability, in this sense, becomes a pragmatic objective: the avoidance of extremes rather than the attainment of an ideal state. The policy mix is evaluated not by its capacity to generate optimal outcomes, but by its ability to prevent cumulative disorder.

Nevertheless, the very need for ever more refined instruments, rules, and institutional safeguards suggests an underlying fragility. Coordination problems persist despite formal separation of powers. Trade-offs reappear despite advances in modelling. Price controls resurface despite repeated demonstrations of their limits. Each of these phenomena points to a deeper issue: the gap between the epistemic ambitions of macroeconomic policy and the nature of the economic processes it seeks to govern.

The standard approach implicitly treats the economy as an object of management, albeit a complex one. Shocks are external disturbances, policy instruments are corrective forces, and institutions are stabilizing constraints.

Even when complexity is acknowledged, it is often framed as a technical challenge to be addressed through better models, improved data, or more sophisticated rules. The question of whether economic order itself emerges from processes that resist centralized interpretation and control remains largely unexamined at this level of analysis.

This becomes particularly evident in the treatment of price controls. Their recurring use is not merely a policy error or a political temptation; it reflects a deeper discomfort with the spontaneous and sometimes disruptive character of price formation. Prices convey information that is not only dispersed but also historically situated and expectation-laden. When policy seeks to override this process in the name of stability, it implicitly substitutes administrative judgment for social interpretation. The resulting distortions are not accidental; they arise from a mismatch between the nature of economic coordination and the means employed to regulate it.

Similarly, the emphasis on rules and institutional commitments, while mitigating certain incentive problems, does not eliminate the interpretative dimension of policy. Rules must be applied, exceptions justified, and objectives redefined as circumstances change. Stability itself is not a fixed condition but a moving target, shaped by evolving expectations, technological change, and institutional memory. What counts as instability in one historical context may be regarded as normal adjustment in another.

At this point, the limits of the standard framework become visible, though not yet fully articulated. The policy mix succeeds in organizing macroeconomic discourse and practice, but it does so by abstracting from the lived, interpretative nature of economic action. It treats expectations as variables to be managed rather than as meanings to be understood. It conceives coordination as an outcome to be engineered rather than as a process that unfolds through time, uncertainty, and entrepreneurial discovery.

This chapter has deliberately refrained from pursuing these issues to their full implications. Its purpose has been to reconstruct the standard understanding of policy mix and macroeconomic stability on its own terms, acknowledging both its internal coherence and its recurring difficulties. The task of critique requires a different level of analysis—one that interrogates not only policy outcomes but also the epistemological and anthropological assumptions underlying macroeconomic governance.

The chapters that follow will undertake this task explicitly. They will question the identification of stability with measurability, the reduction of economic order to aggregate control, and the conflation of policy effectiveness with technical precision. They will explore alternative ways of understanding coordination, not as a problem to be solved by policy design alone, but as an emergent property of social interaction shaped by institutions, narratives, and entrepreneurial action.

For now, it is sufficient to note that the standard policy mix, for all its sophistication, operates at the edge of its own conceptual boundaries. Its recurring reliance on exceptional measures, its sensitivity to institutional credibility, and its difficulty in addressing unintended consequences all point toward a deeper reconsideration of what macroeconomic stability means—and whether it can be meaningfully pursued without first rethinking the nature of economic understanding itself.

Appendix: Macroeconomic Stability and the Policy Mix in
Contemporary Textbooks: A Technical, Modern Treatment

6.A. What "macroeconomic stability" means in contemporary macro

In modern textbooks and policy practice, *macroeconomic stability* is not a single target but a disciplined way of managing unavoidable trade-offs among a small set of core objectives. The canonical post-1990s framework—the "new neoclassical synthesis," implemented in New Keynesian (NK) DSGE models and their semi-structural cousins—treats stability as keeping the economy close to an efficient path in the presence of nominal rigidities, real frictions, and imperfect information.

At an operational level, stability typically means:

1. Inflation stability: inflation near a target (or within a tolerance band), anchored expectations, and limited dispersion across sectors.
2. Real stability: a small and non-persistent output gap (or unemployment gap), avoiding deep recessions and overheating.
3. Financial stability: a financial system resilient enough that credit and asset-pricing dynamics do not amplify shocks into crises. Modern macro textbooks increasingly integrate this explicitly rather than treating finance as "a veil".
4. Fiscal sustainability: public debt dynamics consistent with solvency and political feasibility, so that fiscal policy can stabilize rather than destabilize.
5. External stability (open economy): avoiding disorderly balance-of-payments adjustments, excessive currency mismatch, and runaway risk premia, especially in emerging markets.

The "policy mix" is then the *joint design* of (i) monetary policy, (ii) fiscal policy (automatic stabilizers + discretionary actions + debt management), and increasingly (iii) macroprudential/financial policies. The modern textbook lens insists that these instruments interact via expectations, intertemporal constraints, and institutional credibility; "one instrument–one target" is too naive once you admit multiple frictions and the possibility of regime change (e.g., hitting the effective lower bound, or moving into fiscal dominance).

6.B. The workhorse framework: the three-equation New Keynesian model

Many modern textbooks teach macro stabilization through a "3-equation model" (aggregate demand/IS, Phillips curve, policy rule). Carlin–Soskice popularize this pedagogically and update it to a "modern monetary framework" that connects directly to central-bank practice, while graduate treatments provide the microfoundations.

6.B.1 The output gap and the dynamic IS (aggregate demand)

Let be the output gap (log deviation of output from "natural" or efficient output). A canonical linearized NK IS relation is:

$$x_t = \mathbb{E}_t x_{t+1} - \frac{1}{\sigma}\left(i_t - \mathbb{E}_t \pi_{t+1} - r_t^n\right) + g_t$$

- i_t : nominal policy rate
- π_{t+1}: inflation
- $r_n{}^t$: natural real rate (time-varying, driven by productivity, preferences, global factors)
- σ: intertemporal elasticity parameter (inverse of risk aversion in CRRA setups)
- g_t: demand shifters (fiscal impulse, risk-premium shocks, credit spreads in richer models)

This equation is the technical backbone of the statement: tightening works by raising the real interest rate relative to the natural rate, depressing the output gap. The "policy mix" enters here because fiscal policy and financial conditions can shift and/or drive wedges between the policy rate and broader borrowing costs.

6.B.2 The New Keynesian Phillips Curve (supply/inflation dynamics)

A baseline NKPC is:

$$\pi_t = \beta \mathbb{E}_t \pi_{t+1} + \kappa x_t + u_t$$

- β: discount factor
- κ: slope (increases with price flexibility; decreases with stickiness and strategic complementarities)
- u_t: cost-push / markup / supply shocks

This equation formalizes two crucial stabilization facts:

- Demand-driven inflation: with stable, closing a positive output gap lowers inflation over time.

- Supply shocks create trade-offs: adverse pushes inflation up even as output falls; policy must decide how much to "accommodate" vs "lean against".

Recent empirical debates about a "flatter" Phillips curve (small) matter because they change optimal policy aggressiveness and the inflation–real-activity sacrifice ratio. Modern central-bank research continues to refine these dynamics.

6.B.3 The monetary policy rule (systematic stabilization)

A baseline Taylor-type rule is:

$$i_t = \bar{i} + \phi_\pi \left(\pi_t - \pi^* \right) + \phi_x x_t + \varepsilon_t^i$$

with (the *Taylor principle*) for determinacy in standard NK settings.

Textbook treatments increasingly emphasize that *a rule is a description of systematic behaviour*, not necessarily a mechanical formula. Still, policy evaluation often uses rule families (including "targeted Taylor rules") to discuss robustness and trade-offs.

6.C. WELFARE, LOSS FUNCTIONS, AND "OPTIMAL" STABILIZATION

A major modern move (relative to old IS–LM) is that stabilization can be framed as minimizing a quadratic loss derived (approximately) from microfoundations:

$$\mathscr{L} = \sum_{t=0}^{\infty} \beta^t \left[\left(\pi_t - \pi^* \right)^2 + \lambda x_t^2 \right]$$

- λ summarizes the relative weight on real stabilization vs inflation stabilization, often linked to structural parameters (e.g., the slope κ, degree of price stickiness).

This does two things:

1. It makes transparent that trade-offs are structural: if is small or volatile, disinflation is more costly in terms of output gap volatility.
2. It integrates credibility and expectations: forward-looking terms make commitments (or credible reaction functions) central to outcomes.

This welfare-based view is central to the "new neoclassical synthesis" framing of monetary policy.

6.D. EXTENDING THE CORE: FISCAL POLICY AND THE GOVERNMENT BUDGET CONSTRAINT

A purely monetary 3-equation model is incomplete because fiscal policy affects aggregate demand, debt dynamics, and (in some regimes) inflation determination.

6.D.1 Debt dynamics (accounting identity with macro content)

Let be real public debt as a ratio to GDP (or scaled appropriately). A standard approximation:

$$\Delta b_t \approx (r_t - g_t)\, b_{t-1} - s_t$$

- r_t: effective real interest rate on debt
- g_t: real GDP growth
- s_t: primary surplus (positive surplus reduces debt)

This identity becomes a macroeconomic mechanism because policy affects each term:

- Monetary policy influences r_t (and, via growth, g_t).
- Fiscal stance influences s_t, but also growth and risk premia.
- Credibility influences the spread embedded in r_t.

6.D.2 Fiscal multipliers and state dependence

Modern textbooks treat fiscal multipliers as state-dependent: larger in recessions, under financial stress, and at the effective lower bound (ELB) because monetary policy cannot fully offset. This is one of the deepest reasons the "policy mix" cannot be reduced to "monetary does stabilization, fiscal does long-run structure".

Even in semi-structural NK models, a simple way to see it is through the IS equation: if the central bank raises i_t aggressively in response to fiscal expansion, the net effect on x_t is muted. If the bank is constrained (ELB), fiscal shifts g_t translate more directly into x_t.

6.D.3 The fiscal theory of the price level (regime possibility)

Modern macro also recognizes that inflation may be jointly determined by monetary and fiscal policy depending on the regime. If fiscal policy sets primary surpluses in a way inconsistent with stabilizing debt and monetary policy accommodates, the price level can adjust to ensure real debt sustainability. Even when one does not endorse strong versions, the key lesson is: a credible nominal anchor typically requires coherent fiscal backing.

6.E. MONETARY–FISCAL INTERACTION: COORDINATION, DOMINANCE, AND THE POLICY MIX

A technically useful way to approach monetary–fiscal interaction is to classify policy regimes according to which authority provides the effective nominal anchor and how credibility is distributed between them. In what textbooks typically describe as "normal times," the regime is one of monetary dominance. In this setting, the central bank credibly sets the nominal anchor—usually in the form of an inflation target—and private expectations are firmly aligned with it. Fiscal policy, in turn, adjusts over time so as to satisfy the government's intertemporal budget constraint: primary balances respond to the level of public debt in a way that preserves solvency, rather than challenging the monetary anchor.

Within such a regime, fiscal stabilization is most effective when it operates primarily through automatic stabilizers, allowing tax revenues and transfers to move countercyclically without the need for frequent discretionary intervention. When shocks are unusually large, such as during deep recessions, discretionary fiscal measures can play a useful role, provided they are explicitly temporary and well targeted. Crucially, these short-term interventions must be embedded in a credible medium-term framework, so that rising debt is accompanied by clear and believable plans for consolidation. Credibility in this context is not an abstract virtue but a practical condition for preserving the effectiveness of monetary policy.

A very different configuration emerges under fiscal dominance, or even under the perception of fiscal stress. Here, the fiscal authority fails to credibly stabilize public debt, either because political constraints prevent adjustment or because markets doubt the willingness or ability of governments to do so. In such circumstances, the central bank comes under pressure to keep interest rates artificially low in order to contain debt-servicing costs or to avert an outright fiscal crisis. As a result, the nominal anchor is no longer fully trusted, and inflation expectations risk becoming de-anchored.

Under fiscal dominance, macroeconomic stability becomes significantly harder to achieve. Attempts at disinflation raise real interest rates, worsen debt dynamics, and often increase sovereign spreads, potentially triggering adverse feedback loops. Monetary tightening in this environment can become self-defeating unless it is accompanied by credible fiscal reforms that restore confidence in long-term solvency. Without such reforms, the burden placed on monetary policy alone is not only excessive but also ineffective.

Increasingly, policy analysis has moved beyond this dichotomy to emphasize strategic complementarity and deliberate "mix design" between monetary and fiscal instruments. In a demand-driven downturn, for example, accommodative monetary policy combined with supportive fiscal action can reduce the required adjustment in each instrument, thereby dampening macroeconomic volatility and limiting side effects. Conversely, in an inflationary episode driven by supply constraints, fiscal restraint can ease the task of the central bank by reducing excess demand, improving the disinflation path, and mitigating financial stress associated with aggressive monetary tightening.

Recent research by the European Central Bank has explicitly examined combinations of monetary and fiscal rules and their macroeconomic outcomes in the euro area. This work reflects a broader analytical shift away from treating monetary and fiscal policies in isolation and toward a more explicit evaluation of the policy mix as an integrated stabilization framework.

6.F. OPEN-ECONOMY STABILITY: EXCHANGE RATES, UIP, AND THE "IMPOSSIBLE TRINITY"

For open economies, macro stability must incorporate exchange-rate dynamics, capital flows, and external balance constraints.

A standard building block is uncovered interest parity (UIP) with a risk premium:

$$i_t = i_t^* + \mathbb{E}_t \Delta s_{t+1} + \rho_t$$

- s_t : log nominal exchange rate (domestic price of foreign currency)
- i_t^*: foreign interest rate
- ρ_t: risk premium / wedge (time-varying; can reflect global risk appetite, debt sustainability, political risk)

Policy mix implications:

1. Under a floating rate, monetary policy can target domestic inflation/output, but the exchange rate becomes a fast-moving transmission channel and a source of volatility.

2. Under a fixed/managed rate, monetary policy is partly subordinated to the peg; fiscal and macroprudential tools carry more of the stabilization burden, and reserves become a critical buffer.

3. With high foreign-currency debt, depreciation worsens balance sheets ("original sin"), making external stability central to macro stability.

Modern macroprudential frameworks often arise precisely because open-economy financial channels make pure interest-rate policy insufficient.

6.G. FINANCIAL STABILITY AS A THIRD PILLAR: WHY THE POLICY MIX NOW INCLUDES MACROPRUDENTIAL POLICY

Pre-2008, many textbook accounts implicitly assumed that stabilizing inflation and output was sufficient for stability (the "divine coincidence" in simple NK models, where stabilizing inflation also stabilizes the output gap when shocks are purely demand-side and markets are otherwise efficient).

Post-crisis, mainstream teaching incorporates finance and recognizes that:

- Credit cycles and leverage can build systemic risk even when inflation is low.
- Asset prices affect spending and collateral constraints.
- Monetary policy may face a trade-off between macro stabilization and financial risk ("lean vs clean").

Technical DSGE descriptions used by central banks now routinely include financial blocks (credit spreads, bank capital, occasionally housing). A technical description of a Fed DSGE model illustrates this institutional reality.

A minimal way to represent the new logic in semi-structural form is to add a financial conditions wedge in the IS curve:

$$x_t = \mathbb{E}_t x_{t+1} - \frac{1}{\sigma}\left(i_t - \mathbb{E}_t \pi_{t+1} - r_t^n\right) - \chi\, \text{spread}_t + g_t$$

Macroprudential policy aims to influence spread_t, leverage, and credit growth directly—reducing the need for blunt interest-rate movements that might undershoot inflation goals or impose excessive unemployment costs.

6.H. SHOCK TAXONOMY AND OPTIMAL MIX: DEMAND, SUPPLY, AND FINANCIAL
       DISTURBANCES

A technically disciplined approach to macroeconomic stabilization begins
with a careful diagnosis of the nature of the disturbance hitting the economy.
Modern macroeconomic theory stresses that demand, supply, and financial
shocks operate through different transmission mechanisms, and therefore
call for distinct policy responses. Treating all fluctuations as if they were of
the same type risks either over-reacting or applying the wrong instrument,
thereby magnifying rather than smoothing macroeconomic volatility. The
notion of an "optimal policy mix" is thus inseparable from a clear taxonomy
of shocks.

The policy problem becomes more complex in the presence of adverse
supply or cost-push shocks. These disturbances, often associated with increases
in production costs, energy prices, or disruptions to global value chains, generate upward pressure on inflation while simultaneously depressing output.
The resulting configuration is stagflationary in nature, confronting monetary
policy with a genuine trade-off. Tightening policy can help contain inflation
and prevent expectations from drifting upward, but at the cost of further weakening economic activity. Accommodating the shock, by contrast, can cushion
the output loss but risks validating higher inflation. The appropriate response
depends crucially on the credibility of the policy framework, the degree of
inflation persistence, and the extent to which expectations remain anchored.

In such circumstances, fiscal policy must be designed with particular care.
An expansionary fiscal stance that adds broad-based demand stimulus risks
exacerbating inflationary pressures and forcing monetary policy into a more
aggressive tightening path. As a result, the emphasis shifts toward a neutral or
restraining aggregate fiscal posture, combined with narrowly targeted measures aimed at alleviating the distributional or sectoral impact of the shock.
Temporary and well-focused fiscal relief can mitigate hardship without undermining the overall inflation objective, provided it does not become a substitute
for necessary price adjustment.

Beyond short-run stabilization, structural policies play an important supporting role in shaping the medium-term inflation–output trade-off. Reforms
that enhance competition, improve energy supply and logistics, or increase
labour-market flexibility can reduce cost pressures and raise productive capacity,
thereby improving the economy's ability to absorb shocks with less inflationary fallout. However, modern textbooks are clear that such reforms are not
immediate stabilization tools. Their effects unfold gradually, complementing

but not replacing monetary, fiscal, and macroprudential policies in the short-run management of macroeconomic disturbances.

Financial shocks occupy a distinctive place in modern macroeconomic analysis because they operate primarily through balance sheets, risk premia, and credit conditions rather than through the standard channels of aggregate demand alone. A prototypical financial shock is an abrupt increase in credit spreads, often accompanied by a tightening of leverage or collateral constraints. Such a shock may originate in the banking sector, in capital markets, or through sudden reversals in capital flows, and its defining feature is the impairment of the financial system's capacity to intermediate savings into investment and consumption.

When spreads rise and leverage constraints bind, economic activity contracts. Firms face higher external financing costs and, in some cases, are rationed out of credit markets altogether. Investment declines sharply, not only because borrowing becomes more expensive, but also because internal funds deteriorate as profits fall. Households experience similar pressures, particularly when borrowing constraints tighten in mortgage or consumer credit markets. The resulting drop in spending propagates through income and employment, generating a broad-based fall in output.

The behaviour of inflation following a financial shock is less uniform and depends crucially on the structure of the economy and the nature of the shock. In many advanced economies, the dominant effect of the collapse in demand is disinflationary: lower activity, falling marginal costs, and increased slack in labour markets put downward pressure on prices. However, this pattern is not universal. In emerging market economies, financial shocks are often intertwined with sharp exchange-rate movements. If a sudden stop in capital inflows or a loss of investor confidence leads to a strong currency depreciation, import prices can rise rapidly. In such circumstances, inflation may increase even as output contracts, producing a stagflationary configuration that complicates policy responses. The coexistence of recessionary forces and inflationary pressures illustrates why financial shocks cannot be analysed solely through the lens of standard demand disturbances.

Monetary policy is, in principle, well suited to respond to financial shocks. Lowering policy interest rates reduces borrowing costs, supports asset prices, and alleviates debt-service burdens, thereby cushioning the contraction in spending. Yet financial shocks are precisely those episodes in which the transmission mechanism of monetary policy may be impaired. If banks are undercapitalised, facing liquidity shortages, or unwilling to lend because of heightened risk aversion, reductions in policy rates may not translate into increased credit to the private sector. In such cases, the economy can enter a situation where monetary easing is necessary but insufficient.

This limitation elevates the role of fiscal policy and lender-of-last-resort interventions. Targeted fiscal measures can support aggregate demand directly, bypassing clogged credit channels, while public guarantees or recapitalisations can restore confidence in the financial system. Central banks, acting as lenders of last resort, may provide liquidity to solvent but illiquid institutions, stabilise key funding markets, and prevent fire sales of assets. These interventions are not substitutes for conventional monetary policy, but complements that become essential when financial frictions dominate macroeconomic dynamics.

Beyond immediate stabilisation, financial shocks underscore the importance of macroprudential and resolution tools. When leverage constraints bind across the system, the objective of policy extends beyond short-term demand management to the preservation of financial stability itself. Countercyclical capital buffers, liquidity requirements, and borrower-based measures can mitigate the buildup of vulnerabilities during booms, reducing the severity of subsequent busts. Effective resolution regimes, in turn, allow failing institutions to be restructured or wound down without triggering systemic collapse, limiting the fiscal and macroeconomic costs of crises.

Recent research on inflation dynamics reinforces the complexity of policy design in the presence of financial shocks. Inflation responses are increasingly understood to be state-dependent and potentially nonlinear: the same shock can have different inflationary consequences depending on the degree of slack, the credibility of monetary policy, the extent of exchange-rate pass-through, and the health of the financial system. These insights imply that policy prescriptions cannot rely on simple rules alone. Instead, they require a careful assessment of how financial conditions interact with the inflation process, recognising that the effectiveness of monetary policy, and the balance between monetary, fiscal, and prudential instruments, varies across regimes and institutional contexts.

6.I.   RULES, DISCRETION, CREDIBILITY, AND EXPECTATIONS MANAGEMENT

Modern macroeconomic analysis places the interaction between rules, discretion, credibility, and expectations at the very centre of stabilization policy. A key lesson shared by contemporary textbooks is that what matters most is not the occasional surprise or tactical manoeuvre by policymakers, but the systematic and predictable way in which policy is conducted over time. In forward-looking models of output and inflation, households and firms base their current decisions on expectations about the future path of policy. As a result, anticipated policy actions shape today's output gap, pricing behaviour, and wage setting more powerfully than any one-off intervention. Monetary and fiscal authorities therefore exert influence primarily through the expectations they generate, rather than through isolated discretionary moves.

Credibility emerges as a crucial stabilizing force within this framework. When economic agents believe that policymakers are committed to their stated objectives—most notably price stability—inflation expectations tend to remain anchored even in the face of adverse shocks. Under such conditions, a negative supply disturbance need not trigger self-reinforcing wage–price dynamics, because firms and workers expect inflation to return to target over time. By contrast, when credibility is weak and expectations become unanchored, even relatively modest shocks can give rise to persistent inflationary processes, as precautionary price and wage adjustments amplify the original disturbance. In this sense, credibility acts as a form of macroeconomic capital: once accumulated, it reduces the real cost of stabilization; once lost, it is difficult and costly to rebuild.

Within this expectations-based environment, policy rules retain an important role, but their interpretation has evolved. Simple reaction functions, such as Taylor-type rules, are valued not because they provide mechanical prescriptions, but because they offer a transparent and intelligible description of how policy is expected to respond to changing economic conditions. Their robustness lies in their ability to summarize a contingent strategy—one that reacts systematically to inflation and economic slack—rather than in rigid adherence to a numerical formula. The modern literature on "targeted" or flexible rules reflects this insight, emphasizing that rules serve as communication devices and commitment technologies, guiding expectations while still allowing for informed judgment when circumstances deviate from the norm.

Finally, modern analysis recognizes that credibility and expectations management cannot be separated from institutional design. The structure within which policy is conducted—central bank independence, fiscal rules and budgetary frameworks, and the scope of macroprudential authority—defines the set of feasible stabilization outcomes. Institutions shape not only the incentives faced by policymakers, but also the beliefs of private agents about how policy will respond in future states of the world. In this broader sense, the policy mix extends beyond instruments and targets to include the legal and organizational arrangements that underpin commitment, discipline, and coherence across policy domains.

6.J.   The effective lower bound and unconventional policy: when the mix must change

The effective lower bound on nominal interest rates represents a fundamental constraint on the traditional conduct of monetary policy. When policy rates approach zero, or levels at which further reductions would undermine the functioning of financial markets, central banks lose their primary conventional instrument. In such circumstances, adverse shocks cannot be fully offset by standard rate cuts, and macroeconomic stability can no longer be ensured by monetary policy acting alone in its usual form. The binding nature of the effective lower bound forces a reconfiguration of the policy mix and brings unconventional instruments and broader coordination to the forefront.

At the effective lower bound, the core problem is that the policy rate cannot fall sufficiently to restore aggregate demand to its desired path. Real interest rates may remain too high relative to the economy's depressed state, particularly if inflation expectations decline. To overcome this constraint, policymakers must act on other margins, targeting expectations, financial conditions, and demand more directly. One prominent strategy involves the management of expectations through explicit communication and commitments about the future path of policy. By signalling that interest rates will remain low for an extended period, even after the economy begins to recover, central banks can influence longer-term interest rates and expected real borrowing costs today. This forward-looking dimension of policy aims to stimulate current spending by reshaping beliefs about future financial conditions, rather than by adjusting the current policy rate itself.

In parallel, balance-sheet policies acquire a central role. Large-scale asset purchases, commonly referred to as quantitative easing, operate by compressing term premia, improving liquidity in key markets, and supporting asset prices. By expanding their balance sheets and purchasing government bonds or other securities, central banks can ease financial conditions even when short-term rates are constrained. These measures are designed to restore the link between monetary accommodation and broader financial variables, such as long-term yields and credit spreads, that matter for investment and consumption decisions.

Yet unconventional monetary policies may still face limitations, particularly when financial intermediation is impaired or when households and firms are unwilling to borrow despite favourable financing conditions. In this environment, fiscal policy gains renewed prominence. Public spending increases or targeted tax measures can shift aggregate demand directly, without relying on the interest-rate channel. At the effective lower bound, such fiscal actions tend to be especially powerful, as they are less likely to crowd out private spending and may instead crowd it in by improving expectations about future income and employment. The interaction between fiscal expansion and accommodative monetary policy can further amplify these effects, as central bank actions help stabilise financing conditions and prevent increases in sovereign borrowing costs.

Credit policies also become crucial when the transmission of both monetary and fiscal impulses is obstructed. Measures aimed at restoring the flow of credit, such as targeted lending programmes, guarantees, or regulatory adjustments, can repair broken transmission channels and ensure that policy support reaches the real economy. These interventions acknowledge that, at the effective lower bound, the central challenge is often not the price of credit alone, but its availability and distribution.

The central implication of operating at the effective lower bound is that the relative effectiveness of policy instruments changes. Fiscal policy becomes more potent, while the benefits of coordination between monetary and fiscal authorities increase. Such coordination, however, raises institutional and governance challenges, particularly in systems designed to safeguard central bank independence. Balancing the need for joint action against the risks of fiscal dominance requires careful institutional design and clear mandates. Nevertheless, the experience of economies constrained by the effective lower bound demonstrates that maintaining macroeconomic stability in such regimes depends on a flexible policy mix, in which unconventional monetary tools, active fiscal policy, and credit interventions are combined in a coherent and mutually reinforcing manner.

6.K. PRACTICAL DESIGN OF A STABILIZATION MIX: A COHERENT "REACTION FUNCTION" ACROSS INSTRUMENTS

The practical design of a macroeconomic stabilization mix requires moving beyond the notion of isolated policy tools and instead adopting a unified, state-contingent framework in which different instruments respond coherently to evolving economic conditions. In this perspective, the "policy mix" can be understood as an implicit reaction function shared across monetary, fiscal, and macroprudential policies, where each instrument is guided by clear commitments that depend on the state of the economy and the financial system. What matters is not only the effectiveness of each tool taken in isolation, but the consistency of their joint deployment over the business cycle.

Monetary policy, within this framework, retains responsibility for nominal stabilization. Its central commitment is to return inflation to target over a horizon that balances price stability with real-economic stabilization. This horizon is not fixed mechanically but depends on circumstances, including the size of the output gap and the presence of financial stability concerns. In normal conditions, this implies adjusting policy so as to minimize unnecessary volatility in output and employment while maintaining the credibility of the inflation target. When financial constraints bind or systemic risks emerge, monetary policy may tolerate slower convergence of inflation to target in order to avoid exacerbating financial fragilities, thereby acknowledging that strict inflation control cannot be pursued independently of broader macroeconomic stability.

Fiscal policy, in a coherent stabilization mix, plays a complementary and explicitly countercyclical role. Automatic stabilizers are allowed to operate fully, smoothing fluctuations in disposable income and demand without discretionary intervention. In severe downturns, when private demand collapses and monetary policy faces limits, discretionary fiscal stimulus becomes an essential stabilizing force. Crucially, such stimulus must be embedded in a credible medium-term fiscal framework that reassures households, firms, and investors about debt sustainability once the economy recovers. At the opposite end of the cycle, fiscal policy refrains from procyclical expansion during booms, instead rebuilding fiscal space and avoiding measures that would amplify overheating or asset-price excesses. The credibility of fiscal policy over the cycle is what allows it to act forcefully when conditions deteriorate.

Macroprudential policy completes the stabilization mix by focusing explicitly on financial cycles and systemic risk. During expansions, it leans against excessive leverage, rapid credit growth, and maturity or currency mismatches, thereby dampening the buildup of vulnerabilities that can transform ordinary downturns into crises. When stress materializes, macroprudential policy shifts stance, releasing capital and liquidity buffers to prevent a sudden contraction of credit from amplifying the recession. In this sense, macroprudential tools introduce an additional dimension of countercyclicality, one that operates primarily through balance sheets rather than through aggregate demand.

The stabilizing power of this policy mix derives from its internal consistency. Each instrument is assigned tasks aligned with its comparative advantages, and policy actions are designed to reinforce rather than offset one another. Monetary accommodation is not prematurely neutralized by fiscal tightening when inflation is below target, just as fiscal stimulus is not undermined by aggressive monetary tightening unless inflationary pressures genuinely require it. Similarly, macroprudential easing during stress supports, rather than contradicts, expansionary macroeconomic policies aimed at stabilizing output. When such coherence is achieved, the policy mix functions as an integrated reaction system, capable of adapting to shocks while preserving both macroeconomic and financial stability over time.

6.L. A TECHNICAL SYNTHESIS: WHAT "STABILITY" MEANS IN THE MODERN CONSENSUS

Bringing together the various strands of contemporary macroeconomic analysis, the modern textbook consensus defines macroeconomic stability as the outcome of a structured interaction between private-sector behaviour, nominal frictions, and systematic policy responses. At its core, the economy is understood as being shaped by intertemporal decision-making on the part of households and firms, captured by the IS relation, by nominal rigidities in price and wage setting, summarized by the New Keynesian Phillips Curve, and by policy feedback rules that describe how authorities respond to deviations of inflation and activity from their desired paths. Compared with earlier frameworks, this consensus places much greater emphasis on the explicit role of financial frictions and fiscal constraints, recognizing that credit conditions, balance sheets, and public debt dynamics are integral components of macroeconomic outcomes rather than peripheral considerations.

Within this setting, the notion of a policy mix takes on a precise technical meaning. Stability is no longer associated with the mechanical use of a single instrument, but with the selection of a coherent system of joint rules governing monetary, fiscal, and financial policies. Such a system must simultaneously anchor nominal variables, most importantly inflation expectations, in order to preserve the informational and allocative role of prices. At the same time, it must stabilize real economic activity, limiting excessive fluctuations in output and employment around their potential levels. In addition, modern stabilization policy is expected to contain financial amplification mechanisms, preventing shocks from being magnified through leverage, credit cycles, and balance-sheet effects. Finally, the entire policy configuration must respect the government's intertemporal budget constraint, ensuring that short-run stabilization does not undermine long-run fiscal sustainability and credibility.

A defining feature of the modern consensus is the rejection of one-size-fits-all prescriptions. The appropriate stabilization mix is understood to be contingent on the nature of shocks and on the regime in which the economy operates. Policy responses differ markedly between normal times and periods when the effective lower bound on interest rates is binding, between situations

of fiscal space and episodes of fiscal stress, and between closed and open economies exposed to exchange-rate dynamics and capital flows. Equally important
is the role of expectations: when inflation expectations are well anchored, policy has greater room to maneuver, whereas de-anchored expectations impose
tighter constraints and may require more forceful or coordinated interventions.

Ongoing research continues to refine this framework, particularly with
respect to the empirical behaviour of inflation and the transmission of policy.
Increasing attention is devoted to nonlinearities, state dependence, and the
interaction between macroeconomic conditions and financial stability. These
advances reinforce the idea that stabilization policy is not a fixed engineering
problem with a definitive solution, but an evolving technical discipline. The
modern consensus thus views macroeconomic stability as a dynamic achievement, grounded in theory and evidence, yet constantly adapted in response to
new insights, institutional realities, and the changing structure of the economy.

Lesson 7

A Critique Of Government Intervention: The Calculation And Knowledge Problems

7.1. The Epistemological Foundations of the Socialist Calculation Problem

The critique of government intervention in general and socialism in particular developed by Austrian economists Ludwig von Mises and Friedrich August von Hayek is often misunderstood as a merely technical argument concerning incentives, efficiency, or information processing. In reality, it is none of these things in isolation. At its core, the socialist calculation debate which began in 1920s is an epistemological inquiry into the nature of knowledge, meaning, and rational action within a complex social order. Once this is understood, it becomes evident that the problem of government intervention into the economy is not primarily political, moral, or even economic in the narrow sense, but hermeneutical. Government intervention fails because it presupposes a form of knowledge that cannot exist and a mode of calculation that is conceptually incoherent.

Mises's original intervention in the calculation debate (1920) was not motivated by hostility toward social justice or by ideological attachment to capitalism as such. It emerged from a rigorous analysis of economic rationality itself. Economic action, as Mises insisted, is always action under uncertainty, guided by subjective expectations, oriented toward an unknowable future, and grounded in valuations that cannot be externally imposed. The socialist system, by abolishing private ownership of the means of production, abolishes the very context in which such action becomes intelligible. In doing so, it destroys not merely incentives, but meaning.

Economic calculation, properly understood, is not a computational exercise performed on given data. It is an interpretative practice embedded in a system of market prices that emerge from exchange. Prices are not technical

173

coefficients. They are expressions of historically situated judgments made by acting individuals. They condense dispersed knowledge, expectations, and evaluations into socially meaningful signals. Without markets, these signals do not arise. Without these signals, calculation becomes an empty formalism, severed from reality.

This insight is already present in embryonic form in Mises's 1920 essay on economic calculation, but it becomes fully explicit when read through Hayek's later epistemological contributions, particularly *The Use of Knowledge in Society* (1945). Hayek's central claim is not that planners lack sufficient information in a quantitative sense, but that the kind of knowledge required for coordination is not the sort that can be centralized at all. It is not given, objective, or fully articulable. It is contextual, practical, and often tacit.

The knowledge relevant to economic coordination exists only in fragments, embedded in concrete situations, and often known only to "the man on the spot". This knowledge is inseparable from time, place, and personal interpretation. It is not the knowledge of how to produce something in general, but the knowledge of when, where, and for whom to produce it. Any system that presumes such knowledge can be collected, aggregated, and processed by a central authority commits a category error.

This is why government economic action in general and socialism in particular are not merely impractical, but epistemologically incoherent. Government intervention assumes that economic order can be designed in the same way that a machine is engineered. It treats society as if it were a system of given ends and given means, awaiting optimization. But economic reality is not a mechanical system. It is a process of continuous interpretation, discovery, and revision of plans. Ends are not given; they are formed and transformed through interaction. Means are not fixed; they acquire meaning only within concrete plans of action.

Hayek repeatedly emphasized that the fatal error of socialism lies in its scientistic pretence: the belief that the methods of the natural sciences can be transferred uncritically to the social domain. This theme reaches its clearest expression in his Nobel lecture, *The Pretence of Knowledge* (1974). There, Hayek warns that the attempt to make economics "scientific" by reducing it to measurable magnitudes leads not to greater rigor, but to systematic blindness. What is measurable is treated as important; what is important but not measurable is ignored.

The result is a distorted vision of reality in which complex coordination problems are mistaken for engineering problems. Socialist planning embodies this error in its purest form. By eliminating markets, it eliminates the very process through which relevant knowledge is generated and communicated. It then attempts to replace this process with administrative commands, statistical aggregates, and pseudo-prices that lack any grounding in real exchange.

This point is developed with exceptional clarity in the Austrian reconstruction of the calculation debate, particularly in the work of Jesús Huerta de Soto, who shows that the impossibility of socialism is not merely static but dynamic. Economic calculation is not about solving a system of equations. It is about discovering what the equations themselves should be. This discovery is inseparable from entrepreneurial action. Without entrepreneurship, there is no discovery. Without discovery, there is no knowledge to calculate with.

From this perspective, the debate over "market socialism" appears as an attempt to square the circle. Proposals that retain prices while abolishing private ownership misunderstand what prices are. Prices are not numerical tags that can be administratively assigned. They are outcomes of rivalry, error, speculation, and learning. They presuppose genuine exchange, real profit and loss, and the possibility of failure. To simulate prices without markets is to evacuate them of meaning.

Hayek's later conception of competition as a discovery procedure reinforces this argument. Competition is not a state of affairs; it is a process through which unknown possibilities are revealed. Its value lies precisely in the fact that its outcomes are unpredictable. A system that replaces competition with planning does not merely choose a different method of allocation; it chooses to forgo discovery altogether. It freezes knowledge at a moment in time and then pretends that this frozen snapshot can guide future action.

At this point, the socialist calculation problem reveals its deepest dimension. It is not simply that planners lack sufficient data. It is that the data they would need does not yet exist and can only be created through the very process they suppress. Markets do not merely transmit knowledge; they generate it. Prices are not inputs into calculation; they are the emergent products of interpretative interaction.

In this sense, the market is a hermeneutical institution. It is a social space in which meanings are continuously negotiated, revised, and tested against reality. To abolish it is not to replace one coordination mechanism with another, but to abolish the conditions under which coordination becomes intelligible at all.

7.2. PRICES AS CARRIERS OF MEANING AND THE IMPOSSIBILITY OF NON-MARKET CALCULATION

If the critique of socialism is to be understood in its full depth, prices must be rescued from the impoverished role to which both technocratic economics and socialist planning have reduced them. Within a Hermeneutical Political Economy, prices are not neutral data, nor are they mere informational summaries awaiting mechanical manipulation. They are meaning-bearing social artifacts, generated within a living process of interpretation, contestation, and discovery. To abolish markets is therefore not simply to alter an allocative mechanism; it is to destroy the very language through which economic actors understand and coordinate their actions.

The socialist illusion begins with a deceptively simple move: the assumption that prices are detachable from markets, that they can be imitated, simulated, or replaced by administrative surrogates without loss of substance. This assumption is shared, in different guises, by advocates of central planning, market socialism, algorithmic governance, and contemporary forms of "data-driven" policy. All of them treat prices as if they were *objects* rather than *expressions*, as if they were things that could be engineered rather than meanings that must emerge.

From a hermeneutical standpoint, this is a fundamental category mistake. Prices do not precede action; they are constituted by action. They are not external signals imposed upon agents; they are the sedimented outcomes of countless interpretative judgments made by individuals who confront uncertainty, scarcity, and time. Every market price is the provisional resolution of a multiplicity of subjective expectations, plans, errors, and revisions. It is not a final truth but a temporary interpretation of the state of the world as seen through the eyes of acting persons.

This is why Ludwig von Mises insisted that economic calculation is possible only where there is private ownership of the means of production. Ownership is not merely a legal arrangement; it is the institutional condition that makes responsibility, profit and loss, and genuine choice intelligible. Without ownership, there can be no meaningful exchange; without exchange, no prices; and without prices, no calculation. What disappears is not efficiency in a narrow sense, but economic rationality itself.

The hermeneutical significance of this claim becomes clear once we recognize that calculation is not a technical procedure but a practical interpretation of possible futures. When an entrepreneur compares anticipated revenues with anticipated costs, he is not solving an equation. He is engaging in an act of understanding, projecting herself into an uncertain future, and interpreting present prices as clues about possible courses of action. These prices acquire meaning only because they are embedded in a web of expectations about other actors' interpretations, plans, and likely reactions.

In a socialist system, this web is severed. Administrative prices, shadow prices, or parametric prices may retain numerical form, but they are stripped of interpretative depth. They do not arise from rivalry; they do not incorporate error; they do not reflect genuine opportunity cost as experienced by owners risking their own resources. They are symbols without referents, signs without practices. They resemble language detached from lived speech: grammatically correct perhaps, but devoid of meaning.

This insight connects Mises's calculation argument directly to Hayek's analysis of knowledge. In *The Use of Knowledge in Society*, Hayek makes clear that the economic problem is not one of allocating "given" resources according to known preferences, but of coordinating plans based on knowledge that is not given to anyone in its totality. Prices perform this coordinating role precisely because they condense dispersed, tacit, and often inarticulate knowledge into actionable meanings. They tell actors not *what* to do, but *how* to interpret their situation.

The famous example of tin illustrates this point. When the price of tin rises, users of tin do not need to know whether the cause is a new industrial application, a mine closure, geopolitical tension, or speculative anticipation. The price communicates, in a single meaningful gesture, that tin has become relatively scarcer. This gesture invites interpretation and response: substitution, conservation, innovation. The adjustment that follows is not centrally designed; it is hermeneutically coordinated through the shared understanding embodied in the price change.

What socialism abolishes is precisely this shared interpretative framework. By attempting to replace market prices with administrative calculations, it assumes that meaning can be imposed from above rather than generated from within practice. It presumes that economic significance can be deduced from technical knowledge alone. But technical knowledge—knowledge of production functions, input-output relations, or engineering constraints—is only one layer of economic understanding. It is abstract, general, and context-independent. What it lacks is situated relevance.

Hermeneutical Political Economy insists on the distinction between two fundamentally different kinds of knowledge. On the one hand, there is scientific or technical knowledge: explicit, codifiable, transmissible through instruction. On the other hand, there is practical or entrepreneurial knowledge: tacit, contextual, time-bound, and inseparable from personal experience. Prices are the bridge between these two domains. They translate dispersed practical knowledge into a socially accessible form without ever fully articulating it.

This translation is not mechanical; it is interpretative. Prices do not command; they suggest. They do not dictate outcomes; they invite responses. Their meaning is never fixed, but always contingent upon expectations about future developments. This is why competition, as Hayek later emphasized, must be understood as a discovery procedure. Competition reveals information that did not exist before the competitive process unfolded. It generates meanings that could not have been known in advance.

Socialist planning, by contrast, presupposes that relevant meanings are already known and merely await correct application. It treats the future as if it were an extension of the present, and economic coordination as if it were a problem of optimal control. In doing so, it collapses the temporal dimension of action. It ignores the fact that prices are always oriented toward an uncertain future and that their meaning depends on expectations that are themselves shaped by ongoing market interaction.

From a hermeneutical perspective, this temporal blindness is fatal. Economic life is not a sequence of equilibrium states; it is an unfolding narrative. Prices are narrative devices: they summarize past interactions, reflect present tensions, and point toward possible futures. To freeze them into administrative parameters is to interrupt the narrative and pretend that the story can be continued by decree.

The advocates of market socialism attempted to overcome this difficulty by reintroducing prices without reintroducing markets. They imagined a system in which planners would adjust prices through trial and error until equilibrium conditions were satisfied. But this proposal misunderstands the very nature of error in a market process. Entrepreneurial error is not a deviation from a known optimum; it is an essential moment of discovery. It reveals previously unnoticed possibilities and constraints. It generates new knowledge precisely because it is borne by individuals who face real consequences.

Administrative trial and error lacks this existential dimension. It is error without responsibility, experimentation without ownership. As Huerta de Soto has shown, such systems cannot generate genuine economic knowledge because they suppress the entrepreneurial function itself. Without entrepreneurship, there is no discovery; without discovery, there is nothing to calculate.

Hermeneutical Political Economy thus reframes the socialist calculation problem as a problem of meaning generation. Markets are not efficient because they compute better, but because they *understand* better. They do not solve equations; they create interpretations. They allow individuals to make sense of an ever-changing world by embedding their actions in a shared, though always provisional, symbolic order.

The abolition of markets is therefore an act of semantic destruction. It eliminates the language through which economic actors communicate their valuations, expectations, and discoveries. What remains is a technocratic simulacrum: numbers without narratives, plans without understanding, control without comprehension.

This is why the socialist project, in all its variants, ultimately collapses into arbitrariness. When prices no longer emerge from exchange, they lose their anchoring in lived experience. They become expressions of political power rather than economic meaning. Allocation becomes a matter of authority rather than interpretation. The system may continue to function administratively, but it no longer *knows* what it is doing.

In this light, the impossibility of socialism is not contingent upon computational limits or incentive problems. It is rooted in the nature of human understanding itself. Economic coordination requires a medium through which meanings can emerge, circulate, and be revised. That medium is the price system. To suppress it is to condemn society to blindness, not because it lacks data, but because it lacks understanding.

7.3. Two Kinds of Knowledge: Scientific Mastery and Entrepreneurial Understanding

At the heart of the socialist calculation debate lies a profound confusion about the nature of knowledge itself. This confusion is not accidental; it is constitutive of the socialist worldview and, more broadly, of all technocratic approaches to political economy. Government economic planning – or action – presupposes that the knowledge relevant for coordinating economic life is essentially *scientific* in nature: objective, explicit, measurable, and capable of being centralized. Hermeneutical Political Economy, drawing on Mises and Hayek but pushing their insights further, insists that this presupposition is false. The knowledge that matters most for economic coordination is not scientific mastery but entrepreneurial understanding, a form of knowledge that is irreducibly interpretative, contextual, and embedded in lived experience.

This distinction between two kinds of knowledge is implicit throughout the Austrian critique of socialism, but it becomes fully intelligible only when articulated in hermeneutical terms. Hayek famously distinguished between what may be called technical or scientific knowledge and the practical knowledge of time and place possessed by individuals. Yet this distinction is often misunderstood as a quantitative one, as if the problem were merely that planners do not possess *enough* information. In reality, the problem is qualitative. The two kinds of knowledge differ not in degree but in kind. They belong to different epistemological orders.

Scientific or technical knowledge is abstract and general. It concerns regularities, causal relations, and functional dependencies. It can be written down, taught, transmitted, and stored. It is the knowledge of engineers, statisticians, and natural scientists. In the economic domain, it includes production techniques, accounting identities, input-output tables, and macroeconomic aggregates. This form of knowledge aspires to universality and reproducibility. It seeks to eliminate ambiguity and context-dependence. Entrepreneurial knowledge, by contrast, is concrete and particular. It concerns opportunities rather than laws, meanings rather than mechanisms. It is knowledge of *what might be done*, not merely of *what is*. It is inseparable from judgment, imagination, and expectation. This knowledge cannot be fully articulated because it arises precisely in situations where rules and precedents are insufficient. It is the knowledge of how to act *here and now*, under conditions of uncertainty, with incomplete information, and in anticipation of an unknowable future.

Hermeneutical Political Economy recognizes this second form of knowledge as a form of *understanding* rather than *explanation*. It is closer to what classical philosophy called *phronēsis* than to *epistēmē*. It is not about deducing conclusions from given premises, but about interpreting a situation in order to act meaningfully within it. This is why entrepreneurial knowledge is inherently temporal. It is oriented toward the future and shaped by expectations that can never be fully justified ex ante.

Socialism fails because it systematically privileges the first form of knowledge while denying the epistemic legitimacy of the second. Central planning presupposes that economic coordination can be achieved through scientific mastery alone. It assumes that once the relevant data are collected and processed, correct decisions will follow. But this assumption ignores the fact that entrepreneurial knowledge is not a subset of technical knowledge waiting to be discovered. It is generated only through action itself. It comes into being as individuals interpret signals, experiment, err, and revise their plans.

Mises's insistence that economic calculation requires market prices is often interpreted narrowly, as a claim about numerical computation. In truth, it is a claim about the *conditions under which entrepreneurial understanding becomes possible*. Prices do not merely provide information; they provide orientation. They allow actors to situate themselves within a complex social process and to interpret their own plans in light of others' expectations. This interpretative function cannot be replicated by administrative data because it presupposes genuine exchange and the possibility of profit and loss.

Hayek's contribution deepens this insight by showing that the knowledge relevant for economic coordination is not only dispersed but also tacit. Much of what individuals know cannot be stated explicitly, not because it is mysterious, but because it is embodied in habits, skills, local familiarity, and practical judgment. This tacit dimension is not a defect to be overcome; it is the very source of social coordination. Markets work not despite ignorance, but because they allow individuals to act meaningfully on the basis of partial understanding.

Hermeneutical Political Economy emphasizes that this partiality is not a temporary imperfection that better data or more powerful computation could eliminate. It is an ontological feature of human action. To act is always to interpret a situation from a particular perspective. No actor, individual or collective, can step outside this condition. The dream of a planner who sees the whole is therefore not merely unrealistic; it is conceptually incoherent. There is no "view from nowhere" in economic life.

This is where the socialist aspiration to total knowledge reveals its deepest flaw. By seeking to replace entrepreneurial understanding with scientific control, socialism attempts to substitute interpretation with command. It treats economic life as if it were a closed system governed by known parameters. In doing so, it suppresses the very process through which new meanings emerge. Innovation, adaptation, and discovery become anomalies rather than normal features of economic life.

The advocates of advanced computation, artificial intelligence, and big data often present these technologies as solutions to the knowledge problem identified by Hayek. They argue that what was once dispersed and tacit can now be captured, quantified, and optimized. From a hermeneutical standpoint, this argument merely restates the original error in more sophisticated language. Data are not knowledge. They are records of past actions interpreted through a particular conceptual framework. They do not contain the meanings that actors will attach to future situations.

Entrepreneurial understanding cannot be inferred from data because it concerns possibilities that have not yet been realized. It involves imagining new uses, new combinations, and new interpretations of existing resources. This creative dimension cannot be predicted because it is not determined by prior states. It is precisely the openness of the future that gives entrepreneurial action its meaning. Any system that attempts to close this openness in the name of rational control destroys the conditions of its own rationality.

From this perspective, the socialist calculation problem appears as a special case of a more general epistemological failure: the failure to recognize the interpretative nature of social reality. Economic order is not imposed; it is understood into being through interaction. Coordination is not achieved by aligning variables, but by aligning meanings. Prices serve this function because they are not merely indicators but shared references within a social practice.

Hermeneutical Political Economy thus reframes the Austrian insight in a broader philosophical context. The impossibility of socialism is not a historical contingency, nor a technological limitation, nor a moral objection alone. It is rooted in the structure of human understanding. A system that denies the primacy of entrepreneurial knowledge denies the conditions under which understanding itself can operate.

In this sense, socialism is not only economically inefficient but epistemically violent. It imposes a single interpretative framework upon a pluralistic and evolving reality. It replaces dialogue with decree, learning with compliance, and understanding with administration. What it produces is not order, but a fragile simulacrum of order sustained by coercion rather than comprehension.

The market, by contrast, is an interpretative order. It does not promise certainty, but it allows for meaning. It does not eliminate error, but it makes error instructive. It does not centralize knowledge, but it renders dispersed understanding socially usable. These are not accidental virtues; they are the direct consequence of recognizing the irreducible plurality of perspectives that constitute social life.

7.4.   ECONOMIC CALCULATION AS A DYNAMIC AND HERMENEUTICAL PROCESS: RE-READING MISES

Ludwig von Mises's argument on the impossibility of socialist economic calculation is often presented as if it were a narrow technical objection: without market prices for capital goods, planners cannot perform rational cost–benefit analysis. While this formulation is not incorrect, it radically understates the depth of Mises's insight. When read through the lens of Hermeneutical Political Economy, Mises's calculation argument emerges not as a problem of arithmetic, but as a problem of interpretation over time. Economic calculation is not a static comparison of quantities; it is a dynamic act of understanding, embedded in uncertainty, temporality, and human meaning-making.

Mises's starting point is deceptively simple. In an advanced economy characterized by a complex structure of production, actors must choose among innumerable alternative uses of scarce resources. These choices cannot be made in physical terms alone. Steel cannot be compared to labour hours, nor machinery to land, without a common denominator. Money prices provide this denominator. But what is often overlooked is that money prices do not merely *measure* costs; they *render them intelligible*. They translate heterogeneous means into a common language that allows actors to form expectations about the future.

From a hermeneutical perspective, this translation is crucial. Economic action is always future-oriented. When entrepreneurs calculate, they do not compare known outcomes; they compare imagined futures. They interpret current prices as guides to what others believe, expect, and plan. Calculation is therefore inseparable from anticipation, conjecture, and judgment. It is not a mechanical operation but a narrative construction in which the actor projects a possible course of action and evaluates its plausibility.

Socialism abolishes this process at its root. By eliminating private ownership of the means of production, it eliminates genuine exchange in capital goods. Without exchange, there are no real prices for higher-order goods. Without such prices, there is no meaningful way to interpret the relative scarcity, urgency, or opportunity cost of alternative production plans. What disappears is not only a computational tool but a temporal horizon of meaning.

Mises was acutely aware that the problem of calculation is inseparable from time. Capital goods are not interchangeable inputs; they are elements of a structure that unfolds across stages of production. Decisions made today shape possibilities tomorrow. Calculation therefore requires an understanding of how present choices will resonate through time. This understanding cannot be deduced from technical knowledge alone. It requires entrepreneurial interpretation of uncertain futures.

Hermeneutical Political Economy emphasizes that this interpretative dimension cannot be centralized because it is inherently plural. Different entrepreneurs hold different expectations about the future. They interpret the same price signals differently. This plurality is not a defect but a feature. It is through the clash of interpretations, tested by profit and loss, that coordination emerges. Market prices evolve as interpretations are revised, abandoned, or confirmed.

In a socialist system, this pluralism is replaced by a single authoritative narrative. The planner must impose one interpretation of the future upon society as a whole. Even if this interpretation were internally coherent, it would still be epistemically impoverished. It would suppress alternative perspectives that might reveal errors, overlooked opportunities, or emerging needs. Calculation becomes a bureaucratic ritual rather than a process of discovery.

The attempts to rescue socialism through "calculation in kind", labour-time accounting, or mathematical optimization all fail for this reason. They treat calculation as if it were independent of interpretation. They assume that once physical quantities are known, rational choice follows. But physical quantities acquire economic meaning only within a framework of expectations about future demand, technological change, and relative scarcities. These expectations are not given facts; they are conjectures formed by acting individuals.

Mises's critique of mathematical economics is particularly relevant here. He did not reject mathematics as such, but he rejected its misuse as a substitute for understanding. Equilibrium models describe states in which no further action is required. But economic life is precisely the opposite: it is characterized by constant adjustment, surprise, and error. Calculation is meaningful only because the future is uncertain. To model away this uncertainty is to model away action itself.

From a hermeneutical standpoint, equilibrium is not an explanatory tool but a limiting concept. It describes a world in which interpretation is no longer necessary because all meanings are fixed. Such a world may be analytically convenient, but it is existentially irrelevant. Socialism implicitly aspires to such a world. It seeks to replace interpretation with administration, judgment with rule-following, and uncertainty with control. In doing so, it abolishes the very conditions under which calculation can occur.

The dynamic nature of calculation also reveals why profit and loss are indispensable. Profit is not a reward for efficiency in a mechanical sense; it is a signal that an interpretation of the future has proven more adequate than competing interpretations. Loss is not a punishment; it is information. It tells the actor that her narrative of the future was mistaken. This feedback is essential for learning. It is through loss that erroneous interpretations are discarded and new ones emerge.

In socialism, this feedback mechanism is severed. Without private ownership, losses cannot be meaningfully attributed. Errors are absorbed by the system rather than revealed to the actor. The result is not merely inefficiency but epistemic stagnation. The system loses its capacity to learn because it loses the means by which interpretations are tested against reality.

Hermeneutical Political Economy thus allows us to see Mises's argument in a new light. The impossibility of socialist calculation is not primarily about insufficient data or computational complexity. It is about the suppression of interpretative plurality and temporal openness. Calculation requires a living context in which meanings are continuously generated, contested, and revised. This context is the market.

When markets are abolished, calculation does not become more difficult; it becomes meaningless. Numbers may still be produced, plans may still be drafted, and targets may still be set. But these activities lack orientation. They no longer refer to a shared process of understanding grounded in exchange. They become exercises in power rather than acts of reason.

In this sense, Mises's argument anticipates Hayek's later critique of scientism and the pretence of knowledge. Both thinkers point to the same fundamental error: the belief that social order can be designed without acknowledging the interpretative nature of human action. Hermeneutical Political Economy makes this connection explicit. It shows that economic rationality is not a property of systems but of practices, not of models but of meanings.

The market is not rational because it computes correctly; it is rational because it allows actors to *make sense* of their situation in light of others' actions. It is a space of dialogue rather than design, of understanding rather than command. Economic calculation is the grammar of this dialogue. To abolish it is to reduce economic life to a monologue imposed from above.

7.5. HAYEK'S KNOWLEDGE PROBLEM AS A HERMENEUTICAL PROBLEM

Friedrich August von Hayek's contribution to the socialist calculation debate is commonly summarized under the label of the "knowledge problem". Yet this formulation, while convenient, risks obscuring the radical nature of Hayek's insight. The issue is not simply that knowledge is dispersed, incomplete, or costly to acquire. These are empirical observations, important but secondary. Hayek's deeper claim is epistemological and, when read through the lens of Hermeneutical Political Economy, unmistakably hermeneutical. The problem of socialism is not that planners lack information, but that the kind of knowledge required for social coordination is interpretative, situated, and irreducible to centralized cognition.

Hayek's starting point in *The Use of Knowledge in Society* is a question that appears deceptively technical: what is the economic problem we are trying to solve when we seek to establish a rational economic order? The standard answer, inherited from equilibrium theory, is that we must allocate given means among given ends in an optimal way. Hayek's response is devastating precisely because it rejects the premises of the question. Means are not "given" in any meaningful sense, ends are not fixed, and the relevant knowledge does not exist in a form that could ever be "possessed" by a single mind.

Hermeneutical Political Economy allows us to restate Hayek's argument in clearer philosophical terms. Social reality is not an object to be observed from the outside; it is a web of meanings constituted by acting individuals. Knowledge in such a reality is not a stock of facts but a process of interpretation. Individuals do not merely respond to objective conditions; they interpret situations, form expectations, and act on the basis of meanings that are always provisional and revisable. Coordination emerges not because these interpretations are identical, but because they are mutually adjusted through interaction.

From this perspective, the dispersion of knowledge is not an accidental feature of economic life; it is its very condition of possibility. Knowledge is dispersed because meaning is plural. Each individual occupies a unique position in time and space, confronts a unique set of circumstances, and interprets them through a personal horizon shaped by experience, tradition, and expectation. This horizon cannot be transmitted in full to others, let alone to a central authority. It can only be partially communicated through action.

Prices are the privileged medium of this communication. They do not transmit complete knowledge; they transmit *relevant meaning*. A price change does not explain why conditions have changed; it indicates that they have. It invites interpretation rather than delivering instruction. In doing so, it respects the epistemic autonomy of the actor while enabling coordination. Each individual responds to price signals in light of his own understanding, and it is precisely this diversity of responses that generates order.

Central planning attempts to reverse this process. It assumes that meanings can be made explicit, formalized, and aggregated. It treats interpretation as noise to be eliminated rather than as the substance of social life. In doing so, it commits what Hayek later called the "pretence of knowledge": the belief that because some aspects of reality can be measured and modelled, the whole of reality can be mastered.

Hermeneutical Political Economy highlights the violence implicit in this pretence. To plan centrally is not merely to coordinate resources differently; it is to impose a single interpretative framework upon a pluralistic world. It is to declare one horizon of meaning authoritative and to suppress all others. This is why socialist planning inevitably becomes authoritarian, even when motivated by benevolent intentions. The suppression of interpretative plurality requires coercion.

Hayek's critique of scientism is particularly relevant here. Scientism, as Hayek understood it, is not the application of scientific knowledge to social problems, but the uncritical imitation of the methods of the natural sciences in domains where they are inappropriate. In the natural sciences, phenomena are repeatable, isolable, and governed by stable laws. In social life, phenomena are emergent, context-dependent, and shaped by meaning. To treat the latter as if they were the former is to misunderstand their nature.

The insistence that only measurable knowledge counts as "scientific" leads to a systematic distortion of economic understanding. What can be measured—aggregates, averages, correlations—is treated as causally decisive, while what cannot be measured—expectations, plans, tacit skills, local knowledge—is ignored. Yet it is precisely these unmeasurable elements that drive economic coordination. Planning thus proceeds on the basis of what is accessible rather than what is relevant.

From a hermeneutical standpoint, this is an inversion of rationality. Rational action requires sensitivity to context, not abstraction from it. It requires openness to surprise, not the illusion of control. Hayek's insistence on the limits of knowledge is therefore not a counsel of despair but a call for humility. It is an invitation to design institutions that work with the grain of human understanding rather than against it.

Markets embody this humility. They do not presume to know what individuals want or how resources should be used. They provide a framework within which individuals can discover these things for themselves. They allow meanings to emerge from interaction rather than being imposed from above. This is why Hayek described the market order as a spontaneous order. It is not chaotic; it is ordered precisely because it is not designed.

Hermeneutical Political Economy deepens this insight by emphasizing that spontaneity here does not mean randomness. It means that order arises from the mutual adjustment of interpretations. The market is a conversational process in which actors continuously revise their understanding in light of others' actions. Prices are the grammar of this conversation. To replace them with commands is to silence dialogue.

The failure of socialism, then, is not merely technical or economic. It is epistemological and ultimately anthropological. It rests on a false conception of human beings as passive recipients of information rather than as active interpreters of meaning. It assumes that understanding can be centralized, that judgment can be replaced by rule-following, and that the future can be planned as if it were an extension of the past.

Hayek's knowledge problem exposes the impossibility of these assumptions. But Hermeneutical Political Economy shows why they are not merely mistaken but self-defeating. A system that denies the interpretative nature of knowledge undermines its own capacity to learn. It becomes rigid, brittle, and blind to change. Its failures are not accidental; they are structural.

In this sense, the socialist calculation problem and the knowledge problem are two sides of the same coin. Both point to the same fundamental truth: economic rationality is inseparable from interpretative freedom. Where interpretation is suppressed, calculation loses meaning. Where meaning is imposed, knowledge ceases to grow.

The lesson is not that planning is impossible in any sense. Individuals plan constantly. Firms plan. Households plan. Even governments plan within limited domains. The lesson is that planning cannot replace the market without destroying the epistemic conditions that make planning itself meaningful. Central planning is not an extension of rationality; it is its negation.

7.6. COMPETITION AS DISCOVERY, CREATIVE DESTRUCTION, AND KALEIDIC ORDER

Friedrich Hayek's conception of competition as a discovery procedure represents the decisive completion of the epistemological turn inaugurated by the socialist calculation debate. Once competition is understood not as a static market structure but as an ongoing process of discovery, the impossibility of socialism appears in its most radical and irreducible form. When this insight is placed in dialogue with Joseph Schumpeter's theory of creative destruction and Ludwig Lachmann's radical subjectivism and kaleidic vision of the market, a fully hermeneutical understanding of economic order emerges—one in which markets are seen as meaning-generating processes and planning as an attempt to arrest interpretation itself.

Hayek's claim that competition is a discovery procedure overturns the conventional view of markets as mechanisms that merely allocate known resources according to known preferences. Competition, as Hayek insists, is valuable precisely because its outcomes are unpredictable. If all relevant facts were already known, competition would be superfluous. Its function is not to compute an optimum but to reveal information that does not yet exist. This revelation is not accidental; it is constitutive of the market process itself. Through rivalry, experimentation, and error, actors uncover possibilities, constraints, and valuations that could not have been anticipated ex ante.

Hermeneutical Political Economy highlights the interpretative nature of this discovery. What competition discovers are not "facts" in the positivist sense, but meanings: new ways of understanding resources, technologies, and consumer needs. Entrepreneurs do not simply respond to given signals; they reinterpret the world. They imagine new combinations, reframe existing goods, and challenge prevailing expectations. The market is therefore not a neutral arena but a dynamic field of interpretation in which meanings are continuously contested and revised.

This is precisely where Schumpeter's theory of creative destruction enters the picture. For Schumpeter, capitalism is not characterized by equilibrium but by incessant disruption. Innovation does not merely add new products to an existing structure; it destroys old structures and replaces them with new ones. Creative destruction is not a side effect of competition; it is its essence. The economic system advances not by perfecting what already exists, but by redefining what counts as valuable.

From a hermeneutical standpoint, creative destruction is a process of semantic transformation. Innovations change the meaning of resources, skills, and even consumer desires. What was once central becomes peripheral; what was once marginal becomes decisive. These shifts cannot be predicted because they involve changes in interpretation rather than adjustments to known parameters. The entrepreneur is not a calculator of probabilities but a creator of narratives about possible futures.

Socialism is fundamentally incompatible with this process. Central planning presupposes stability of meanings. It requires that technologies, preferences, and production methods be sufficiently well-defined to allow for coherent planning. Creative destruction undermines this stability. It introduces discontinuities that cannot be assimilated into a comprehensive plan. To tolerate genuine innovation is to tolerate the invalidation of prior calculations. To plan is therefore to resist creative destruction.

This resistance is not merely conservative; it is epistemic. By suppressing innovation, socialism suppresses the discovery of new meanings. It freezes the interpretative horizon of society and condemns it to stagnation. Schumpeter himself recognized this tension, noting that socialism might achieve a form of administrative efficiency at the cost of entrepreneurial dynamism. Hermeneutical Political Economy clarifies why this trade-off is illusory. Without entrepreneurial interpretation, there is no genuine efficiency, only bureaucratic routine.

The contribution of Lachmann radicalizes this insight by rejecting any residual notion of market convergence toward equilibrium. For Lachmann, expectations are inherently divergent. Individuals interpret the world differently, and these interpretations need not converge over time. The market is therefore not a system tending toward harmony but a kaleidic order: a pattern that changes with every turn, producing new configurations without settling into a final form.

This kaleidic vision is profoundly hermeneutical. It recognizes that economic order is not the outcome of shared beliefs but of mutual adjustment among conflicting interpretations. Coordination does not require agreement; it requires compatibility. Prices, contracts, and institutions allow individuals with different expectations to coexist and interact without resolving their differences. Order emerges not from consensus but from the disciplined interaction of plural meanings.

Socialism cannot accommodate this pluralism. It requires convergence of expectations because it requires unified plans. Divergence appears as disorder rather than as a source of discovery. The kaleidic nature of the market thus appears, from the planner's perspective, as chaos. What is in fact an interpretative order is misrecognized as randomness. The response is to impose coherence by force, replacing spontaneous coordination with administrative alignment.

Hayek's discovery procedure, Schumpeter's creative destruction, and Lachmann's kaleidic order converge on a single insight: economic order is not designed; it is interpreted into existence. It arises from the interaction of agents who do not share a common plan, a common understanding, or a common vision of the future. What they share is a framework—private property, contract, and prices—that allows their interpretations to confront one another productively.

Hermeneutical Political Economy emphasizes that this confrontation is not pathological; it is generative. Disagreement is not a problem to be solved but a condition to be cultivated. It is through disagreement that new meanings emerge. Competition is the institutionalization of disagreement. It allows rival interpretations to be tested against reality, not by persuasion or authority, but by success and failure.

The socialist system, by contrast, seeks to eliminate disagreement by replacing it with authoritative interpretation. The planner's vision becomes the official meaning of economic reality. Alternative interpretations are dismissed as errors or inefficiencies. But in suppressing disagreement, socialism suppresses discovery. It becomes epistemically closed, incapable of learning from its own failures because it lacks mechanisms for interpreting failure as meaningful information.

In this sense, the impossibility of socialism is inseparable from its hostility to interpretation. It seeks certainty where uncertainty is constitutive, stability where change is essential, and unity where plurality is irreducible. The market, understood hermeneutically, embodies the opposite virtues. It embraces uncertainty, channels plurality, and transforms conflict into coordination.

Competition, creative destruction, and kaleidic order are not anomalies to be corrected by policy. They are the very substance of economic life. Any attempt to replace them with planning is an attempt to replace understanding with control. The result is not a higher rationality but a collapse of meaning.

7.7. THE PRETENCE OF KNOWLEDGE, SCIENTISM, AND POLICY HUBRIS

The socialist calculation debate does not belong to the past. Its deepest error—the confusion of scientific mastery with social understanding—has merely reappeared under new guises. What Friedrich August von Hayek famously called the *pretence of knowledge* is today embedded in the everyday language of policy analysis, macroeconomic management, and evidence-based governance. Hermeneutical Political Economy allows us to see why this pretence is not a contingent intellectual mistake but a structural temptation of modern policymaking, and why it produces not merely inefficiency but epistemic hubris.

Hayek's Nobel lecture was not a polemic against science; it was a warning against scientism. Scientism, in his precise sense, is the uncritical transfer of the methods and ambitions of the natural sciences into domains governed by meaning, interpretation, and human action. It is the belief that because certain variables can be measured, modelled, and correlated, the social world itself can be mastered through technique. The tragedy Hayek identified is that this belief appears most compelling precisely where it is least justified: in complex systems whose essential features are not observable, quantifiable, or repeatable.

Hermeneutical Political Economy clarifies the philosophical root of this tragedy. Social reality is not constituted by variables but by known meanings. It is not governed by laws in the same sense as physical reality but by expectations, plans, and interpretations that are constantly revised. To impose a scientific posture upon such a reality is not to illuminate it, but to flatten it. What cannot be measured is treated as irrelevant; what can be measured is elevated to causal primacy. The result is a systematic distortion of understanding.

This distortion becomes policy hubris when the limits of knowledge are not merely ignored but denied. Policymakers come to believe that because they can model aggregates, forecast trends, and simulate outcomes, they can steer society toward desired ends. The humility implicit in Hayek's epistemology is replaced by confidence in expertise. Planning re-enters through the back door, no longer under the banner of socialism, but under that of optimization, stabilization, and governance.

The danger here is not simply that policies may fail. Failure is inevitable in a world of uncertainty. The danger is that failure becomes unintelligible. When policy is grounded in a scientistic worldview, deviations from expected outcomes are interpreted not as signals of flawed understanding but as evidence of insufficient control. The response is therefore not learning but escalation: more data, more regulation, more intervention. Each failure reinforces the belief that the solution lies in greater mastery rather than greater humility.

Hermeneutical Political Economy reveals why this dynamic is

self-reinforcing. Once policymakers adopt a single authoritative interpretative framework, alternative interpretations are marginalized. Dissent is recoded as ignorance or irrationality. Local knowledge is dismissed as anecdotal. Entrepreneurial judgment is treated as noise. The plurality of meanings that constitutes social life is progressively silenced. What remains is a technocratic monologue, increasingly detached from lived reality.

This is the modern form of the socialist error. It no longer insists on comprehensive planning of production, but it presumes comprehensive intelligibility of outcomes. It no longer abolishes markets outright, but it treats them as instruments to be corrected, nudged, or overridden whenever they deviate from policy objectives. Prices are tolerated only insofar as they align with administrative goals. When they do not, they are blamed for "failures" that are in fact failures of understanding.

The hermeneutical insight here is decisive. Policy is not an extension of economic theory; it is an art exercised under radical uncertainty. To treat it as a science is to confuse explanation with control. Economic theory can illuminate patterns, constraints, and tendencies, but it cannot deliver prescriptions that bypass interpretation. Every policy action is itself an interpretation of social reality, and its consequences depend on how others interpret it in turn.

Hayek's critique of scientism thus converges with a broader critique of moral authority in policy. When policymakers believe they possess superior knowledge, they also assume superior legitimacy to decide what outcomes are desirable. The epistemic claim slides into a moral claim. This is why technocratic governance so easily becomes paternalistic. If experts know better, then resistance must be irrational; if resistance is irrational, it may be overridden.

Hermeneutical Political Economy rejects this move at its root. It insists that no authority can legitimately claim epistemic supremacy over a complex social order. Knowledge is not hierarchical in the way power is. It is dispersed, contextual, and often contradictory. The attempt to centralize it does not elevate understanding; it suppresses it. Institutional humility is therefore not a moral concession but an epistemic necessity.

This humility has concrete institutional implications. It means designing rules rather than outcomes, frameworks rather than plans. It means accepting that policy cannot aim at precise targets without distorting the interpretative processes that generate economic order. It means recognizing that unintended consequences are not anomalies but signals of misunderstood reality. Above all, it means resisting the temptation to treat society as an object of administration rather than as a field of meaning.

The pretence of knowledge is seductive because it offers certainty in a world of uncertainty. It promises control where only interpretation is possible. But this promise is illusory. The more policymakers attempt to master complexity through technique, the more they undermine the very processes through which complexity becomes intelligible. The result is not rational governance but epistemic fragility.

In this sense, the socialist calculation debate culminates not in a technical conclusion but in a philosophical one. The limits of knowledge are not obstacles to be overcome; they are conditions to be respected. Economic order does not arise from superior intelligence but from institutional arrangements that allow imperfect understanding to coordinate itself. The market is such an arrangement. Planning, in its hubristic form, is not.

7.8. Why Computation, Big Data, and Artificial Intelligence Do Not Solve the Knowledge Problem

The contemporary resurrection of planning ambitions rarely presents itself under the old banners of socialism or government intervention in the economy. Instead, it appears clothed in the language of computation, data science, algorithmic governance, and artificial intelligence. What earlier generations of planners could not calculate, it is now claimed, machines can. What was once dispersed and tacit, it is argued, can now be captured, quantified, and optimized. In this way, the socialist calculation problem is declared obsolete—not because its premises were mistaken, but because technology has allegedly rendered them irrelevant.

Hermeneutical Political Economy reveals why this claim is not merely false, but conceptually confused. The appeal to computation does not overcome the knowledge problem identified by Mises and Hayek; it reinstates it at a higher level of abstraction, while obscuring its true nature even further. The core error remains unchanged: the belief that economic coordination is a problem of information processing rather than of meaning generation.

Big data and artificial intelligence operate on representations of the past. They analyze recorded actions, observed correlations, and measurable outcomes. Their strength lies precisely in identifying patterns within large datasets. But patterns are not meanings, and correlations are not interpretations. The knowledge that matters for economic coordination is not knowledge of what has been done, but understanding of what *might* be done. It concerns possibilities that have not yet materialized, preferences that have not yet been articulated, and interpretations that have not yet been formed.

Entrepreneurial knowledge is therefore fundamentally non-algorithmic. It does not consist in selecting the optimal option from a known set, but in imagining options that are not yet known. No amount of data can reveal a genuinely novel use for an existing resource, because novelty is not latent in data; it is created by interpretation. Algorithms can recombine existing elements according to predefined rules, but they cannot supply the meaning that makes a new combination economically relevant.

This limitation is not a temporary technological constraint. It is structural. Algorithms require a defined problem space. They optimize given objectives. But economic life is characterized precisely by the continuous redefinition of objectives. What counts as success, value, or efficiency is not fixed; it is contested and revised through market interaction. Prices change not merely because conditions shift, but because meanings shift. No algorithm can anticipate such shifts without presupposing them.

Hermeneutical Political Economy insists that economic coordination depends on open-ended interpretation, not closed-form optimization. The future is not a statistical distribution waiting to be sampled; it is an indeterminate horizon shaped by creative action. Attempts to model it as a probability space mistake uncertainty for risk. They treat the unknown as if it were merely unknown data, rather than unknowable meaning.

This distinction is crucial. Risk can be insured against; uncertainty cannot. Markets exist precisely to cope with uncertainty, not by eliminating it, but by allowing actors to experiment, fail, and learn. Profit and loss are not inefficiencies in this process; they are its epistemic engines. They tell us which interpretations of the future were more adequate and which were not. Algorithms, by contrast, learn only from labelled outcomes within predefined frameworks. They cannot reinterpret the framework itself.

The promise of algorithmic planning also rests on a misunderstanding of tacit knowledge. Tacit knowledge is not merely knowledge that has not yet been codified; it is knowledge that cannot be codified without loss of meaning. Skills, judgments, local familiarity, and situational awareness are embodied in practice. They are expressed through action rather than through description. To record their outputs is not to capture their substance.

When planners claim that digital technologies can now "aggregate dispersed knowledge", they confuse aggregation with understanding. Aggregation produces summaries; understanding requires interpretation. A centralized system may possess more data than any individual, but it lacks the situated perspective from which data become meaningful. It does not know *why* actors act as they do, nor how they will reinterpret situations in response to new circumstances.

Moreover, algorithmic governance introduces a new layer of epistemic rigidity. Once policy decisions are encoded into models, they acquire an aura of objectivity that shields them from critique. Outcomes produced by algorithms are treated as neutral results rather than as the expressions of specific assumptions and value judgments. This intensifies policy hubris by disguising interpretation as computation.

Hermeneutical Political Economy unmasks this disguise. Every model embodies a particular interpretation of reality. Every algorithm reflects choices about what to measure, how to classify, and which objectives to optimize. These choices are not technical; they are normative and interpretative. When such choices are centralized and automated, they become harder to contest, not easier. The result is not more rational governance, but epistemic closure.

The socialist temptation thus returns in digital form. Planning is no longer justified by ideological certainty but by technical prowess. The planner is replaced by the engineer; the five-year plan by the predictive model. Yet the underlying aspiration remains the same: to replace the open-ended interpretative process of the market with a controllable system of administration.

This aspiration fails for the same reasons it always has. It presumes that coordination can be achieved without entrepreneurial discovery, that meanings can be stabilized long enough to be optimized, and that the future can be managed as if it were a dataset. In doing so, it suppresses the very processes through which economic knowledge is generated.

The irony is that digital technologies themselves thrive in market environments precisely because they rely on decentralized experimentation. Innovation in artificial intelligence, software, and data analytics has advanced not through central planning, but through entrepreneurial rivalry, creative destruction, and failure. The attempt to use these technologies to abolish the market misunderstands the conditions of their own emergence.

Hermeneutical Political Economy therefore insists on a clear boundary. Technology can assist human action, but it cannot replace interpretation. Data can inform judgment, but they cannot substitute for it. Computation can support coordination, but it cannot generate the meanings upon which coordination depends.

The knowledge problem identified by Mises and Hayek is not a problem of insufficient processing power. It is a problem of human understanding in a world of radical uncertainty. No increase in computational capacity can alter this condition. To believe otherwise is to succumb once again to the pretence of knowledge, this time reinforced by silicon rather than ideology.

7.9. HERMENEUTICAL POLITICAL ECONOMY AND THE IRREDUCIBILITY OF MARKETS

If the preceding parts have dismantled the epistemological pretensions of social-ism, technocratic planning, and algorithmic governance, what remains to be articulated is the positive alternative. Hermeneutical Political Economy is not merely a critique of planning; it is a theory of economic order grounded in the nature of human understanding. It explains why markets are not contin-gent historical arrangements, nor inferior substitutes for rational design, but irreducible institutions of meaning. Their indispensability lies not in efficiency alone, but in their capacity to render a complex, uncertain world intelligible to acting persons.

At the most fundamental level, Hermeneutical Political Economy begins from the insight that economic life is not a problem to be solved, but a reality to be interpreted. Human beings do not encounter the economy as an objective system governed by transparent laws; they encounter it as a field of possibil-ities whose significance must be understood before action is possible. Choice presupposes meaning. Calculation presupposes interpretation. Coordination presupposes a shared, though never fully articulated, symbolic order.

Markets provide precisely this order. They do not impose meanings from above; they allow meanings to emerge from interaction. Prices, profits, losses, contracts, and competition form a grammar through which individuals com-municate their interpretations of scarcity, urgency, and opportunity. This grammar is not designed; it evolves. It is not precise; it is expressive. It does not eliminate uncertainty; it makes uncertainty actionable.

From this perspective, the irreducibility of markets becomes evident. Any attempt to replace markets with planning is an attempt to replace an interpre-tative institution with an administrative one. It assumes that meanings can be fixed ex ante, that relevant knowledge can be centralized, and that the future can be treated as a technical problem. Hermeneutical Political Economy shows why these assumptions contradict the very structure of human action.

Economic understanding is always situated. It arises within particular con-texts and horizons that cannot be detached from the actor. This is why the idea of a "collective mind" capable of performing economic calculation for society as a whole is a fiction. There is no social subject that can interpret the world in place of individuals. There are only individuals whose interpretations must somehow be coordinated. Markets are the institutional answer to this coordination problem.

The crucial point is that markets coordinate without requiring consensus.

They do not presuppose shared values, identical expectations, or common plans. They presuppose only that individuals are free to act on their own interpretations and to bear the consequences of those actions. Coordination emerges not because actors agree, but because incompatible interpretations are disciplined through profit and loss. In this sense, markets are not harmonious by design; they are orderly through contestation.

Hermeneutical Political Economy therefore rejects the widespread belief that disagreement, volatility, and instability are pathologies to be corrected by policy. These phenomena are not failures of the market process; they are expressions of its interpretative vitality. They signal that meanings are being revised in response to new circumstances. To suppress them in the name of stability is to suppress learning.

This insight has profound implications for the role of policy. Policy cannot aspire to optimize outcomes without undermining the interpretative processes that generate those outcomes. When policymakers attempt to steer prices, suppress losses, or guarantee returns, they do not merely redistribute resources; they distort meanings. They interfere with the signals through which actors understand their situation. The result is not better coordination, but confusion.

Hermeneutical Political Economy thus reframes the proper role of institutions. Institutions should not aim at producing specific economic results, but at preserving the conditions under which interpretation can occur. Private property, freedom of contract, and open competition are not ideological commitments; they are epistemic necessities. They allow individuals to form, test, and revise interpretations in a shared social space. This is also why markets cannot be fully subordinated to moral or political objectives without losing their epistemic function. When prices are treated as instruments of moral correction rather than as expressions of relative scarcity and preference, they cease to communicate meaning. The economy becomes opaque. Policymakers may achieve symbolic victories, but at the cost of intelligibility. Moral intentions cannot substitute for understanding.

The socialist project fails because it seeks to replace interpretation with authority. It assumes that someone can know what should be produced, how it should be produced, and for whom, independently of the process through which these questions acquire meaning. Hermeneutical Political Economy shows that this assumption is not merely false but incoherent. Meaning cannot be commanded. It must be discovered.

In this light, the impossibility of socialism is not an empirical hypothesis awaiting falsification. It is a theoretical conclusion derived from the nature of human understanding. Wherever markets are suppressed, interpretation is suppressed. Wherever interpretation is suppressed, calculation becomes meaningless. And wherever calculation becomes meaningless, coordination collapses into arbitrariness.

Markets are therefore not instruments of policy; they are preconditions of intelligible action. They do not guarantee justice, prosperity, or stability. What they guarantee is something more fundamental: the possibility of learning in a world of ignorance. They allow society to cope with uncertainty not by mastering it, but by living with it intelligently.

Hermeneutical Political Economy thus offers a radically different vision of economic rationality. Rationality is not the ability to compute optimal solutions; it is the ability to act meaningfully under uncertainty. Institutions are rational not because they produce desired outcomes, but because they respect the limits of knowledge. In this sense, the market is the most rational institution precisely because it does not pretend to be omniscient.

With this understanding in place, the final task of this chapter is to draw the threads together and articulate the broader philosophical lesson of the socialist calculation debate. This will be the aim of the concluding part.

7.10. Concluding Synthesis: Knowledge, Humility, and the Conditions of Human Flourishing

The socialist calculation debate, when reconstructed through the lens of Hermeneutical Political Economy, reveals itself as far more than a historical controversy about economic systems. It is a decisive confrontation between two radically different conceptions of human knowledge, action, and social order. At stake is not merely the feasibility of planning, but the intelligibility of economic life itself. The impossibility of socialism emerges not as a contingent empirical failure, but as a necessary consequence of misunderstanding the nature of human understanding.

Throughout this chapter, we have seen that the core error of socialism lies in its epistemological ambition. Socialism presupposes that economic order can be consciously designed, that relevant knowledge can be centralized, and that the future can be rendered tractable through calculation. Against this presupposition, the contributions of Mises and Hayek—deepened by Schumpeter and Lachmann—demonstrate that economic coordination is an interpretative achievement, not a technical solution. It arises from the interaction of agents who do not know the whole, who disagree about the future, and who must nonetheless act.

Hermeneutical Political Economy allows us to articulate this insight with philosophical clarity. Human action is always situated, temporal, and meaning-laden. Individuals do not respond to objective data; they interpret situations within horizons shaped by experience, expectation, and imagination. Knowledge in such a world is not a stock of information but a process of understanding. It is generated through action, revised through feedback, and communicated through symbolic institutions—above all, through prices.

Markets are irreducible because they institutionalize this process of understanding. They do not eliminate ignorance; they make ignorance manageable. They do not suppress disagreement; they channel it productively. They do not promise certainty; they enable learning. Prices, profits, and losses form a language through which individuals orient themselves in a world they cannot fully comprehend. To abolish this language is to condemn society to silence, or worse, to the monologue of authority.

The calculation problem identified by Mises thus appears in its true dimension. Without market prices for capital goods, economic calculation is not merely difficult; it is meaningless. Calculation is not an abstract comparison of quantities but an interpretative act that presupposes a living context of exchange. Where this context is absent, numbers lose their referential power. Planning becomes ritual rather than reason.

Hayek's knowledge problem completes this argument by showing that the relevant knowledge for coordination is not merely dispersed but tacit, contextual, and often inarticulate. No authority can possess it in its totality because it does not exist as a totality. It exists only in fragments, embedded in practice. The attempt to centralize it is therefore not a technical challenge but a conceptual impossibility. It is the attempt to transform understanding into information.

Schumpeter's creative destruction and Lachmann's kaleidic order reveal why this impossibility is dynamic rather than static. Economic life is not a system tending toward equilibrium but a process of continuous reinterpretation. Innovation transforms meanings, disrupts expectations, and invalidates prior calculations. Order persists not because interpretations converge, but because institutions allow divergent interpretations to coexist and be tested. Socialism, by contrast, seeks stability of meaning and therefore suppresses the very forces that generate progress.

The modern revival of planning through computation, artificial intelligence, and big data does not escape this critique. It intensifies it. By mistaking pattern recognition for understanding and optimization for judgment, algorithmic governance reproduces the pretence of knowledge in digital form. It amplifies policy hubris while further distancing decision-makers from the lived realities they seek to control. Technology does not overcome the knowledge problem because the problem is not technological. It is hermeneutical.

Hermeneutical Political Economy therefore leads to a decisive conclusion: economic rationality is inseparable from epistemic humility. Rational institutions are not those that claim superior knowledge, but those that acknowledge the limits of knowledge and work within them. Markets embody such humility. Planning, when it aspires to replace markets, embodies its negation.

This conclusion also carries a broader anthropological implication. Socialism fails because it misconceives the human person. It treats individuals as passive recipients of information rather than as active interpreters of meaning. It reduces action to execution and judgment to compliance. In doing so, it undermines not only economic coordination but human agency itself. The suppression of markets is therefore inseparable from the suppression of freedom—not merely political freedom, but the freedom to understand and to act.

The lesson of the socialist calculation debate is thus neither cynical nor fatalistic. It does not deny the possibility of improvement, reform, or institutional learning. On the contrary, it grounds these possibilities in a realistic understanding of human limits. Progress does not come from mastering complexity but from respecting it. Social order does not arise from superior intelligence but from institutions that allow imperfect knowledge to correct itself.

Hermeneutical Political Economy articulates this insight as a general theory of social order. It affirms that understanding precedes control, that meaning precedes measurement, and that humility precedes rationality. In this sense, the market is not merely an economic arrangement but a moral and epistemic achievement. It embodies a way of living together without presuming omniscience.

The impossibility of socialism, finally, is not a verdict against human aspirations for justice, coordination, or flourishing. It is a warning against pursuing these aspirations through means that negate the very conditions of their realization. A society that seeks to flourish must first seek to understand—and must recognize that understanding itself is a shared, fragile, and ongoing accomplishment.

With this, the socialist calculation debate reaches its true conclusion: not in the assertion of market superiority as an ideology, but in the recognition of human finitude as the foundation of social order.

Lesson 8

Understanding Inflation And Its Link With Fiscal Policy And Unemployment

8.1. Defining Inflation: From Price Phenomena to Monetary Disorder

Inflation is among the most frequently invoked and least carefully defined concepts in contemporary political economy. In public discourse, it is almost invariably equated with rising prices; in political rhetoric, it is presented as an external shock, an accident of history, or the result of morally suspect behaviour by producers, traders, or consumers; in policy debates, it is treated as a technical variable to be managed by expert discretion. Yet beneath this apparent familiarity lies a profound conceptual confusion.

Traditional textbooks distinguish between *demand-pull inflation* and *cost-push inflation*. The former refers to a situation in which aggregate demand exceeds potential output, driven by an increase in total demand for goods and services beyond the economy's productive capacity. According to standard accounts, this may result from higher consumption, credit expansion, or deficit-financed public spending. Cost-push inflation, by contrast, is typically described as a rise in prices caused by increases in production costs that outpace gains in productivity, or by higher prices of key inputs such as raw materials, energy, or transport. However, these definitions can be regarded as a misuse of the term *inflation*.

Inflation is not merely a statistical outcome, nor a neutral change in an index of prices. It is a monetary and institutional phenomenon, deeply embedded in the structure of economic coordination, expectations, and social order.

From a hermeneutical perspective, inflation cannot be understood simply as an observable increase in prices. Prices are *signs*, not causes. They are expressions of underlying processes of exchange, valuation, and monetary mediation. To confuse inflation with price increases is to mistake symptom for essence, surface for structure. This confusion is not accidental. It reflects a deeper transformation in economic language, whereby monetary responsibility has been progressively displaced from institutions onto anonymous "forces", and ultimately onto society itself.

The widespread identification of inflation with rising prices is reflected even in standard reference sources. Popular definitions describe inflation as a general increase in the average level of prices and a corresponding decline in purchasing power. Such definitions, while descriptively convenient, already embed a theoretical choice: they define inflation by its effects, not by its cause. This move is not innocent. It allows the causal structure of inflation to remain opaque, contestable, and politically malleable.

From the standpoint of classical monetary theory, and from the tradition running from Hume to Mises, Hayek, Friedman, Alchian, and Yeager, this definitional shift represents a fundamental error. Inflation, properly understood, refers to a disorder in the monetary system, specifically to an expansion of monetary demand beyond the growth of real output. Prices respond to this disorder, but they do not define it. To reverse this order of explanation is to deprive political economy of its diagnostic capacity.

Milton Friedman was acutely aware of this semantic slippage. His insistence that inflation is "always and everywhere a monetary phenomenon" was not a rhetorical flourish, but an attempt to restore conceptual clarity in a discipline increasingly seduced by macroeconomic aggregates divorced from institutional reality. Inflation, in Friedman's framework, arises when the quantity of money grows more rapidly than the economy's capacity to produce goods and services. Prices rise because money has lost its coordinating function, not because production costs have mysteriously conspired against consumers.

This point was reinforced by Armen Alchian, whose evolutionary and institutional perspective added an additional layer of clarity. Alchian distinguished sharply between one-time price level adjustments and persistent inflationary processes. A drought, a war, or a technological disruption may cause prices to rise, but such events do not constitute inflation in the proper sense. They reflect changes in scarcity conditions. Inflation, by contrast, requires a continuing monetary impulse, sustained over time, altering not only prices but the structure of relative prices, expectations, and economic calculation.

Yeager's contribution further deepens this analysis by emphasising the role of monetary disequilibrium. Inflation emerges when the supply of money exceeds the demand to hold it at existing prices and incomes. In such a situation, economic agents attempt to rid themselves of excess balances by increasing spending, thereby bidding up prices. This process is not mechanical; it is interpretative. Agents respond to monetary signals, revise expectations, and adjust plans. Inflation, in this sense, is not merely an excess of money, but a breakdown in the alignment between money as an institution and money as a medium of intertemporal coordination.

What unites these perspectives is the rejection of the idea that inflation can be explained by reference to costs, bargaining power, or sectoral shocks alone. These factors may influence individual prices, but they cannot generate a general and sustained rise in prices without an accommodating monetary framework. To claim otherwise is to attribute causal power to agents who lack control over the monetary medium itself.

This insight is particularly important in a fiat money system, where money is no longer anchored to a commodity constraint and where the supply of base money is determined by political and institutional decisions. In such a system, inflation cannot be understood as an emergent property of market interaction alone. It is, necessarily, a policy phenomenon, even when it is mediated through complex financial mechanisms.

The COVID-19 period offers a paradigmatic illustration of this conceptual confusion. Rising prices were widely attributed to supply chain disruptions, energy shocks, or geopolitical tensions. While these factors undeniably affected relative prices, they cannot account for the sustained increase in the general price level observed across advanced economies. What was largely absent from public discussion was the unprecedented expansion of monetary aggregates, facilitated by fiscal deficits monetised through central bank balance sheets. The narrative of "cost-push inflation" served, once again, as a convenient veil obscuring monetary responsibility.

From a hermeneutical standpoint, this misattribution is not merely an analytical error; it is a failure of interpretation. It reflects an unwillingness to confront the institutional origins of monetary disorder and a preference for explanations that disperse responsibility across impersonal forces. Inflation is thus transformed from a policy outcome into a natural disaster, from a monetary phenomenon into a moralised story of greed, speculation, or misfortune.

Yet inflation is neither mysterious nor inevitable. It is the result of identifiable choices embedded in specific institutional arrangements. As Boettke, Salter, and Smith argue in their analysis of money and the rule of law, discretionary monetary regimes systematically undermine predictability, generality, and accountability. When monetary policy is insulated from clear rules and constitutional constraints, inflation becomes not an accident but a recurring feature of governance.

This institutional perspective aligns closely with the argument developed by Hearn and Ferlito, where inflation is explicitly linked to unemployment and macroeconomic instability. Inflation distorts relative prices, misguides investment decisions, and ultimately generates unemployment once the artificial stimulus dissipates. The price level may rise first, but the deeper cost is borne in the structure of production and the coherence of economic plans.

To define inflation, therefore, is not merely to describe a statistical regularity. It is to take a position on the nature of money, the limits of policy, and the moral responsibility of institutions. In *Hermeneutical Political Economy*, inflation must be understood as a failure of monetary interpretation, a breakdown in the shared expectations that allow money to function as a medium of coordination rather than a tool of expediency.

Therefore, inflation's "original and proper meaning is an excessive increase in the quantity of money, leading in turn to an increase in prices" (Hayek). Similarly, we may say that inflation is produced by "a more rapid increase in the quantity of money than in the quantity of goods and services available for purchase, and such an increase raises prices in terms of that money" (Friedman).

In the sections that follow, this chapter will reconstruct the intellectual origins of the cost-push narrative, expose its analytical inconsistencies, and re-establish inflation as a monetary phenomenon rooted in institutional design and political incentives. Only by restoring this conceptual clarity can political economy reclaim its critical function and resist the technocratic temptation to treat inflation as a variable to be "managed" rather than a disorder to be prevented.

8.2. THE MYTH OF COST-PUSH INFLATION AND THE KEYNESIAN REINTERPRETATION OF MONETARY DISORDER

If inflation is, as argued in the previous section, a monetary phenomenon rooted in the institutional management of money, the persistence of the idea of cost-push inflation presents a theoretical puzzle. Why did a doctrine emerge that attributes a general and sustained rise in prices to increases in production costs, wage pressures, or external shocks, despite its incompatibility with monetary theory? The answer cannot be found merely in analytical error. It lies instead in the historical evolution of macroeconomic policy, the political incentives embedded in discretionary governance, and a profound shift in the way economic causality came to be interpreted after the Keynesian revolution.

The concept of cost-push inflation is strikingly absent from the pre-Keynesian tradition. Classical economists, including Ricardo, Mill, and Marshall, were well aware that changes in costs affect relative prices and profit margins, but none suggested that rising costs could, by themselves, generate a general inflationary process. Even Keynes himself, despite his emphasis on aggregate demand and nominal rigidities, never advanced a theory of cost-push inflation in *The General Theory*. Where Keynes discussed wages and costs, he did so in the context of relative price adjustments and employment, not as an autonomous source of sustained inflation. As Hutchison observed, the idea that cost pressures could drive a continuous rise in the general price level is not present in Keynes's own analytical framework.

The emergence of cost-push inflation as a central explanatory device must therefore be understood as a post-Keynesian development, closely linked to the attempt to reconcile Keynesian policy prescriptions with empirical outcomes that increasingly contradicted them. This reconciliation took place not at the level of theory alone, but through a reinterpretation of historical experience, most notably during the macroeconomic turbulence of the 1960s and 1970s.

The United Kingdom offers a paradigmatic case. Throughout the 1960s, Keynesian economists and policymakers sought to operationalise counter-cyclical fiscal policy in pursuit of full employment and stable growth. The underlying vision was one of macroeconomic fine-tuning: government demand management would smooth fluctuations, close output gaps, and maintain employment near its socially desirable level. Yet this ambition was constrained by the international monetary order of the time. Under the Bretton Woods system and its associated fixed exchange rates, domestic expansion was limited by external balance considerations. Fiscal stimulus tended to increase imports, worsen the current account, and place pressure on the exchange rate. When these pressures became unsustainable, expansionary policies were reversed.

The result was a pattern of policy oscillation that came to be known as the stop–go cycle. Expansionary measures were introduced when unemployment rose or elections approached, only to be abruptly withdrawn when balance-of-payments constraints tightened. This cycle was not merely an unfortunate by-product of imperfect policy execution; it reflected a fundamental incompatibility between discretionary demand management and an externally anchored monetary regime. Yet rather than questioning the feasibility of fine-tuning itself, Keynesian analysis treated these interruptions as exogenous constraints, temporary obstacles to an otherwise sound strategy.

The collapse of the Bretton Woods system in 1971 appeared to remove these obstacles. With the suspension of the gold exchange standard and the transition to floating exchange rates, governments were no longer bound by the discipline of external convertibility. Monetary sovereignty seemed complete. Keynesian policymakers interpreted this institutional shift as an opportunity to pursue expansionary fiscal policies without fear of external imbalance. In the United Kingdom, as in many other advanced economies, ambitious growth and employment targets were set, often explicitly aiming at sustained annual growth rates of around five percent.

What followed, however, was not the promised era of stable prosperity, but a sequence of accelerating inflation, rising unemployment, and stagnant output. By the mid-1970s, the UK economy exhibited all the defining features of stagflation. Inflation reached levels exceeding twenty percent per year, unemployment rose sharply, and growth collapsed. The Keynesian promise of full employment without inflation was not merely unfulfilled; it appeared fundamentally inverted.

Confronted with this outcome, Keynesian economists faced a theoretical dilemma. According to their framework, persistent unemployment signalled deficient aggregate demand. Yet inflation was accelerating even as output remained below potential. The standard demand-pull explanation of inflation was therefore unavailable. To preserve the coherence of the Keynesian system, an alternative explanation was required—one that could account for rising prices without conceding a monetary origin. Cost-push inflation provided precisely such an explanation.

Rising oil prices, increasing wage demands, and import price pressures resulting from currency depreciation were invoked as autonomous forces driving inflation. These factors were undeniably present. The oil shocks of the 1970s did raise energy costs; wage negotiations did reflect social and political tensions; exchange rate movements did affect import prices. But the crucial interpretative move was to treat these cost increases not as relative price adjustments within a monetary framework, but as independent drivers of general inflation.

This move had profound analytical consequences. By redefining inflation as a response to cost pressures, responsibility was shifted away from monetary and fiscal policy. Inflation became an externally imposed constraint, something that "happened" to the economy rather than something generated by institutional choices. Governments could thus maintain expansionary policies while attributing inflation to forces beyond their control.

The British government's 1975 pamphlet *Attack on Inflation: A Policy for Survival* epitomises this narrative. Distributed to households nationwide, the document explicitly rejected the attribution of inflation to monetary expansion. Instead, it emphasised world commodity prices, oil shocks, and wage pressures as primary causes. The monetary dimension of inflation was conspicuously absent. This omission was not accidental. Acknowledging monetary responsibility would have implied a need for fiscal restraint, monetary discipline, and a reconsideration of the full-employment policy paradigm itself.

From the standpoint of monetary theory, the cost-push explanation is deeply flawed. As Friedman repeatedly emphasised, individual prices can rise for many reasons, but a general and sustained rise in prices requires a monetary accommodation. Without an increase in the quantity of money, cost increases in one sector must be offset by reduced spending elsewhere. In a barter economy, or in a monetary economy with a fixed money supply, widespread cost increases would manifest not as inflation but as unemployment, bankruptcies, and reallocations of resources. Inflation only occurs when monetary policy validates these cost pressures by expanding nominal demand.

Yeager's framework of monetary disequilibrium clarifies this point further. When costs rise, firms may attempt to raise prices, but whether they succeed depends on the availability of monetary purchasing power. If money supply growth is constrained, higher prices in one area necessitate lower prices or reduced quantities elsewhere. Inflation emerges only when excess money balances enable agents to accommodate higher prices without reducing other expenditures. In this sense, cost-push inflation is not a cause but a symptom of prior monetary expansion.

Alchian's distinction between transient price shocks and persistent inflation is again instructive. A one-time increase in oil prices may raise the general price level temporarily, but it does not constitute inflation unless it is followed by continued monetary expansion. History provides no example of sustained inflation without sustained growth in money relative to output. Conversely, every episode of prolonged inflation has been accompanied by accommodative monetary policy.

The persistence of the cost-push narrative thus reflects not empirical necessity but theoretical expediency. It allows policymakers to interpret inflation in a way that preserves discretionary authority while deflecting accountability. In hermeneutical terms, it represents a reinterpretation of economic phenomena designed to stabilise a particular policy worldview rather than to explain reality.

This reinterpretation has enduring consequences. By treating inflation as a cost phenomenon, economic discourse shifts attention away from monetary institutions and toward microeconomic actors. Trade unions, multinational corporations, energy producers, or "speculators" become convenient scapegoats. Inflation is moralised rather than analysed. The structural conditions that enable inflation—central bank discretion, fiscal dominance, and the erosion of monetary rules—remain unexamined.

Moreover, the cost-push narrative obscures the temporal structure of inflation. Monetary expansion operates with lags, as Friedman emphasised. The effects of money creation may not manifest immediately in prices, particularly when velocity is unstable or when financial intermediaries absorb liquidity. When inflation eventually emerges, it is tempting to attribute it to contemporaneous cost shocks rather than to prior monetary decisions. This temporal mismatch reinforces the illusion that inflation is exogenous and unpredictable.

From the perspective of *Hermeneutical Political Economy*, the rise of cost-push inflation theory exemplifies a broader pattern: the substitution of interpretative convenience for causal understanding. Economic phenomena are re-described in ways that align with prevailing policy commitments, even when such descriptions undermine explanatory coherence. Inflation becomes a narrative of pressure and constraint rather than a diagnosis of institutional failure.

The myth of cost-push inflation thus serves a dual function. Analytically, it fills a gap created by the failure of Keynesian demand management to deliver its promised outcomes. Politically, it legitimises continued intervention by portraying inflation as a problem requiring further control rather than restraint. In doing so, it entrenches a cycle of policy activism that exacerbates, rather than resolves, monetary disorder.

In the next section, the analysis will move beyond the critique of cost-push inflation to re-establish the monetary nature of inflation in positive terms. By examining the relationship between money, velocity, expectations, and institutional design, the chapter will show how inflation emerges as a systemic phenomenon rooted in monetary disequilibrium, and why attempts to suppress its symptoms without addressing its causes inevitably fail.

8.3. INFLATION AS A MONETARY PHENOMENON: MONEY, VELOCITY, EXPECTATIONS, AND DISEQUILIBRIUM

Once the myth of cost-push inflation has been set aside, the task of political economy is no longer merely critical but constructive. If inflation is not caused by rising costs, bargaining power, or sectoral shocks, then it must be explained in terms of the monetary processes that govern exchange, coordination, and expectation formation in a complex economy. To say that inflation is a monetary phenomenon is not to offer a slogan, but to commit oneself to a specific causal architecture—one in which money is understood as an institution mediating time, uncertainty, and social cooperation.

At the centre of this architecture lies the relationship between money and nominal expenditure. Inflation emerges when the flow of monetary spending grows more rapidly than the economy's capacity to supply goods and services at existing prices. This proposition, most famously articulated by Milton Friedman, is deceptively simple. Its simplicity, however, conceals a rich and subtle analysis of how monetary impulses propagate through the economy, how expectations are formed, and how institutional arrangements shape the transmission of policy decisions into economic outcomes.

Friedman's insistence that inflation is "always and everywhere a monetary phenomenon" must be understood in its proper context. He did not deny that real shocks affect prices, nor did he claim that money operates mechanically or instantaneously. On the contrary, Friedman repeatedly emphasised that the relationship between money and prices is neither precise nor immediate. Changes in the quantity of money affect nominal income with long and variable lags, typically ranging from several months to more than a year. These lags are not a technical inconvenience; they are central to understanding why inflation is so often misunderstood and misattributed.

Because monetary expansion operates with delays, inflation tends to appear disconnected from its causes. By the time prices begin to rise across the economy, the monetary decisions that set the process in motion may be politically distant, institutionally opaque, or analytically forgotten. This temporal separation creates fertile ground for alternative explanations, particularly those that focus on visible, contemporaneous events such as energy shocks or supply disruptions. Yet from a monetary perspective, these events merely shape the pattern of price adjustments; they do not explain the persistence or generality of inflation.

To grasp this dynamic, it is helpful to move beyond the crude equation-of-exchange caricature often associated with monetarism and instead consider the deeper logic of monetary coordination. Money is not merely a numéraire or a stock variable. It is a medium through which agents form plans, compare alternatives, and coordinate actions over time. Inflation, therefore, is not simply "too much money", but a breakdown in the alignment between money supply and money demand.

This is where Yeager's contribution becomes indispensable. Yeager reframed inflation as a problem of monetary disequilibrium, emphasising that what matters is not the quantity of money in isolation, but the relationship between the supply of money and the public's demand to hold it. When the quantity of money exceeds the amount that individuals wish to hold at prevailing prices and incomes, excess balances emerge. Agents attempt to rid themselves of these balances by increasing expenditure, thereby bidding up prices. Inflation, in this view, is the macroeconomic manifestation of countless micro-level attempts to restore desired money holdings.

Crucially, this process is interpretative rather than mechanical. Individuals do not respond to money growth as such; they respond to perceived opportunities, constraints, and expectations. They interpret changes in their cash balances, asset prices, and income streams, and adjust their behaviour accordingly. Inflation is thus inseparable from expectation formation. Once agents come to expect continuing price increases, their demand for real money balances falls further, increasing velocity and reinforcing the inflationary process.

This interaction between money supply, money demand, and velocity highlights the inadequacy of explanations that focus exclusively on one component of the monetary system. The familiar expression of aggregate monetary demand as the product of money stock and velocity captures an important insight: inflation can be driven not only by increases in the quantity of money, but also by changes in the rate at which money circulates. Yet velocity itself is not an independent causal force. It reflects agents' expectations about the future value of money, the stability of prices, and the credibility of monetary institutions.

Hyperinflation provides the most dramatic illustration of this dynamic. In such episodes, rapid money creation initially drives prices upward. As confidence in the currency erodes, individuals seek to minimise their holdings of money, accelerating its circulation. Velocity rises sharply, amplifying inflation far beyond what would be implied by money growth alone. The collapse of money demand becomes both a symptom and a driver of monetary disorder. Inflation, in this sense, is as much a crisis of trust as it is a quantitative imbalance.

Conversely, during deflationary episodes or periods of monetary contraction, velocity tends to fall as individuals seek to increase their money holdings. The same institutional logic operates in reverse. What changes is not the essence of money, but the interpretation agents place on its future purchasing power. Inflation and deflation are thus mirror images of monetary disequilibrium, reflecting shifts in the relationship between money, expectations, and institutional credibility.

Alchian's analysis reinforces this perspective by stressing the importance of persistence and adaptation. Inflation is not defined by a one-time adjustment in prices, but by a continuing process that reshapes behaviour over time. Economic agents adapt to inflation by shortening planning horizons, altering contractual arrangements, and reallocating resources in ways that prioritise nominal gains over productive efficiency. These adaptations, while individually rational, collectively undermine the coordinating function of the price system.

From this standpoint, inflation is not merely an increase in prices, but a systemic disturbance that alters the informational content of market signals.

Prices no longer reliably reflect relative scarcities or consumer preferences; they become contaminated by monetary noise. Hayek's insight into the price system as a mechanism for communicating dispersed knowledge is particularly relevant here. When inflation becomes volatile or unpredictable, the informational role of prices is compromised. Entrepreneurs find it increasingly difficult to distinguish changes in relative demand from changes in the general price level. Investment decisions become speculative rather than calculative.

This is why inflation cannot be treated as a neutral or purely nominal phenomenon. Even when average prices rise at a seemingly moderate rate, the underlying distortions in relative prices can be profound. Monetary expansion does not affect all prices simultaneously or proportionally. It enters the economy through specific channels—financial markets, government spending, credit expansion—and reshapes relative prices as it spreads. These distributional and structural effects are central to understanding the real consequences of inflation.

Friedman acknowledged this point, even as he emphasised the long-run neutrality of money. In the short and medium term, monetary disturbances have real effects precisely because they disrupt the process of relative price adjustment. Inflation, therefore, cannot be evaluated solely by its impact on an index of consumer prices. Its true cost lies in the misallocation of resources, the erosion of long-term planning, and the degradation of economic calculation.

This insight connects directly to the institutional analysis developed in *Money and the Rule of Law*. Discretionary monetary regimes, by their very nature, generate uncertainty about future policy actions. Even when central banks articulate explicit targets or frameworks, the absence of binding rules leaves room for reinterpretation, exception, and political pressure. Agents must therefore form expectations not only about economic fundamentals, but about the behaviour of monetary authorities. Inflation becomes, in part, a product of institutional ambiguity.

From a hermeneutical perspective, this ambiguity undermines the shared understanding that money requires to function as a stable medium of coordination. Money is a social institution grounded in trust, predictability, and generality. When monetary policy becomes contingent, reactive, and opaque, the interpretative framework within which agents operate is destabilised. Inflation is one manifestation of this deeper interpretative breakdown.

The experience of the COVID-19 period once again illustrates these dynamics. Massive monetary expansion was initially absorbed by financial markets, asset prices, and bank reserves. Consumer prices remained relatively stable, reinforcing the belief that inflation was unlikely or controllable. When price pressures eventually emerged, they were attributed to supply-side factors, even as monetary aggregates had grown at historically unprecedented rates. The lagged and uneven transmission of monetary impulses created the illusion that inflation was decoupled from money.

Yet once expectations shifted and velocity began to recover, inflation accelerated across a broad range of goods and services. The monetary explanation did not lose relevance; it merely required patience and institutional awareness. Inflation appeared not because supply chains were disrupted, but because monetary demand had been expanded far beyond the economy's productive capacity, and because confidence in the stability of money had been implicitly weakened.

In this sense, inflation is best understood as a failure of monetary interpretation. It arises when the signals conveyed by monetary policy are inconsistent, when institutional commitments lack credibility, and when agents revise their expectations in response to perceived instability. Monetary expansion is the initiating impulse, but expectations and velocity determine the path and intensity of the process.

The monetary nature of inflation thus cannot be reduced to a single variable or equation. It is a dynamic, institutionally embedded process that unfolds over time, shaped by policy decisions, expectations, and the interpretative frameworks through which agents make sense of economic reality. To deny this complexity is to fall back into the superficial language of price indices and cost pressures, abandoning the deeper task of political economy.

In the next section, the analysis will turn explicitly to the relationship between inflation and unemployment. Building on the monetary theory developed here, it will show how inflation distorts relative prices, misdirects resources, and ultimately generates unemployment rather than curing it. The critique of the Phillips Curve and the alleged inflation–employment trade-off will emerge not as an empirical anomaly, but as a logical consequence of monetary disequilibrium and institutional misdesign.

8.4. INFLATION, RELATIVE PRICES, AND UNEMPLOYMENT: THE COLLAPSE OF THE PHILLIPS CURVE ILLUSION

If inflation is properly understood as a monetary phenomenon rooted in institutional design and monetary disequilibrium, its relationship with unemployment must be reconsidered from the ground up. The conventional macroeconomic narrative, dominant for much of the post-war period, framed inflation and unemployment as opposing evils, linked by a stable trade-off. According to this view, policymakers could choose a point along a curve:

higher inflation would buy lower unemployment, while price stability would come at the cost of idle labour. This idea, crystallised in the Phillips Curve, became one of the most influential and damaging simplifications in the history of macroeconomic thought.

From a hermeneutical standpoint, the Phillips Curve represents not merely an empirical error, but a profound misinterpretation of economic signals. It transformed a historically contingent correlation into a policy-relevant law, abstracted from its institutional context and stripped of its causal foundations. The result was a policy framework that treated inflation as an instrument and unemployment as a technical variable, rather than as outcomes of complex processes of coordination and miscoordination.

The original Phillips Curve, as presented by A.W. Phillips, was a statistical relationship between wage inflation and unemployment observed in the United Kingdom over a specific historical period. It did not purport to describe a universal law, nor did it explicitly link price inflation to employment. It merely noted that periods of low unemployment tended to coincide with faster wage increases, while high unemployment was associated with wage moderation or decline. This relationship was descriptive, not causal, and it operated within a particular institutional environment characterised by stable monetary arrangements and limited inflationary expectations.

The Keynesian reinterpretation of the Phillips Curve fundamentally altered its meaning. Wages were treated as a proxy for prices, and the observed correlation was elevated into a general macroeconomic trade-off between inflation and unemployment. Inflation was reimagined as the "price" society must pay for lower unemployment, while unemployment became a cost imposed by price stability. This reinterpretation required a crucial conceptual leap: it assumed that nominal disturbances could systematically influence real variables in a predictable and controllable manner.

This assumption stood in direct tension with monetary theory. From the perspective of Friedman and the monetarist tradition, any apparent trade-off between inflation and unemployment could only be temporary. Monetary expansion might reduce unemployment in the short run by creating unanticipated increases in nominal demand, thereby encouraging firms to hire more workers at existing wages. But once expectations adjusted and workers demanded higher nominal wages to compensate for rising prices, the real effects would dissipate. Unemployment would return to its underlying level, determined by real factors such as preferences, institutions, and the structure of production.

Friedman's introduction of the natural rate of unemployment was not a concession to equilibrium fetishism, but a way of reasserting causality. Unemployment is not primarily a monetary phenomenon; it reflects the degree of coordination between labour supply and labour demand across sectors and over time. Monetary policy can obscure this coordination temporarily, but it cannot sustainably improve it. Attempts to exploit an inflation–unemployment trade-off merely distort price signals and delay necessary adjustments.

Hayek's contribution adds a deeper structural dimension to this critique. Inflation does not affect all prices simultaneously or proportionally. Monetary expansion enters the economy through specific channels, altering relative prices and changing the pattern of demand. Some sectors expand artificially, while others lag behind. Employment rises in favoured sectors, creating the illusion of general improvement, but this expansion rests on distorted signals. Labour is drawn into lines of production that are not aligned with underlying consumer preferences or resource constraints.

As inflation progresses, these distortions intensify. Entrepreneurs misinterpret nominal signals as real ones, committing resources to projects that appear profitable only under inflationary conditions. Labour follows capital into these sectors, reinforcing the pattern of misallocation. Unemployment may temporarily fall, but this reduction is fragile and deceptive. It depends on the continuation of monetary expansion and the maintenance of false price signals.

When monetary expansion slows or expectations adjust, the underlying miscoordination is revealed. Projects that relied on inflationary financing become unviable, investment collapses, and labour is released from sectors that cannot sustain employment. Unemployment rises, often exceeding its pre-inflationary level. The economy experiences stagnation or recession, not because demand is insufficient in the aggregate, but because labour and capital are in the wrong places.

This dynamic explains the phenomenon of stagflation, which proved fatal to the Phillips Curve framework. The coexistence of high inflation and high unemployment in the 1970s was not an anomaly requiring ad hoc explanations; it was the logical outcome of prolonged monetary distortion. Inflation had not cured unemployment; it had postponed and magnified it.

From Yeager's perspective, this outcome reflects persistent monetary disequilibrium. Inflation disrupts the process by which relative prices guide labour allocation. Workers and firms struggle to distinguish changes in real demand from changes in the value of money. Contracts become shorter, labour markets more volatile, and planning horizons shrink. Unemployment emerges not as a lack of demand, but as a failure of coordination under monetary noise.

The Keynesian response to stagflation was to double down on the cost-push narrative. Inflation was blamed on unions, oil producers, and external shocks, while unemployment was attributed to insufficient aggregate demand. This bifurcation allowed policymakers to pursue expansionary policies while explaining their failures as the result of exogenous constraints. Yet this explanation ignored the central role of monetary policy in generating both inflation and unemployment through distorted signals.

From a hermeneutical standpoint, the Phillips Curve episode illustrates the danger of reifying statistical regularities into policy doctrines. The observed correlation between wages and unemployment was treated as a stable relationship independent of expectations, institutions, and monetary regimes. In doing so, economists and policymakers mistook an artefact of interpretation for a structural feature of the economy.

Unemployment, like inflation, must be understood as a process rather than a variable. It reflects the ongoing attempt of individuals to align their plans with those of others in a context of uncertainty. Monetary stability facilitates this process by providing a reliable framework for calculation and expectation formation. Monetary instability, by contrast, undermines coordination and generates unemployment as a systemic outcome.

Inflation therefore does not offer a remedy for unemployment; it creates the conditions under which unemployment becomes more persistent and more socially destructive. By distorting relative prices and obscuring real scarcities, inflation delays necessary adjustments and channels labour into unsustainable activities. When correction eventually occurs, it does so violently, producing social dislocation and political pressure for further intervention.

This pressure, in turn, reinforces the cycle of discretionary policy. Governments faced with rising unemployment and inflation are tempted to intervene more aggressively, expanding spending, manipulating credit, and imposing controls. Each intervention further degrades the informational content of prices and deepens miscoordination. Inflation and unemployment become intertwined symptoms of institutional failure.

In the framework of *Hermeneutical Political Economy*, this outcome is not accidental. It reflects a fundamental misunderstanding of the economy as a machine to be fine-tuned rather than a process of interpretation and coordination. The Phillips Curve promised control where humility was required. Its collapse revealed the limits of technocratic ambition and the necessity of institutional restraint.

The next section will confront these issues directly by examining how inflation is addressed in practice. It will explore the policy responses available once inflation has taken hold, the dilemmas they create, and the institutional reforms required to prevent inflationary dynamics from recurring. In doing so, it will shift the focus from diagnosis to remedy, while maintaining the critical perspective developed throughout this chapter.

8.5. ADDRESSING INFLATION: MONETARY RESTRAINT, RULES, AND THE LIMITS OF DISCRETION

Once inflation has taken hold, political economy enters a phase in which choices are no longer neutral. Inflation is not a condition that can be painlessly reversed, nor is it a purely technical malfunction to be corrected by fine adjustments. It is the cumulative result of prior monetary and fiscal decisions, sedimented into expectations, contracts, and patterns of production. Any attempt to address inflation must therefore confront not only its immediate symptoms but the institutional logic that generated it. This confrontation is invariably costly, politically contentious, and socially disruptive—precisely because inflation itself represents a prolonged evasion of those costs.

Hayek was unsparing in his assessment of the options available to governments once inflationary dynamics become entrenched. He identified three broad paths: allowing inflation to accelerate until it destroys the monetary system; suppressing its visible effects through price and wage controls; or decisively halting monetary expansion and accepting the necessary correction. The first path leads to monetary collapse, the second to economic repression, and only the third—however painful—offers the possibility of restoring a functioning price system.

These options are not merely theoretical. They reflect recurring historical responses to inflationary crises, each grounded in a distinct interpretative stance toward economic order. Accelerating inflation is the path of denial, where governments attempt to outrun the consequences of past policies by doubling down on monetary expansion. Price controls represent the path of coercion, where political authority substitutes command for coordination. Monetary restraint, by contrast, is the path of recognition: it acknowledges that inflation has distorted the structure of production and that restoring coherence requires allowing relative prices and employment patterns to adjust.

From a hermeneutical perspective, the appeal of the first two options is easily understood. Inflation creates social tension by eroding purchasing power and redistributing wealth in opaque ways. Governments confronted with rising discontent are tempted to seek immediate relief through visible action. Accelerating inflation postpones the reckoning by sustaining nominal incomes, while controls offer the illusion of stability by freezing prices. Both approaches rely on the hope that interpretation can override reality—that economic meaning can be legislated or deferred.

Yet both approaches ultimately fail because they deepen the very misco-ordination they seek to conceal. Accelerating inflation destroys confidence in money as a medium of exchange and a store of value. As expectations adjust, velocity rises, contracts shorten, and economic calculation becomes increasingly speculative. Price controls, on the other hand, sever the link between prices and scarcity. Shortages, queues, black markets, and declining quality emerge as alternative mechanisms of allocation. Inflation does not disappear; it becomes repressed, expressing itself through non-price channels.

Historical experience repeatedly confirms Hayek's warning that repressed inflation is often more destructive than open inflation. When prices are pre-vented from adjusting, the economy loses its primary signalling mechanism. Entrepreneurs cannot distinguish between profitable and unprofitable activities, consumers cannot express preferences through prices, and labour cannot real-locate efficiently. The result is a progressive disorganisation of economic life, accompanied by expanding bureaucratic control and diminishing individual autonomy.

The third option—terminating the increase in the quantity of money—forces the underlying distortions into the open. When monetary expansion stops, sectors that depended on inflationary financing contract, asset prices adjust, and unemployment rises. This outcome is politically painful because it reveals the misdirection of labour and capital that inflation had masked. Yet this pain is not the cause of the problem; it is the delayed conse-quence of earlier policies. To confuse the cure with the disease is one of the most persistent errors in inflationary politics.

Friedman was particularly clear on this point. Slower growth, recession, and higher unemployment are not remedies for inflation; they are the costs of reversing inflation. He famously compared disinflation to giving up alcohol: the discomfort is real, but it reflects the body's adjustment to sobriety, not the harm of sobriety itself. Inflation, by contrast, is intoxicating in the short run and destructive in the long run. The political difficulty lies in persuading societies to endure short-term pain for long-term stability.

This difficulty is magnified by the discretionary nature of modern mon-etary institutions. Central banks operating under discretionary mandates face intense pressure to smooth outcomes, avoid recessions, and respond to political demands. Even when they commit rhetorically to price stability, the absence of binding constraints allows priorities to shift in response to perceived emergencies. Inflation control becomes contingent, reversible, and therefore less credible.

Here the institutional analysis developed in *Money and the Rule of Law* becomes central. Boettke, Salter, and Smith argue that discretionary monetary regimes suffer from both knowledge and incentive problems. Central bankers lack the information required to fine-tune monetary conditions in real time, and they operate within political environments that reward short-term accommodation over long-term discipline. Constrained discretion, despite its appeal, collapses into discretion when constraints are neither precise nor enforceable.

From a hermeneutical standpoint, discretion undermines the shared expectations that money requires to function as a coordinating institution. When monetary policy is unpredictable, agents must interpret not only economic signals but also policy intentions. Inflation expectations become endogenous to political communication, forward guidance, and credibility management. Monetary policy shifts from rule-following to narrative construction, where words are expected to substitute for constraints.

Yeager's analysis reinforces the case for rules by highlighting the fragility of money demand under uncertainty. When agents cannot rely on stable monetary conditions, their demand for real balances becomes volatile. Small policy surprises can trigger large shifts in velocity, amplifying inflationary or deflationary pressures. In such an environment, discretionary intervention often exacerbates instability rather than containing it.

The alternative is not technocratic perfection, but institutional humility. Monetary stability does not require omniscience; it requires predictability, generality, and restraint. Rules achieve this not by eliminating discretion entirely, but by confining it within narrow, transparent boundaries. A credible commitment to limiting monetary expansion reduces the need for continuous intervention by anchoring expectations and stabilising money demand.

Friedman's advocacy of a monetary growth rule reflected this logic. While the specific parameters of such a rule remain open to debate, its underlying principle is clear: remove money creation from short-term political pressures and align it with the long-term growth of the economy. Hayek, more sceptical of gradualism, ultimately went further, questioning whether any monopoly issuer of money could resist the temptation of cheap credit and fiscal accommodation.

This scepticism led Hayek to propose a radical institutional alternative: competition among currencies. By allowing individuals to choose which monies they use for contracts and accounting, governments would be deprived of their monopoly over money creation. Monetary discipline would emerge not from benevolence or expertise, but from competitive pressure. Issuers of depreciating currencies would lose users; those maintaining stability would gain trust.

While such proposals may appear utopian, their hermeneutical significance is profound. They shift the locus of monetary meaning from political authority to social practice. Money becomes once again an institution grounded in consent, usage, and trust, rather than an instrument of policy. Inflation, under such conditions, would no longer be a collective fate imposed from above, but a choice individuals could exit.

Short of currency competition, fiscal discipline remains indispensable. As Buchanan and Wagner argued, inflation is inseparable from deficit finance. Governments that systematically spend beyond their revenues create irresistible pressure for monetary accommodation. Balanced budget rules, debt constraints, and constitutional limits on fiscal expansion are therefore not ancillary to monetary stability; they are its precondition.

From the perspective of *Hermeneutical Political Economy*, these institutional constraints are not merely technical devices. They embody a normative commitment to humility in governance. They recognise that economic order is not the product of control, but of coordination, and that the role of policy is to preserve the conditions under which individuals can form coherent plans.

Inflation, in this sense, is a moral as well as an economic failure. It reflects the abandonment of restraint in favour of expediency, the substitution of short-term political gains for long-term social trust. Addressing inflation requires more than tightening policy; it requires re-embedding monetary institutions within a framework of rules that command legitimacy and limit discretion.

The final section of this chapter will draw these threads together. It will return to the hermeneutical foundations laid at the outset and reflect on inflation as a challenge to liberal democracy itself—one that tests the capacity of societies to accept limits, honour commitments, and resist the seduction of control.

8.6. Conclusion: Inflation, Monetary Meaning, and the Fragility of Liberal Order

Inflation is often treated as a technical disturbance, a fluctuation in an index to be corrected by calibrated policy responses. This chapter has argued that such a view is radically insufficient. Inflation is not merely a change in prices, nor even a narrowly defined monetary imbalance. It is a systemic failure of monetary meaning, a breakdown in the institutional and interpretative framework that allows money to coordinate plans, transmit knowledge, and sustain social cooperation over time.

From the outset, the analysis has insisted on restoring the proper definition of inflation as a monetary phenomenon. Inflation arises when monetary demand expands more rapidly than real output, whether through direct increases in the quantity of money, through accommodative credit creation, or through institutional arrangements that undermine confidence in the stability of money. Rising prices are not the cause of inflation; they are its manifestation. To invert this causal relationship is to deprive political economy of its explanatory power and to obscure responsibility for monetary disorder.

The persistence of alternative explanations—most notably the doctrine of cost-push inflation—cannot be understood as an innocent analytical error. It reflects a deeper transformation in economic interpretation, one that shifts attention away from monetary institutions and toward proximate, visible events. Supply shocks, wage pressures, and commodity prices become explanatory substitutes for monetary expansion, allowing inflation to be framed as an external constraint rather than a policy outcome. This interpretative move has proven politically convenient, but intellectually corrosive.

By reconstructing the historical emergence of the cost-push narrative, particularly in the context of post-war Keynesian policy and the stagflationary crises of the 1970s, the chapter has shown how inflation theory adapted to protect discretionary governance from falsification. When inflation and unemployment appeared together, the failure of demand management was reinterpreted as evidence of new kinds of inflation rather than as a refutation of the underlying paradigm. The result was a proliferation of explanations that multiplied symptoms while leaving causes unexamined.

Against this backdrop, the monetary theory of inflation articulated by Friedman, Alchian, and Yeager offers not merely a competing hypothesis, but a restoration of causal coherence. Inflation is understood as a process unfolding through time, shaped by expectations, institutional credibility, and the alignment—or misalignment—between money supply and money demand. Velocity, expectations, and relative prices are not auxiliary considerations; they are the channels through which monetary disorder expresses itself in real economic life.

This perspective also clarifies the relationship between inflation and unemployment. The alleged trade-off enshrined in the Phillips Curve dissolves once inflation is recognised as a source of miscoordination rather than stimulus. Monetary expansion may temporarily obscure unemployment by distorting signals and encouraging unsustainable patterns of production, but it cannot eliminate the underlying coordination problem. On the contrary, by mis-directing labour and capital, inflation ultimately generates higher and more persistent unemployment once the illusion fades.

Unemployment, in this framework, is not primarily a consequence of insufficient aggregate demand, but of disrupted alignment between plans. Inflation contributes to this disruption by degrading the informational content of prices and undermining the reliability of monetary calculation. The resulting stagnation is not a paradox; it is the predictable outcome of prolonged monetary distortion.

When the analysis turns from diagnosis to remedy, the limits of discretion become unmistakable. Inflation cannot be cured by rhetoric, fine-tuning, or selective intervention. Once inflation has taken hold, societies face a constrained set of choices, none of which are painless. Attempts to accelerate inflation or suppress its symptoms through controls merely postpone and magnify the eventual adjustment. Monetary restraint, though politically costly, is the only path that restores the coordinating function of the price system.

Yet even monetary restraint, if pursued within a discretionary framework, remains fragile. Without credible rules, policy commitments are contingent, reversible, and vulnerable to political pressure. Expectations remain unstable, and money demand volatile. The chapter has therefore emphasised the necessity of embedding monetary policy within a rule-based institutional order—one that prioritises predictability, generality, and restraint over short-term expediency.

From a hermeneutical standpoint, this institutional argument is not merely technical. It speaks to the conditions under which money can function as a shared social language. Money, like law, derives its coordinating power from common understanding and trust. When monetary institutions become instruments of discretionary control, that shared understanding erodes. Inflation is one expression of this erosion, but its deeper cost lies in the weakening of social cooperation and the expansion of coercive governance.

The proposals advanced by Hayek—whether in the form of strict monetary rules or currency competition—should be understood in this light. They are not blueprints for technocratic optimisation, but attempts to re-anchor money within a framework that limits power and restores responsibility. Similarly, the emphasis on fiscal discipline reflects the recognition that monetary stability cannot be sustained in isolation from political incentives. Persistent deficits and debt create irresistible pressure for monetary accommodation, undermining even the most well-intentioned central banks.

In the final analysis, inflation poses a challenge not only to economic efficiency, but to liberal democracy itself. By redistributing wealth opaquely, distorting incentives, and provoking demands for control, inflation erodes the moral and institutional foundations of a free society. It invites the expansion of discretionary power under the guise of necessity, gradually replacing coordination with command.

Hermeneutical Political Economy insists that such outcomes are not inevitable. They arise from choices—conceptual, institutional, and political. To understand inflation is therefore to confront the limits of policy ambition and the necessity of humility in governance. Economic order cannot be engineered; it must be cultivated through institutions that respect complexity, uncertainty, and the interpretative nature of human action.

Inflation, properly understood, is a warning. It signals not merely excess money, but excess confidence in the capacity of authority to control outcomes without consequences. To heed that warning is to reaffirm the principles of restraint, rule-governed institutions, and responsibility that underpin a stable and humane economic order.

LESSON 9

Monetary Policy, Government Spending And Business Cycles

9.1. HERMENEUTICAL FOUNDATIONS: CYCLES, TIME, AND THE MEANING OF POLICY

Economic fluctuations are as old as market societies themselves. Periods of expansion and contraction, optimism and retrenchment, innovation and re-coordination appear as recurring features of economic life. Yet the way in which these fluctuations are interpreted has changed profoundly over time. In contemporary macroeconomic discourse, business cycles are predominantly framed as technical deviations from an assumed equilibrium path, to be corrected through calibrated interventions by monetary and fiscal authorities. In this view, cycles are not expressions of the inner logic of a market economy unfolding in time, but malfunctions of an otherwise stable mechanism. Policy thus presents itself as an external corrective force, endowed with the epistemic authority to diagnose, stabilize, and steer aggregate outcomes.

Hermeneutical political economy rejects this mechanistic image at its root. It does not deny the existence of recurrent economic crises, nor does it romanticize instability. Rather, it insists that cycles must be understood as meaningful processes emerging from human action under conditions of time, uncertainty, and imperfect knowledge. Economic life is not governed by timeless equations but unfolds historically, shaped by expectations, narratives, institutional frameworks, and the interpretative judgments of entrepreneurs, consumers, savers, and policymakers. Within this perspective, the business cycle is not a statistical pattern to be smoothed, but a temporal process to be interpreted.

This interpretative stance has decisive implications for the analysis of monetary policy and government spending. If cycles are meaningful processes rather than mechanical deviations, then policy interventions are not neutral technical adjustments. They are themselves interpretative acts, embedded in narratives about stability, growth, employment, and social welfare. Monetary and fiscal policies do not merely "respond" to cycles; they reshape the structure of expectations and the allocation of capital, thereby influencing the very dynamics they claim to control.

The starting point of this chapter, therefore, must be methodological rather than technical. Before asking how monetary policy or government spending affect business cycles, one must clarify what kind of phenomena cycles are, and what kind of knowledge economic agents—and policymakers in particular—can realistically possess. This requires revisiting the relationship between time, capital, and coordination that lies at the heart of Austrian and hermeneutical economics.

In *Economics: An Interpretative Science of Human Flourishing*, the economy has been defined not as a closed system tending toward equilibrium, but as an open process of meaning formation, in which individuals interpret signals, revise plans, and discover new possibilities through entrepreneurial action. Capital, within this framework, is not a homogeneous stock measured in monetary units, but a complex, time-structured constellation of heterogeneous goods whose value depends on subjective expectations about future uses. Production is therefore inseparable from time, and coordination is always provisional, exposed to revision as new information emerges.

Business cycles must be situated within this temporal and interpretative structure. Fluctuations are not accidental disturbances imposed from outside the economic process; they reflect changes in intertemporal coordination. At times, these changes arise from genuine shifts in preferences, technologies, or entrepreneurial discovery. At other times, they are induced by institutional distortions, particularly those affecting money, credit, and interest rates. To conflate these fundamentally different sources of fluctuation under a single notion of "the business cycle" is to obscure more than it reveals.

It is precisely at this point that the distinction between natural cycles and monetary cycles becomes essential. Natural cycles emerge from the endogenous dynamics of a market economy operating under uncertainty. They are rooted in innovation, learning, error correction, and the continuous reinterpretation of plans over time. In a world without perfect foresight, even well-functioning markets cannot avoid periods of miscoordination. Entrepreneurial errors are discovered only ex post, and their correction necessarily involves phases of contraction and reallocation. These cycles are not pathologies to be eliminated, but expressions of the economy's adaptive capacity.

Monetary cycles, by contrast, originate from systematic distortions in the intertemporal signals that guide production decisions. When the rate of interest is manipulated through credit expansion disconnected from genuine saving, the price system conveys misleading information about the availability of real resources. Entrepreneurs are induced to undertake projects that appear profitable under distorted monetary conditions but cannot be sustained once these conditions change. The resulting boom is not a phase of genuine prosperity, but a period of growing intertemporal inconsistency. The subsequent bust represents not a failure of the market, but an unavoidable process of re-coordination.

This distinction, which draws on but also extends the Austrian theory of the business cycle, cannot be fully grasped without abandoning the equilibrium-centric mindset of mainstream macroeconomics. Hayek already emphasized that the essential problem of the trade cycle lies not in fluctuations of aggregate demand or the general price level, but in changes in the structure of relative prices and the allocation of resources across time. Monetary disturbances affect production by altering the intertemporal pattern of investment, lengthening or reshaping the structure of production in ways that are inconsistent with underlying time preferences.

Yet Hayek's contribution is often misunderstood when it is reduced to a purely technical theory of overinvestment. At its core, his analysis is epistemic. The problem is not that entrepreneurs are irrational, but that they are misled by distorted signals. Interest rates, in a market economy, perform a communicative function: they summarize dispersed information about time preferences, risk, and resource availability. When this signal is manipulated, coordination breaks down—not because agents fail to optimize, but because optimization itself becomes epistemically compromised.

Mises deepened this insight by situating monetary disturbances within a broader theory of human action. In *Human Action*, he insisted that economic phenomena must be understood as the unintended consequences of purposeful behaviour under uncertainty. The trade cycle is not an autonomous force acting upon individuals, but the outcome of specific institutional arrangements governing money and credit. Expansionary policies do not suspend the logic of scarcity; they merely postpone its manifestation, often at the cost of greater dislocation later.

From a hermeneutical perspective, what is most striking in Mises's analysis is his rejection of the idea that policy can substitute for market processes of interpretation and adjustment. There is no Archimedean point from which policymakers can observe the economy as a whole and calibrate interventions accordingly. Knowledge is fragmented, contextual, and often tacit. Attempts to stabilize the economy through aggregate management therefore rest on an illusion of control that ignores the interpretative nature of economic coordination.

This illusion is particularly evident in the way time is treated in conventional policy discourse. Time is reduced to a sequence of periods indexed by data releases and forecast horizons. Policy operates through lags that are assumed to be measurable and manageable. Yet economic time is not clock time. It is lived time, shaped by expectations, commitments, and irreversible decisions. Investments, once undertaken, cannot be costlessly reversed. Capital goods are specific to particular production plans, and their value depends on future states of the world that are fundamentally uncertain.

Natural cycles emerge precisely because economic actors must act in the present based on interpretations of an unknowable future. Errors are inevitable, but they are also instructive. They generate learning, adaptation, and institutional evolution. To suppress these processes in the name of stability is to undermine the very mechanisms through which markets coordinate over time.

Monetary policy, however, often presents itself as a tool for eliminating uncertainty rather than coping with it. By targeting interest rates, inflation expectations, or asset prices, central banks seek to anchor beliefs and smooth outcomes. In doing so, they implicitly claim an epistemic superiority over market participants. Yet this claim is difficult to reconcile with the hermeneutical insight that meaning and coordination emerge from decentralized interpretation, not from centralized design.

The problem is not merely that policymakers may make mistakes. It is that the institutional framework within which monetary policy operates systematically biases interpretation. When expansionary measures are repeatedly deployed to counteract downturns, agents come to expect intervention as a permanent feature of the economic environment. Risk perceptions are altered, leverage increases, and investment horizons lengthen in ways that are contingent on continued policy support. What appears as stabilization in the short run may therefore generate fragility in the long run.

This dynamic cannot be captured by models that abstract from capital heterogeneity and intertemporal structure. It requires an interpretative analysis attentive to how policy narratives shape expectations and behaviour. Monetary policy does not merely change prices; it changes the stories economic actors tell themselves about the future. These stories, in turn, influence saving, investment, and consumption decisions in ways that feed back into the cycle.

Government spending must be analyzed within the same hermeneutical framework. Fiscal policy is often justified as a countercyclical tool designed to compensate for insufficient private demand. Yet this justification presupposes a view of the economy as an aggregate system that can be fine-tuned through expenditure flows. It overlooks the fact that government spending, like any other form of spending, reallocates resources across time and sectors. It does not create resources *ex nihilo*, but redirects them according to political priorities rather than entrepreneurial judgment.

From the standpoint of natural cycles, fiscal intervention may disrupt processes of re-coordination by sustaining activities that would otherwise be restructured or abandoned. From the standpoint of monetary cycles, deficit-financed spending often interacts with accommodative monetary policy to prolong distortions in the capital structure. The combination of low interest rates and expansive public expenditure blurs the distinction between productive investment and politically driven allocation.

At a deeper level, government spending introduces an additional interpretative layer into the economy. Decisions about which sectors to support, which projects to fund, and which risks to socialize are embedded in normative judgments about social value. These judgments are not neutral, nor can they be reduced to efficiency criteria. They reflect particular visions of growth, employment, and welfare that compete with entrepreneurial interpretations of consumer preferences.

Hermeneutical political economy does not deny the legitimacy of political choice. It insists, however, that political action must be recognized as qualitatively different from market coordination. When fiscal policy is framed as a technical instrument for managing cycles, its normative and interpretative dimensions are obscured. This obscurity contributes to the illusion that policy can replace the market's discovery process rather than complement it.

So far, we have sought to establish the conceptual ground on which a critical analysis of monetary policy and government spending must be built. Business cycles are not homogeneous phenomena, and policy is not an external corrective force standing outside the economic process. Cycles reflect the temporal structure of capital and the interpretative nature of coordination. Monetary policy and fiscal activism, far from neutralizing instability, often reshape it by altering the signals and narratives through which agents form expectations.

In the following parts of this chapter, this framework will be applied more concretely. Part 2 will examine how monetary policy generates and amplifies the monetary cycle through interest rate manipulation and credit expansion. Part 3 will turn to government spending and fiscal activism as sources of cyclical distortion. Part 4 will analyze the interaction between monetary and fiscal policies and their role in suppressing, rather than accommodating, the economy's natural processes of adjustment.

What must be retained at this stage is a fundamental inversion of perspective. Stability is not achieved by suppressing fluctuation, but by allowing meaningful processes of error correction and re-coordination to unfold. Policy that ignores this insight risks transforming natural cycles into chronic instability, and adaptive markets into fragile systems dependent on permanent intervention.

9.2. MONETARY POLICY AND THE MONETARY CYCLE: INTEREST, CREDIT, AND THE DISTORTION OF TIME

If Part 1 established that business cycles must be understood as meaningful processes unfolding in time, Part II turns to the specific role of monetary policy in generating a particular kind of cyclical dynamic: the monetary cycle. This cycle is not simply a fluctuation amplified by money, nor a neutral response to exogenous shocks. It is a distinct phenomenon arising from the systematic manipulation of the intertemporal signals that coordinate production across time. At its core lies a distortion of meaning: a misinterpretation of scarcity, patience, and future-oriented plans induced by monetary intervention.

In mainstream macroeconomics, monetary policy is typically presented as a stabilizing device. By adjusting short-term interest rates, managing liquidity, and shaping expectations, central banks are said to smooth fluctuations, anchor inflation, and guide the economy toward its potential output. The implicit image is that of a pilot correcting deviations from a predetermined flight path. From a hermeneutical perspective, this image is deeply misleading. It assumes that the economy has a knowable trajectory, that equilibrium is an observable benchmark, and that interest rates can be treated as policy instruments rather than as communicative prices emerging from human interaction.

Austrian monetary theory, as developed by Mises and Hayek, challenges this image by reinterpreting the interest rate as a time-coordinating signal, not a policy lever. The interest rate is not merely the cost of borrowing; it is the price that mediates between present and future, between saving and investment, between consumption foregone and production extended. To manipulate this signal is therefore not to fine-tune the economy, but to interfere with the process through which economic actors interpret time and scarcity.

Hayek's early work on the trade cycle insisted that the central problem of monetary theory lies not in changes in the general price level, but in changes in the structure of relative prices, especially those governing the allocation of resources across stages of production. Monetary expansion, when transmitted through the credit system, does not affect all prices uniformly. It enters the economy at specific points, typically through financial markets and investment goods industries, altering profitability signals and reshaping production plans.

This insight cannot be understood without a theory of capital that treats it as heterogeneous and time-structured. Production is not a single act, but a sequence of stages extending from the most remote inputs to final consumption. Each stage is linked to others through expectations about future demand and relative prices. The interest rate coordinates these stages by indicating how much society is willing to defer consumption. When this rate emerges from voluntary saving, it reflects genuine intertemporal preferences. When it is pushed downward by credit expansion, it conveys a false message.

The false message at the heart of the monetary cycle is deceptively simple: it suggests that more real resources are available for long-term investment than is actually the case. Entrepreneurs, responding rationally to lower borrowing costs and rising asset prices, undertake projects that are more roundabout, more capital-intensive, and more time-consuming. From the standpoint of individual decision-makers, these investments appear justified. From the standpoint of the economy as a whole, however, they represent an intertemporal inconsistency.

This inconsistency is not immediately visible, because the early phase of the monetary expansion is typically accompanied by prosperity. Employment rises, profits increase, optimism spreads. This phase is often celebrated as evidence of successful policy. Yet the apparent prosperity rests on a fragile foundation. The expansion has not been financed by an increase in real saving, but by the creation of additional purchasing power. Consumption does not fall accordingly; in many cases, it rises. The economy is thus pulled in two incompatible directions: toward longer production processes and sustained or even increased present consumption.

From a hermeneutical standpoint, what matters here is not simply the allocation of resources, but the interpretation of signals. Entrepreneurs interpret low interest rates as a sign of greater future-oriented willingness to save. Consumers interpret rising incomes and asset values as a signal of increased wealth. Policymakers interpret stable consumer price indices as confirmation that inflation is under control. Each interpretation is internally coherent, yet collectively inconsistent.

Mises emphasized that such inconsistencies cannot be resolved through monetary means alone. In *Human Action*, he argued that credit expansion sets in motion processes that must eventually reverse, because it cannot abolish scarcity or alter time preferences. The boom generated by monetary expansion is therefore unsustainable by its very nature. Its end is not caused by mysterious psychological shifts or external shocks, but by the gradual realization that resources are insufficient to complete all initiated projects.

The bust phase of the monetary cycle represents the painful process of re-coordination. Projects that appeared profitable under distorted conditions are revealed as malinvestments. Capital goods specific to these projects lose value, workers must relocate, and balance sheets deteriorate. From a mainstream perspective, this phase is interpreted as a failure of demand, a collapse of confidence, or a financial shock. From a hermeneutical-Austrian perspective, it is the moment when meaning catches up with reality, when misinterpretations induced by policy are corrected through loss and restructuring.

It is precisely at this juncture that contemporary monetary policy intervenes most aggressively. Rather than allowing the economy to reallocate resources and revise plans, central banks often respond to downturns with further monetary easing. Interest rates are reduced even more, liquidity is expanded, and unconventional measures are deployed to support asset prices and credit flows. The stated objective is to prevent deflation, stabilize expectations, and restore growth. The unintended consequence is to extend and deepen the distortion of intertemporal coordination.

This pattern reveals a fundamental asymmetry in modern monetary regimes. Booms are attributed to market efficiency or structural strength; busts are attributed to market failure requiring policy correction. The possibility that the boom itself was policy-induced is systematically downplayed. As a result, monetary policy becomes trapped in a cycle of its own making, responding to the consequences of previous interventions with ever more intrusive measures.

From a hermeneutical perspective, this dynamic can be described as a self-reinforcing narrative. Each intervention reshapes expectations, leading agents to anticipate future support and adjust behaviour accordingly. Risk-taking increases, leverage rises, and investment horizons lengthen. What begins as an attempt to stabilize the economy evolves into a regime of permanent intervention, in which market participants no longer interpret price signals as expressions of scarcity, but as contingent on policy commitments.

The interest rate, in this context, loses its communicative function. It no longer summarizes dispersed information about time preferences and resource availability. Instead, it becomes a policy signal, interpreted through the lens of central bank communication strategies. Forward guidance, quantitative easing, and balance sheet policies are explicitly designed to shape expectations. Yet expectations shaped by authority differ fundamentally from expectations emerging through market interaction. They are less adaptive, more synchronized, and therefore more prone to systemic error.

Hayek warned against precisely this danger when he emphasized the limits of centralized knowledge. The price system, he argued, is valuable not because it produces equilibrium outcomes, but because it enables decentralized learning. When monetary policy overrides this system, it replaces a process of discovery with a process of coordination by command. The result is not greater stability, but a different and often more fragile form of order.

The monetary cycle thus differs qualitatively from the natural cycle discussed in Part 1. Natural cycles arise from entrepreneurial experimentation and learning. They are localized, heterogeneous, and self-correcting. Monetary cycles are systemic, synchronized, and driven by institutional incentives that encourage uniform interpretation. When credit expansion affects the entire financial system, errors are not isolated; they become correlated. The eventual correction is therefore broader and more disruptive.

This distinction has profound implications for how crises are interpreted. If downturns are seen primarily as failures of aggregate demand, policy responses will focus on restoring spending. If they are understood as phases of re-coordination following monetary distortion, policy responses should aim at removing impediments to adjustment. The hermeneutical approach does not deny the social costs of crises, but it insists that these costs cannot be eliminated by suppressing the signals through which coordination occurs.

Monetary policy, in this light, appears less as a stabilizing force and more as a source of interpretative interference. By altering the meaning of interest rates, it affects not only investment decisions but the temporal horizon of economic actors. Short-term gains are privileged over long-term sustainability, not because agents are myopic, but because the institutional framework rewards behaviour consistent with policy-induced signals.

This observation also helps explain why modern monetary regimes tend to produce asset price inflation rather than consumer price inflation. When credit expansion is channelled through financial markets, it raises the prices of assets whose valuation depends heavily on discount rates and future expectations. Consumer prices may remain stable for extended periods, leading policymakers to conclude that inflation is under control. Yet beneath this surface stability, the capital structure becomes increasingly fragile.

From a hermeneutical standpoint, focusing exclusively on consumer price indices reflects a narrow conception of meaning. Prices are treated as data points rather than as signals embedded in a broader narrative of production and time. Asset prices, credit spreads, and balance sheet structures are not peripheral phenomena; they are central to understanding how monetary policy reshapes the economy's temporal orientation.

The monetary cycle, then, is not merely a technical failure of policy calibration. It is the outcome of a deeper epistemic problem: the attempt to manage an interpretative process through centralized control. By treating money and credit as neutral instruments rather than as carriers of meaning, policymakers underestimate the extent to which their actions transform the very framework within which economic decisions are made.

Part 2 has sought to reconstruct the monetary cycle as a distortion of intertemporal meaning rather than as an aggregate fluctuation. Interest rate manipulation and credit expansion interfere with the communicative function of prices, inducing coordinated errors that cannot be resolved without painful adjustment. Attempts to prevent this adjustment through further intervention risk transforming episodic cycles into chronic instability.

In Part 3, the analysis will be extended to government spending and fiscal activism. While monetary policy distorts the interpretation of time through interest rates, fiscal policy reshapes meaning through political allocation and debt finance. Together, they form a policy mix that profoundly alters the dynamics of business cycles and the prospects for sustainable coordination.

9.3. Government Spending, Fiscal Activism, and the Politicization of the Cycle

If monetary policy reshapes the business cycle by distorting the intertemporal signal conveyed by interest rates, government spending intervenes at a different but complementary level. Fiscal activism does not primarily alter the price of time; it redefines the *ownership, direction, and interpretation of resources* through political decision-making. In doing so, it transforms business cycles from processes of market coordination and re-coordination into arenas of political stabilization, distributional conflict, and narrative management.

In orthodox macroeconomic theory, government spending is typically justified as a countercyclical instrument. When private demand is deemed insufficient, public expenditure is expected to fill the gap, stabilizing output and employment. This reasoning presupposes that spending, regardless of its source or direction, is functionally equivalent at the aggregate level. Money spent by the state is assumed to substitute for money not spent by private actors, with little regard for differences in motivation, information, or temporal orientation.

Hermeneutical political economy challenges this equivalence at its foundation. Spending is never merely a flow of money; it is always an *act of interpretation*. To spend is to assign meaning to resources, to decide which ends are worth pursuing, which projects should be sustained, and which time horizons deserve priority. When these decisions are made through the political process, they reflect not the emergent judgments of entrepreneurial actors responding to price signals, but the institutional logic of public authority, electoral incentives, and bureaucratic planning.

From this perspective, government spending is not simply an economic variable; it is a political reallocation of meaning. It redirects resources away from uses validated through voluntary exchange toward uses justified by political narratives—growth, employment, social justice, national development, or crisis response. These narratives are not neutral descriptions of economic reality; they are interpretative frameworks that compete with market-based interpretations of value and scarcity.

This distinction becomes especially significant during periods of cyclical downturn. In the aftermath of a monetary boom, when malinvestments are revealed and re-coordination becomes necessary, fiscal activism often steps in to arrest the adjustment process. Projects that would otherwise be liquidated are sustained through subsidies, public procurement, or direct state ownership. Employment that would shift across sectors is frozen through public hiring or wage support schemes. Losses that would discipline capital allocation are socialized through deficits and debt.

Such interventions are commonly defended as pragmatic responses to social hardship. Hermeneutical political economy does not deny the human costs of adjustment, nor does it dismiss the moral motivations behind fiscal intervention. What it insists upon is that postponing economic meaning does not eliminate it. By sustaining activities that no longer correspond to genuine consumer preferences or viable production structures, government spending delays the reinterpretation of capital and labour that is necessary for recovery.

Mises was explicit on this point. In his analysis of interventionism, he argued that government spending financed through borrowing or monetary expansion cannot restore coordination; it can only redistribute purchasing power and obscure the underlying scarcity of real resources. Fiscal policy does not create capital; it reallocates it according to political criteria. When such reallocation contradicts market signals, it deepens rather than resolves cyclical maladjustments.

The Keynesian tradition, by contrast, interprets the cycle primarily through the lens of aggregate demand. In this view, recessions persist because private actors fail to spend, trapped by pessimistic expectations or liquidity constraints. Government spending is therefore framed as a catalyst that restores confidence and reactivates idle resources. Yet this framework abstracts from the *structure* of production and the *heterogeneity* of capital. It treats idle resources as homogeneous and readily re-deployable, ignoring the specificity of skills, machinery, and organizational knowledge.

From a hermeneutical standpoint, this abstraction is not merely a simplification; it is a misinterpretation of economic reality. Idle resources are idle for a reason: they are embedded in production plans that have lost their meaning under current conditions. Reassigning them through public spending does not automatically restore coherence; it imposes a new, politically defined meaning that may or may not align with future consumer demand.

The problem is compounded when government spending is financed through persistent deficits. Deficit finance extends the temporal horizon of fiscal intervention by shifting the burden of current spending into the future. This shift is not neutral. It alters expectations about taxation, inflation, and policy continuity, influencing private decision-making in ways that are difficult to anticipate or control.

Debt, in this sense, is not merely a financial instrument; it is a claim on future interpretation. It presupposes that future taxpayers will accept the political narratives that justified current spending, or at least that they will be compelled to honour them. When debt accumulates, fiscal policy becomes increasingly oriented toward maintaining credibility and refinancing obligations, rather than facilitating genuine economic re-coordination.

The interaction between fiscal activism and the monetary cycle is particularly destabilizing. When monetary policy suppresses interest rates and fiscal policy expands spending simultaneously, the signals guiding investment and consumption are doubly distorted. Low interest rates encourage long-term projects, while government spending sustains demand patterns that may not be consistent with underlying preferences. The result is a prolonged suspension of adjustment, often accompanied by rising public and private leverage.

In such a regime, the distinction between public and private investment becomes blurred. Public spending crowds into sectors favoured by policy—often infrastructure, energy, housing, or strategic industries—while private actors adjust their plans to align with expected government support. This alignment is not necessarily inefficient in the short run; it can generate growth spurts and employment gains. Over time, however, it entrenches dependency on policy continuity and amplifies the systemic consequences of policy reversal.

From a hermeneutical perspective, this dynamic reflects a deeper transformation of the economic order. Market coordination relies on the continuous reinterpretation of price signals. Fiscal activism replaces this process with narrative coordination, in which coherence is sought through shared expectations about policy support rather than through relative prices. Stability becomes a function of credibility rather than adaptability.

This shift has important implications for the nature of crises. In an economy dominated by fiscal and monetary intervention, downturns are no longer perceived as phases of re-coordination but as failures of policy resolve. The political imperative becomes one of preventing visible contraction at almost any cost. As a result, each cycle tends to be met with stronger intervention, larger deficits, and more comprehensive stabilization programs.

The long-term consequence is not the elimination of cycles, but their transformation. Natural cycles, characterized by localized errors and decentralized adjustment, give way to policy-driven cycles marked by synchronized expansions and contractions. When adjustment eventually occurs—often triggered by inflationary pressures, fiscal constraints, or loss of policy credibility—it does so on a larger scale, with more pervasive social and economic disruption.

Hayek warned that such dynamics would lead to a progressive erosion of the market order. When government spending is used systematically to override price signals, the informational function of the market is weakened. Economic actors become less responsive to relative prices and more attentive to policy announcements. Investment decisions are increasingly shaped by regulatory and fiscal considerations rather than by entrepreneurial judgment.

This erosion is not necessarily visible in conventional macroeconomic indicators. GDP may grow, employment may remain high, and inflation may appear contained. Yet beneath these aggregates, the economy's capacity for adaptation deteriorates. Capital becomes misaligned with consumer preferences, labour skills stagnate in protected sectors, and innovation is channelled toward rent-seeking rather than value creation.

From the standpoint of hermeneutical political economy, the crucial question is not whether government spending can "stimulate" the economy, but whether it respects the interpretative processes through which coordination emerges. Fiscal policy that treats the economy as a machine to be kept running overlooks the fact that economic vitality depends on the freedom to revise plans, abandon failing projects, and reassign meaning to resources.

This does not imply that all government spending is necessarily destabilizing. The issue is not the size of the state per se, but the logic according to which fiscal intervention is justified and deployed. Spending that aims to preserve flexibility, reduce institutional rigidities, or support the conditions for entrepreneurial discovery differs fundamentally from spending designed to maintain existing structures regardless of their economic viability.

However, contemporary fiscal activism is rarely framed in these terms. It is more often presented as an emergency response to cyclical weakness, legit-imized by aggregate indicators and short-term political imperatives. In such a context, government spending becomes a tool for suppressing symptoms rather than addressing causes.

Part 3 has argued that fiscal policy, when understood hermeneutically, is a powerful force in shaping business cycles—not by smoothing them, but by redefining their meaning and trajectory. By reallocating resources through political narratives and debt finance, government spending interacts with mon-etary policy to suspend re-coordination and amplify systemic fragility.

In Part 4, the analysis will bring together monetary policy and government spending within a unified interpretation of the modern policy mix. The focus will shift to crisis management, chronic instability, and the suppression of the natural cycle, showing how the attempt to eliminate fluctuation ultimately undermines the economy's capacity for sustainable adjustment.

9.4. THE POLICY REGIME, CRISIS MANAGEMENT, AND THE SUPPRESSION OF THE NATURAL CYCLE

When monetary policy and government spending are considered in isolation, their destabilizing effects can still be misunderstood as contingent errors of cali-bration or execution. It is only when they are analyzed together—as a coherent policy regime—that their deeper consequences for the business cycle become fully visible. Contemporary economies are not shaped by discrete interventions, but by a persistent interaction between monetary accommodation and fiscal expansion, sustained by a shared narrative of stabilization. This interaction does not merely influence cyclical dynamics; it restructures the meaning of crisis, adjustment, and time within the economic order.

In Parts 2 and 3, monetary policy was shown to distort intertemporal coordination by manipulating the interest rate, while fiscal activism was shown to reallocate resources through political narratives and debt finance. In combi-nation, these two dimensions form what is commonly described as the policy mix. In orthodox macroeconomic discourse, the policy mix is evaluated in terms of effectiveness, credibility, and coordination between authorities. From a hermeneutical perspective, however, the decisive question is not whether policies are coordinated, but what kind of coordination they replace.

Market coordination emerges from decentralized interpretation. Entrepreneurs, consumers, and investors continuously revise their plans in response to relative prices, profits and losses, and evolving expectations. This process is inherently imperfect, but it is adaptive. Errors are localized, feedback is immediate, and learning occurs through failure as much as through success. The natural cycle reflects this process: expansions driven by discovery and innovation, contractions driven by error correction and reallocation.

The modern policy regime seeks to substitute this open-ended process with a managed form of coordination. Monetary policy anchors expectations through interest rate targets and communication strategies; fiscal policy sustains demand and employment through spending programs and transfers. Together, they aim to prevent visible breakdowns in aggregate indicators. In doing so, they transform crises from moments of reinterpretation into problems of policy resolve.

This transformation is most evident in the concept of crisis management. In contemporary discourse, crises are framed as exceptional events requiring extraordinary measures. Yet as policy intervention becomes permanent, crisis management itself becomes routine. Each downturn is met with faster, larger, and more comprehensive interventions, justified by the experience of past episodes and the fear of systemic collapse. What was once exceptional becomes normalized, and normalization reshapes expectations.

From a hermeneutical standpoint, crisis management is not simply a set of tools; it is a narrative practice. Policymakers interpret economic signals, construct stories about causality and risk, and communicate these stories to the public. These narratives, in turn, influence behaviour. When crises are consistently attributed to exogenous shocks or market failures, intervention appears not only justified but necessary. The possibility that policy itself has contributed to the buildup of fragility is marginalized.

This narrative asymmetry has profound implications for the cycle. Booms are rarely interpreted as problematic unless they manifest as visible inflation. Asset price inflation, leverage, and capital misallocation are often reinterpreted as signs of confidence or financial deepening. Busts, by contrast, are framed as intolerable disruptions requiring immediate action. The cycle thus becomes one-sided: expansion is accepted, contraction is resisted.

The resistance to contraction is not merely political; it is epistemic. Allowing the natural cycle to unfold requires acknowledging that previous interpretations were mistaken—that investments undertaken under certain expectations were errors. This acknowledgment carries economic, social, and political costs. It challenges narratives of competence and control. Policy regimes oriented toward stabilization therefore develop strong incentives to delay or disguise this recognition.

Monetary policy plays a crucial role in this delay. By lowering interest rates and expanding liquidity in response to downturns, central banks seek to preserve asset values and credit relationships. Fiscal policy complements this effort by sustaining incomes and demand, often targeting sectors most affected by adjustment. Together, these measures aim to bridge the economy from one expansion to the next without passing through a visible re-coordination phase.

Yet bridging is not the same as healing. The underlying inconsistencies in the capital structure remain unresolved. Projects that are viable only under accommodative conditions continue to absorb resources. Firms that would otherwise exit are kept alive through cheap credit or public support. Labor remains tied to activities whose economic meaning has eroded. The natural cycle is not eliminated; it is suppressed.

Suppression, however, is not neutral. It alters the temporal horizon of economic actors. When adjustment is repeatedly postponed, expectations adjust accordingly. Entrepreneurs come to rely on policy support; investors price assets based on anticipated intervention; households form consumption plans under the assumption of continued stabilization. The economy becomes increasingly policy-dependent, not because agents are irrational, but because policy has become a dominant interpretative framework.

This dependency transforms the nature of risk. In a market-driven environment, risk is primarily entrepreneurial: the risk that a particular interpretation of the future proves incorrect. In a policy-driven environment, risk becomes systemic and political: the risk that policy narratives change, that constraints emerge, or that credibility is lost. The distribution of risk shifts from decentralized actors to the system as a whole.

The accumulation of public and private debt intensifies this shift. Debt extends commitments into the future, binding future choices to past interpretations. When both monetary and fiscal policies encourage leverage, the economy becomes increasingly sensitive to changes in interest rates, inflation expectations, and policy credibility. Adjustment, when it eventually occurs, is therefore more abrupt and more disruptive.

From the standpoint of hermeneutical political economy, this outcome represents a tragic irony. Policies designed to reduce instability end up amplifying fragility. By suppressing small and frequent adjustments, they prepare the ground for larger and less manageable crises. The cycle does not disappear; it is displaced in time and magnified in scale.

This logic is consistent with the Austrian insight that interventionism generates cumulative effects. Mises argued that partial interventions tend to create problems that invite further intervention, leading to an escalating cycle of control. In the context of business cycles, this escalation manifests as a progressive deepening of policy involvement in credit markets, labour markets, and capital allocation.

Hayek, for his part, emphasized that the greatest danger lies not in overt planning, but in the gradual erosion of the price system's coordinating function. When prices increasingly reflect policy decisions rather than relative scarcity, they lose their capacity to convey knowledge. Economic actors are left navigating an environment shaped by administrative signals rather than by market feedback.

The suppression of the natural cycle thus entails a loss of economic meaning. Prices, profits, and losses become ambiguous indicators, interpreted through the lens of policy expectations. Entrepreneurial discovery is crowded out by regulatory arbitrage and rent-seeking. Innovation shifts from value creation to compliance and subsidy capture. The economy may continue to grow in measured terms, but its capacity for genuine adaptation declines.

This diagnosis does not imply a call for abrupt withdrawal of all policy support. Hermeneutical political economy is not a doctrine of mechanical non-intervention. It is an appeal for epistemic humility. It recognizes that policymakers operate under severe knowledge constraints and that attempts to manage complex adaptive systems through aggregate control are prone to unintended consequences.

A policy regime consistent with this humility would distinguish between supporting adjustment and preventing it. It would aim to reduce institutional rigidities, facilitate reallocation, and allow price signals to regain their communicative function. It would resist the temptation to equate stability with the absence of fluctuation and prosperity with the maintenance of existing structures.

In this sense, the distinction between natural and monetary cycles acquires normative significance. Natural cycles reflect the economy's capacity to learn and adapt. Monetary cycles reflect institutional distortions that misguide interpretation. The task of policy is not to eliminate cycles altogether, but to avoid transforming natural fluctuations into policy-induced instability.

Chapter 9 has sought to reinterpret monetary policy, government spending, and business cycles through a hermeneutical lens. It has argued that cycles are meaningful processes rooted in time and interpretation, that monetary policy distorts these processes by manipulating intertemporal signals, and that fiscal activism politicizes resource allocation and delays re-coordination. Together, these forces form a policy regime that suppresses the natural cycle and replaces adaptive coordination with managed fragility.

Lesson 10

Policy, Entrepreneurship And Innovation

10.1. Innovation as an Interpretative Process

The relationship between policy, innovation, and entrepreneurship cannot be properly understood within the confines of a mechanistic or technocratic vision of the economy. Innovation is not an output variable to be engineered, entrepreneurship is not a residual factor to be incentivised, and policy is not an optimisation problem to be solved through technical calibration. All three belong to the realm of human action and, as such, must be analysed within an interpretative framework that recognises meaning, expectations, uncertainty, and historical time as constitutive elements of economic life. Any attempt to detach innovation policy from this hermeneutical foundation risks transforming public intervention into an exercise in social engineering, substituting judgment with measurement and creativity with compliance.

In the preceding chapters, economics has been redefined as an interpretative science of understanding rather than a predictive science of control. Human action has been presented as purposeful behaviour unfolding in real time, shaped by expectations that are constantly revised through experience. Capital has been interpreted as a structure of meanings rather than a stock of physical goods, while business cycles have been explained as the outcome of interpretative discoordination, particularly when monetary policy distorts the signals guiding entrepreneurial judgment. Chapter 10 extends this interpretative framework to the domain of innovation and entrepreneurship, confronting directly the growing ambition of governments to "manage" innovation through policy instruments.

Innovation, when viewed hermeneutically, is not reducible to technological novelty or measurable R&D outcomes. It is the concrete manifestation of a successful reinterpretation of reality: a new way of seeing products, processes, markets, or institutional arrangements. Entrepreneurs are not innovators because they possess superior technical knowledge, but because they interpret reality differently and act upon those interpretations with commitment and leadership. Policy, in turn, operates within the same interpretative universe. It can either facilitate or obstruct entrepreneurial discovery, depending on whether it respects or suppresses the open-ended nature of the market process.

This perspective departs sharply from mainstream innovation economics, which tends to frame innovation as a function of inputs—research expenditure, human capital, subsidies, or clusters—and entrepreneurship as a behavioural response to incentives. Such approaches implicitly assume that innovation can be planned ex ante and that the role of policy is to correct market failures identified through quantitative indicators. Yet this vision neglects the epistemic problem at the heart of innovation: the impossibility of knowing in advance which ideas will succeed, which technologies will scale, and which business models will transform society. Innovation, precisely because it introduces novelty, cannot be forecast using existing data.

In other works, we have emphasised that economic development is not the result of optimal allocation within a given structure, but of endogenous transformation arising from within the market process. This insight finds its most powerful expression in Joseph Schumpeter's theory of economic development, where innovation appears as a disruptive force that breaks the circular flow of routine economic life. However, even Schumpeter's framework risks being misinterpreted when innovation is treated as a mechanical outcome of investment or technological progress. What must be recovered is the subjective, interpretative dimension of innovation: the act of seeing differently and acting decisively under uncertainty.

From a hermeneutical standpoint, innovation is inseparable from the entrepreneur's interpretative act. Before any product is launched, any process redesigned, or any market created, there is a moment of understanding—an insight that reconfigures the meaning of existing resources and opportunities. This insight is not derived from statistical analysis but from judgment exercised in historical time. It is therefore misleading to speak of "innovation systems" as if they were machines producing predictable outputs. What exists instead are institutional environments that either allow or constrain entrepreneurial interpretation and experimentation.

This distinction is crucial for policy analysis. When policy is conceived as an engineering tool aimed at producing innovation outcomes, it inevitably over-steps its epistemic limits. It assumes that policymakers can identify promising sectors, technologies, or firms ex ante, despite lacking access to the dispersed, tacit, and context-specific knowledge that entrepreneurs possess. In doing so, policy risks crowding out genuine entrepreneurial discovery and replacing it with rent-seeking behaviour oriented toward subsidy capture rather than market validation.

The hermeneutical critique of innovation policy does not imply a rejection of policy as such. Rather, it demands a redefinition of policy as an art of prudential action rather than a science of optimisation. Policy operates within uncertainty and must therefore be guided by humility, not by the illusion of control. Its role is not to select winners, but to shape an institutional framework within which entrepreneurial interpretation can unfold freely and competitively.

This insight resonates with the Products, Processes and Policies (PPP) Neo-Schumpeterian framework developed by the author of this textbook and his colleagues, which expands the traditional focus on products and processes to include policies as a third, endogenous dimension of innovation. Crucially, however, policies are not innovative because they generate measurable outputs, but because they alter the interpretative conditions under which entrepreneurs act. A policy innovation is meaningful only insofar as it enables new entrepreneurial interpretations to emerge and be tested by the market.

The danger arises when policy innovation becomes detached from market feedback. In such cases, policy ceases to be an enabling framework and becomes a substitute for entrepreneurial judgment. The state begins to act as if it were the entrepreneur, allocating capital, directing research, and defining strategic priorities. This substitution is not merely inefficient; it is epistemically incoherent. Without the discipline of profit and loss, policy cannot distinguish between productive innovation and wasteful experimentation. What appears innovative in bureaucratic terms may prove sterile in market terms.

Understanding innovation as an interpretative process also sheds new light on the relationship between innovation and competition. In the mainstream view, competition is often reduced to price rivalry within given technological constraints. In contrast, the Schumpeterian—and more radically, hermeneutical—perspective recognises competition as a discovery process driven by divergent interpretations of the future. Entrepreneurs compete not merely by lowering prices, but by proposing alternative meanings: new products, new organisational forms, new ways of satisfying human needs.

This dynamic conception of competition implies that innovation cannot

be separated from entrepreneurial freedom. Where entry is restricted, experimentation regulated, or failure penalised, innovation stagnates—not because
incentives are insufficient, but because interpretation is constrained. Policy
that aims to promote innovation must therefore begin by safeguarding
the openness of the market process, rather than by multiplying targeted
interventions.

At this stage, it becomes clear that the core tension explored in this chapter
is not between markets and policy per se, but between two competing visions
of economic order. One vision treats innovation as an outcome to be managed
through technocratic instruments; the other recognises innovation as an emergent property of human action unfolding within an institutional framework
shaped by rules, norms, and expectations. Hermeneutical political economy
aligns decisively with the latter.

In this section we have thus established the conceptual foundations necessary to analyse policy, innovation, and entrepreneurship without falling into
the traps of determinism and technocracy. Innovation has been reinterpreted
as a subjective, meaning-driven process; entrepreneurship as an act of leadership under uncertainty; and policy as a prudential activity constrained by
epistemic limits. The next part will deepen this analysis by returning explicitly
to Schumpeter's trinomial—entrepreneurship, innovation, and finance—and
by integrating it with your distinction between investment as potency and
innovation as act, preparing the ground for a systematic critique of contemporary innovation policy.

10.2. Entrepreneurship, Investment and the Passage from Potency to Act

If innovation is to be understood as an interpretative process, then entrepreneurship must be recognised as its human carrier. Innovation does not occur
autonomously, nor does it arise mechanically from technological progress,
institutional design, or policy incentives. It is always mediated by individuals
who interpret reality, envision alternative futures, and act under conditions
of uncertainty. Entrepreneurship, in this sense, is not a profession, a sector, or
a statistical category; it is a function within the market process, inseparable
from judgment, leadership, and responsibility.

Within hermeneutical political economy, entrepreneurship cannot be
reduced to opportunity recognition in a static environment. Opportunities
are not "out there", waiting to be discovered like physical objects; they are constituted through interpretation. Entrepreneurs do not merely respond to given
data but actively reconfigure the meaning of existing resources, technologies,

and social needs. This act of reinterpretation is what transforms latent possibilities into concrete economic change. Entrepreneurship, therefore, is not a reaction but an initiative, not adaptation but transformation.

This conception finds its classical articulation in Joseph Schumpeter's theory of economic development, yet it must be read carefully to avoid the distortions introduced by later, overly formalised interpretations. For Schumpeter, development is not an incremental process occurring within equilibrium, but a qualitative transformation that disrupts the circular flow of routine economic life. Innovation introduces discontinuity, breaking established patterns and forcing the system to reorganise itself around new combinations. Such transformations cannot be generated by ordinary economic actors operating within habitual routines; they require leadership.

Entrepreneurship, in Schumpeter's original sense, is inseparable from leadership. The entrepreneur is not defined by ownership of capital, technical expertise, or inventiveness, but by the capacity to carry out new combinations and to impose a new direction upon the economic system. This capacity is not primarily intellectual but volitional. It involves the courage to act without guarantees, to mobilise resources in the face of resistance, and to sustain commitment when outcomes remain uncertain. The entrepreneur, in this sense, is not a calculator of probabilities but a bearer of conviction.

This emphasis on leadership resonates deeply with the hermeneutical framework developed in earlier chapters. Acting under uncertainty means acting without full knowledge of future states of the world. Entrepreneurial judgment is therefore irreducible to optimisation. It is an act of interpretation grounded in subjective expectations, shaped by personal experience, institutional context, and historical time. What distinguishes the entrepreneur from the routine manager is not superior information, but a different way of seeing reality.

Yet entrepreneurship alone is insufficient to bring innovation into existence. Interpretation must be translated into action, and action requires resources. This brings us to the central role of investment and finance, which Schumpeter identified as the indispensable complement to entrepreneurship. New combinations cannot be financed out of existing flows of income, because they disrupt established production structures rather than reproduce them. Innovation requires the mobilisation of purchasing power in advance of realised returns. It therefore presupposes the availability of credit.

In Schumpeter's theory, the banker plays a role as fundamental as that of the entrepreneur. By creating purchasing power, financial institutions enable entrepreneurs to withdraw resources from existing uses and reallocate them toward new combinations. Credit, in this sense, is not a neutral intermediary but a constitutive element of economic development. Without it, entrepreneurship remains a mere aspiration; with it, interpretation gains material force.

The PPP Neo-Schumpeterian framework deepens this insight by introducing the distinction between investment as potency and innovation as act. Investment represents the realm of possibility: resources committed to an uncertain future, guided by expectations rather than certainties. Innovation represents the actualisation of that possibility: the moment when investment is validated by the market through successful coordination of production and demand. This distinction is not merely analytical; it is ontological.

Drawing on the Aristotelian and Thomistic tradition, potency refers to the capacity-to-be, while act refers to realised being. Investment, as potency, embodies the entrepreneur's interpretation of the future, mediated by financial support. Innovation, as act, emerges only when that interpretation proves capable of coordinating dispersed plans and satisfying human needs more effectively than existing arrangements. The passage from potency to act is therefore neither automatic nor guaranteed. It is contingent upon market validation.

This framework allows us to overcome a persistent confusion in contemporary policy discourse, where investment is often treated as synonymous with innovation. Public authorities frequently equate increased spending—whether on R&D, infrastructure, or subsidies—with innovative outcomes. Yet investment without successful entrepreneurial interpretation remains mere potential. It may generate activity, employment, or technological artefacts, but it does not necessarily generate innovation in the economic sense. Innovation requires that new combinations prove themselves within the competitive market process.

Competition, in this context, must be understood in its Schumpeterian sense, not as price rivalry among homogeneous firms, but as a struggle between alternative interpretations of the future. Entrepreneurs compete by proposing different visions of how resources can be combined to create value. The market selects among these visions through profit and loss, rewarding those interpretations that achieve superior coordination and penalising those that fail. This selection mechanism is indispensable, because it provides the only reliable feedback on whether investment has successfully passed from potency to act.

From a hermeneutical standpoint, profit and loss are not merely financial indicators; they are signals within an interpretative process. Profit confirms that an entrepreneurial interpretation has aligned production with consumer valuations; loss indicates a misinterpretation of reality. These signals are meaningful precisely because they emerge from voluntary exchange and real scarcity. When policy intervenes in ways that distort these signals, it interferes with the very process through which innovation is recognised and consolidated.

This insight has profound implications for innovation policy. When governments attempt to substitute market validation with administrative criteria—such as technological readiness levels, strategic priorities, or social objectives—they risk conflating potency with act. Projects may be funded, scaled, and celebrated as innovative without ever undergoing the disciplining test of the market. In such cases, policy does not merely fail to promote innovation; it actively obscures the distinction between successful and unsuccessful interpretations.

The temptation to bypass market validation is particularly strong in sectors characterised by high uncertainty, long time horizons, or strong ideological narratives, such as green technologies, digital transformation, or strategic industries. Yet it is precisely in such contexts that entrepreneurial judgment and competitive selection are most needed. The greater the uncertainty, the less justified is the belief that policymakers can identify successful innovations ex ante.

This does not imply that all policy involvement in innovation is illegitimate. Rather, it requires a clear conceptual separation between enabling conditions and substitutive action. Policy can shape the institutional environment within which entrepreneurship and investment operate—by protecting property rights, ensuring monetary stability, enforcing contracts, and maintaining openness to competition. These conditions do not determine which innovations will succeed, but they preserve the interpretative openness of the market process.

By contrast, when policy attempts to direct investment toward predefined outcomes, it assumes knowledge it cannot possess. It replaces entrepreneurial interpretation with bureaucratic judgment, and market selection with political discretion. The result is not innovation but politicised investment, in which success is measured by compliance with policy objectives rather than by genuine economic coordination.

The hermeneutical framework thus reveals a fundamental asymmetry between entrepreneurship and policy. Entrepreneurs act within the market process, bearing the consequences of their interpretations through profit and loss. Policymakers act outside the market process, insulated from direct feedback and guided by abstract indicators. When policy attempts to perform entrepreneurial functions, it does so without the epistemic and moral discipline that entrepreneurship requires.

This asymmetry also explains why innovation cannot be commanded, accelerated, or guaranteed by policy. Innovation emerges from the interaction of subjective interpretations within a competitive framework that no single actor controls. It unfolds in real time, through trial and error, success and failure.

Attempts to compress this process into predefined targets or timelines reflect a misunderstanding of its nature.

Part 2 has thus clarified the central role of entrepreneurship and investment within the interpretative process of innovation. Entrepreneurship has been presented as leadership under uncertainty, investment as potency, and innovation as act validated by market coordination. This framework prepares the ground for a deeper analysis of the role of policy, which will be undertaken in the next part. There, the focus will shift explicitly to policies as institutional interpretations, examining when they can genuinely support innovation and when they become obstacles to entrepreneurial discovery.

10.3. Policy as Interpretation: Institutions, Humility, and the Limits of Innovation Policy

To advance the analysis of policy, innovation, and entrepreneurship within a hermeneutical political economy, it is necessary to abandon the widespread conception of policy as a neutral technical apparatus designed to optimise outcomes. Policy, like entrepreneurship, is an activity undertaken by human agents operating under uncertainty, guided by interpretations of reality rather than by exhaustive knowledge. The crucial difference lies not in the presence or absence of interpretation, but in the position from which interpretation is exercised and the feedback mechanisms through which it is corrected.

Policy is itself an interpretative act. Policymakers do not respond to objective facts as such; they respond to meanings attributed to economic phenomena, institutional narratives, statistical representations, and political priorities. In this sense, policy belongs fully to the hermeneutical universe described in the earlier chapters of this book. The error of technocratic governance lies precisely in the denial of this fact: in the belief that policy can be depersonalised, rendered automatic, and insulated from judgment through rules, models, and indicators.

When policy is framed as innovation policy, this denial becomes particularly acute. Innovation is treated as an outcome to be engineered, accelerated, or steered through targeted interventions. Governments speak of innovation roadmaps, strategic sectors, technological missions, and national champions, implicitly assuming that the direction of economic development can be identified ex ante and implemented through administrative coordination. Such an approach reflects a mechanistic view of the economy that is fundamentally incompatible with the interpretative nature of human action.

From a hermeneutical perspective, the first task is therefore to reinterpret the role of policy itself. Policy does not create innovation in the same sense that entrepreneurs do. It cannot generate new combinations, because it does not engage directly in the market process of interpretation, experimentation, and validation. What policy can do is shape the institutional framework within which entrepreneurial interpretations are formed and tested. This distinction is decisive.

Institutions are not neutral constraints imposed upon economic actors; they are carriers of meaning. Property rights, contract enforcement, monetary regimes, regulatory norms, and fiscal structures communicate expectations about permissible actions, risk-taking, and reward. They influence how entrepreneurs interpret opportunities and how investors assess uncertainty. In this sense, institutions are not external to the innovation process; they are part of its interpretative environment.

This insight aligns with the broader argument developed in *Economics: An Interpretative Science of Human Flourishing*, where institutions are understood as sedimented interpretations of social order rather than as purely technical arrangements. Institutions embody historical judgments about trust, responsibility, and cooperation. When they are stable, transparent, and predictable, they reduce interpretative noise and allow entrepreneurial judgment to focus on substantive innovation rather than on defensive adaptation.

The central policy question, therefore, is not how to stimulate innovation directly, but how to preserve the institutional conditions that allow entrepreneurial interpretation to flourish. These conditions include secure property rights, openness to competition, freedom of entry and exit, monetary stability, and a legal system that treats failure as a learning process rather than as a moral or political transgression. Such conditions do not prescribe specific outcomes; they preserve openness.

By contrast, innovation policy in its contemporary form often seeks to replace openness with direction. Policymakers identify priority sectors, allocate subsidies, design tax incentives, and establish public–private partnerships aimed at achieving predefined objectives. While these interventions are typically justified in the language of market failure, coordination failure, or externalities, they rest on a deeper presumption: that policymakers possess the interpretative capacity to foresee which innovations will be socially valuable.

This presumption conflicts directly with the epistemic insights of hermeneutical political economy. If innovation is the emergence of the genuinely new, then its content cannot be known in advance. The attempt to guide innovation toward predetermined ends necessarily favours what is already intelligible within existing conceptual frameworks. Radical innovation, by definition, escapes such frameworks. It appears anomalous, implausible, or even irrational when judged by prevailing standards.

The history of economic development provides ample evidence of this pattern. Transformative innovations were rarely the result of policy foresight; they emerged from entrepreneurial reinterpretations that challenged dominant assumptions. Policy, when it played a positive role, did so retrospectively—by removing barriers, recognising new practices, or adapting institutions to accommodate changes already underway. When policy attempted to lead, it often entrenched obsolete technologies or misallocated resources on a massive scale.

This asymmetry reflects a fundamental difference in learning mechanisms. Entrepreneurs learn through market feedback, absorbing losses and adjusting plans accordingly. Policymakers learn, if at all, through political processes that are slow, indirect, and often insulated from failure. The absence of a clear profit-and-loss mechanism means that policy errors persist longer and on a larger scale than entrepreneurial errors. In the domain of innovation, this persistence can be particularly damaging, as it locks resources into unproductive paths and crowds out alternative interpretations.

The Neo-Schumpeterian PPP framework offers a nuanced way to think about policy without collapsing into either laissez-faire dogmatism or technocratic activism. By recognising policies as a third dimension of innovation—alongside products and processes—it acknowledges that institutional change can itself be innovative. However, this recognition must be carefully qualified.

Policy innovations are not equivalent to entrepreneurial innovations. They do not arise from market experimentation, nor are they validated through competitive selection. Their legitimacy depends on a different criterion: whether they enhance or suppress the interpretative openness of the economic system. A policy is innovative in the proper sense only if it expands the space for entrepreneurial interpretation, reduces artificial barriers, and restores alignment between action and responsibility.

Examples of such policy innovations include the simplification of regulatory frameworks, the removal of entry restrictions, the clarification of property rights, and the de-politicisation of credit allocation. These changes do not dictate outcomes; they modify the rules of the game in ways that allow new strategies, technologies, and business models to emerge organically. In this sense, policy innovation is meta-innovation: it innovates the conditions under which innovation occurs.

The opposite tendency is equally evident in contemporary governance. Policies that multiply compliance requirements, fragment markets, subsidise incumbents, or politicise investment decisions narrow the interpretative horizon of entrepreneurs. They encourage conformity rather than creativity, risk aversion rather than experimentation. Even when such policies are motivated by laudable objectives—sustainability, inclusion, resilience—their effect may be to substitute administrative judgment for entrepreneurial discovery.

This substitution is often justified through the language of urgency. Climate change, digital transformation, or geopolitical competition are invoked as reasons to suspend the normal discipline of the market and to accelerate innovation through centralised direction. Yet urgency does not eliminate uncertainty; it intensifies it. The more complex and uncertain the environment, the more dangerous it becomes to concentrate interpretative authority in the hands of policymakers.

Hermeneutical political economy thus calls for a renewed emphasis on humility in policy design. Humility does not mean inaction; it means recognising the limits of what policy can know and control. It means preferring rules over discretion, general frameworks over targeted interventions, and institutional learning over strategic planning. Above all, it means respecting the market as a process of discovery rather than as a system to be optimised.

In this light, the most important contribution of policy to innovation may be negative rather than positive: the restraint from interfering with entrepreneurial judgment, the willingness to allow failure, and the courage to dismantle policies that no longer serve their enabling function. Such restraint is politically difficult, precisely because it resists the visible action bias that dominates contemporary governance. Yet it is intellectually necessary.

Part 3 has reframed policy as an interpretative activity embedded within institutional structures, subject to epistemic limits and moral responsibilities. It has argued that innovation policy, when conceived as engineering, conflicts with the hermeneutical nature of economic development, while policy understood as institutional craftsmanship can support entrepreneurial discovery. The next part will bring these insights together by analysing the interaction between policy, innovation, and business cycles, showing how misguided innovation policy can amplify monetary and real distortions rather than fostering sustainable growth.

10.4. Innovation, Policy, and the Dynamics of Natural and Monetary Cycles

The relationship between innovation policy and business cycles can only be fully understood once innovation is placed within the temporal structure of the market process. Innovation does not unfold in a timeless equilibrium; it emerges in historical time, through sequences of expectations, investments, successes, and failures. For this reason, the interaction between policy and innovation cannot be separated from the dynamics of economic cycles. Indeed, one of the most neglected consequences of contemporary innovation policy is its tendency to amplify cyclical distortions rather than to foster sustainable development.

Earlier chapters have introduced the distinction between the natural cycle and the monetary cycle. The natural cycle arises from the endogenous rhythm of entrepreneurial discovery, investment, error, and correction. It is inseparable from real time and from the interpretative processes through which entrepreneurs continuously revise their plans. The monetary cycle, by contrast, emerges when monetary and financial interventions distort the price system, altering the signals upon which entrepreneurial judgment relies. This distinction proves decisive when analysing innovation policy.

In a natural cycle, innovation is embedded within a learning process. Entrepreneurs interpret market signals, commit resources to uncertain projects, and receive feedback through profit and loss. Some innovations succeed and reshape the structure of production; others fail and release resources for alternative uses. This process is neither smooth nor painless, but it is coherent. It allows the economy to adapt to new knowledge and changing preferences without accumulating systemic imbalances.

Innovation, in this context, is self-limiting. Because investment is constrained by real savings and disciplined by market validation, the pace and direction of innovation reflect the underlying structure of consumer preferences and resource availability. The natural cycle therefore embodies a form of temporal coordination: expectations, investment, and consumption remain aligned through decentralized judgment.

The monetary cycle disrupts this coordination by altering the temporal structure of investment. When credit is expanded beyond the limits imposed by voluntary saving, entrepreneurs receive distorted signals about the availability of resources and the sustainability of long-term projects. Investment decisions that appear profitable under artificially low interest rates may prove unsustainable once monetary conditions change. This is the classical Austrian insight into boom-and-bust dynamics, which remains fully applicable to contemporary innovation-driven economies.

Innovation policy interacts with this monetary distortion in particularly problematic ways. When governments seek to promote innovation through subsidised credit, public guarantees, or central-bank-supported financing schemes, they reinforce the illusion of abundance created by monetary expansion. Innovation projects that would not pass the test of market discipline are sustained by policy support, delaying the moment of correction and increasing the scale of eventual adjustment.

The result is not merely inefficient investment, but structural miscoordination. Resources are channelled into sectors favoured by policy narratives—often labelled as "strategic," "future-oriented," or "mission-critical"—without adequate regard for their compatibility with the broader structure of production. Entrepreneurs, responding rationally to distorted incentives, adapt their interpretations accordingly. They orient their plans not toward consumer demand, but toward policy signals.

This phenomenon illustrates a crucial hermeneutical point: entrepreneurs do not respond to "markets" or "policies" as abstract entities; they respond to meanings. When policy communicates that certain activities will be protected, subsidised, or prioritised, it reshapes entrepreneurial interpretation. Investment flows toward compliance rather than discovery, toward alignment with administrative criteria rather than with consumer valuations.

In such an environment, innovation loses its grounding in the natural cycle and becomes entangled with the monetary cycle. The apparent acceleration of innovation during the boom phase is often celebrated as evidence of successful policy. New firms emerge, capital expenditures rise, and technological activity intensifies. Yet beneath this surface dynamism lies a fragile structure of expectations dependent on continued policy support and monetary accommodation.

When conditions eventually change—through inflationary pressures, fiscal constraints, or political shifts—the fragility is exposed. Projects once hailed as innovative are revealed as unsustainable. The correction phase then takes the form not only of bankruptcies and layoffs, but of a broader loss of trust in innovation itself. Society becomes sceptical of entrepreneurial risk-taking, and political pressure mounts for further intervention, perpetuating the cycle.

This dynamic helps explain why periods of aggressive innovation policy are often followed by disillusionment. The failure lies not in innovation as such, but in the attempt to detach it from market validation and temporal discipline. Innovation forced into existence through policy shortcuts lacks the resilience required to survive changing conditions. It is innovation in appearance, not in substance.

The distinction between natural and monetary cycles also clarifies the ethical dimension of innovation policy. In the natural cycle, entrepreneurial losses are borne by those who make the decisions. Responsibility and judgment remain aligned. In the policy-driven monetary cycle, losses are socialised through

public budgets, inflation, or financial repression. This separation of decision
and responsibility undermines the moral foundations of the market process.

Hermeneutical political economy insists that sustainable innovation requires
coherence between interpretation, action, and consequence. When policy
intervenes in ways that sever this coherence, it corrodes both economic coordination and moral accountability. Entrepreneurs become less attentive to reality
and more attentive to political signals; policymakers become less accountable
for outcomes and more focused on narrative management.

This does not imply that innovation must be slow or conservative. On
the contrary, the natural cycle can accommodate profound transformations.
What it cannot accommodate is the suppression of error correction. Innovation
flourishes where failure is possible and instructive, not where it is postponed
or disguised by policy support. The natural cycle is dynamic precisely because
it allows mistakes to be recognised and corrected early.

The interaction between innovation policy and monetary conditions therefore requires particular caution. Policies that appear benign in a stable monetary
environment can become destabilising when combined with credit expansion.
Conversely, policies that respect market discipline can mitigate the disruptive
effects of monetary interventions by preserving interpretative clarity.

A hermeneutically informed innovation policy would therefore begin not
with sectoral strategies or funding programmes, but with an assessment of the
monetary and financial context in which innovation unfolds. Without monetary stability, even well-designed institutions struggle to support sustainable
entrepreneurship. Inflation, interest-rate manipulation, and financial repression
obscure the signals that guide long-term investment, making innovation policy
both less effective and more dangerous.

Part 4 has shown that innovation cannot be analysed independently of
business cycles. When innovation policy aligns with the natural cycle, it can
support learning and adaptation. When it reinforces the monetary cycle, it
amplifies miscoordination and fragility. The next and final part will draw these
threads together, offering a synthetic perspective on policy, innovation, and
entrepreneurship as elements of a broader civilizational order, and articulating
the normative implications of hermeneutical political economy for the future
of innovation governance.

10.5. INNOVATION, POLICY, AND HUMAN FLOURISHING: A HERMENEUTICAL SYNTHESIS

The preceding parts of this chapter have reconstructed the relationship between policy, innovation, and entrepreneurship within a hermeneutical framework that rejects both technocratic engineering and naïve laissez-faire. Innovation has been interpreted as an emergent, meaning-driven process rooted in human action; entrepreneurship as leadership exercised under genuine uncertainty; policy as an interpretative and prudential activity constrained by epistemic limits; and business cycles as temporal expressions of coordination or miscoordination within the market process. Part 5 brings these elements together into a synthetic vision, clarifying the normative implications of hermeneutical political economy for innovation governance and, more broadly, for human flourishing.

At the centre of this synthesis lies a decisive methodological claim: innovation is not a policy objective to be maximised, but a by-product of a social order that respects freedom, responsibility, and the open-ended character of human creativity. When innovation is elevated to an explicit target of governance, it is inevitably reified, measured, and instrumentalised. The result is a paradoxical impoverishment of innovation itself. What is lost is not technological capability, but meaning.

Hermeneutical political economy insists that economic development cannot be detached from the question of what it means to act, choose, and create within a shared world. Innovation, in this light, is not merely about doing things differently, but about doing them in ways that respond to human purposes as they are interpreted and reinterpreted over time. It is therefore inseparable from human flourishing, understood not as the accumulation of outputs, but as the expansion of meaningful possibilities for action.

This perspective challenges the dominant narrative of innovation governance, which tends to conflate progress with acceleration and novelty with improvement. In contemporary discourse, innovation is often treated as an unquestioned good, irrespective of its content or consequences. Policies are evaluated according to their capacity to increase the rate of innovation, measured through patents, start-ups, or investment flows. Yet such metrics say little about whether innovation enhances human agency or merely reorganises dependency.

A hermeneutical approach restores a qualitative dimension to the analysis. It asks not only whether innovation occurs, but how it occurs and under what institutional conditions. Does innovation emerge from entrepreneurial judgment tested by market feedback, or from administrative selection insulated from failure? Does it expand the range of meaningful choices available to individuals, or does it constrain them through standardisation and control? These questions cannot be answered through quantitative indicators alone; they require interpretation.

Entrepreneurship occupies a privileged place within this interpretative order because it embodies the unity of vision, action, and responsibility. The entrepreneur is not merely an agent of economic change, but a moral actor who commits resources to uncertain futures and bears the consequences of error. This unity is essential for the integrity of the market process. When entrepreneurship is displaced by policy-driven investment, this unity is broken. Decisions are taken without corresponding responsibility, and responsibility is diffused without clear decision-makers.

The erosion of this unity has implications that extend beyond efficiency. It affects the moral ecology of the economy. When losses are systematically socialised and success is politically mediated, entrepreneurial judgment is weakened. Risk-taking becomes strategic rather than creative, oriented toward regulatory advantage rather than toward the satisfaction of human needs. Innovation, under such conditions, becomes performative rather than substantive.

Hermeneutical political economy thus reveals a deep affinity between innovation and freedom. Innovation presupposes the freedom to interpret reality differently and to act upon those interpretations without prior authorisation. It also presupposes the freedom to fail, to learn, and to try again. Policies that restrict this freedom in the name of innovation undermine the very process they claim to support.

This does not imply a withdrawal of policy from economic life. Rather, it calls for a reorientation of policy toward institutional craftsmanship. The task of policy is not to guide innovation toward predefined ends, but to maintain the conditions under which entrepreneurial interpretation remains possible. This includes protecting property rights, ensuring monetary stability, preserving competitive openness, and resisting the politicisation of credit and investment.

Such a vision demands intellectual humility. Policymakers must acknowledge that they operate within the same uncertainty that entrepreneurs face, but without access to the same feedback mechanisms. The appropriate response to this asymmetry is restraint, not ambition. Prudential policy recognises that the most important contributions to innovation often come from unexpected directions and that institutional rigidity is more damaging than the absence of strategic coordination.

The distinction between natural and monetary cycles reinforces this conclusion. Sustainable innovation unfolds within a temporal structure that allows expectations, investment, and consumption to remain aligned through decentralized learning. When policy interferes with this structure—whether through monetary distortion or targeted innovation programmes—it risks transforming innovation into a cyclical artefact rather than a durable achievement. The short-term appearance of dynamism masks long-term fragility.

From the standpoint of human flourishing, this fragility is not merely economic. It erodes trust in institutions, scepticism toward entrepreneurship, and the social legitimacy of the market order. When innovation repeatedly fails to deliver on its promises, not because of entrepreneurial error but because of policy distortion, society becomes receptive to calls for further control. A vicious circle emerges in which innovation policy generates the very instability it seeks to prevent.

Hermeneutical political economy offers a way out of this circle by reconnecting innovation with meaning. It reminds us that economic life is not a machine to be optimised, but a living process shaped by interpretation, memory, and expectation. Innovation, in this sense, is an expression of human creativity operating within institutional constraints that must themselves be open to revision. Policy plays a role in this process not by commanding outcomes, but by preserving openness.

In concluding this chapter, it is important to emphasise that the argument advanced here is not anti-innovation, anti-policy, or anti-state. It is anti-illusion. It rejects the illusion that innovation can be planned without judgment, that policy can substitute for entrepreneurship, and that progress can be measured without understanding. Against these illusions, hermeneutical political economy affirms the dignity of human action as the source of economic development.

Innovation worthy of the name emerges when individuals are free to interpret the world, to experiment with new combinations, and to bear responsibility for their choices. Policy contributes to this process when it respects its own limits and focuses on cultivating the institutional soil rather than engineering the harvest. Only under these conditions can innovation serve not merely growth, but human flourishing.

With this synthesis, Chapter 10 completes the arc developed throughout *Hermeneutical Political Economy*. Innovation, entrepreneurship, policy, money, and cycles are revealed as interdependent moments of a single interpretative process unfolding in historical time. Understanding this unity is the precondition for designing policies that do not merely act upon the economy, but participate prudently in the ongoing drama of human creativity and coordination.

Lesson 11

Getting Policy Right: Incentives, Institutions And Humility

11.1. Introduction

This book has advanced a single, persistent claim: economic life is not a mechanical system to be engineered, but an interpretative, historically unfolding process shaped by meaning, expectations, institutions, and entrepreneurial creativity. Political economy, when properly understood, is therefore not a science of control but a science of understanding, while policy is an art of prudence exercised under conditions of radical uncertainty. The purpose of this final chapter is to draw together the threads developed throughout the book and to articulate what it means, in practical and normative terms, to "get policy right" within a hermeneutical framework.

Getting policy right does not mean selecting the correct policy instrument, optimising a target variable, or calibrating an intervention to an estimated coefficient. It means recognising the limits of policy knowledge, aligning incentives with social cooperation, embedding decision-making within robust and general institutions, and exercising humility in the face of complexity. Policy success, in this sense, is less about achieving predefined outcomes than about creating and preserving the conditions under which individuals and communities can interpret, adapt, and flourish over time.

11.2. Incentives and the moral neutrality of policy tools

Any discussion of policy must begin with incentives, not because incentives exhaust human motivation, but because they shape the context within which meaning-laden human action unfolds. Individuals act purposefully, guided by expectations, beliefs, and interpretations of their circumstances. Policy interventions alter these circumstances by modifying relative costs and benefits, thereby influencing the pattern of action without ever determining it mechanically.

A hermeneutical political economy rejects the naïve belief that policymakers can "design" outcomes by manipulating incentives as if human agents were programmable units. Yet it also rejects the equally naïve belief that incentives are irrelevant or that intentions alone can substitute for institutional structure. Incentives are morally neutral; they do not tell individuals what to value, but they do influence how values are pursued. A tax, a subsidy, a regulation, or a monetary expansion does not compel behaviour in a deterministic sense, but it changes the narrative environment in which decisions are made.

This insight bridges Austrian political economy with contemporary public policy analysis. Modern policy studies increasingly recognise that policy outcomes emerge from complex interactions among multiple actors, institutions, and interpretations rather than from linear implementation chains. However, much of this literature remains descriptively sophisticated but normatively agnostic. Hermeneutical political economy adds a crucial layer by insisting that incentives must be evaluated not only in terms of efficiency or effectiveness, but in terms of their compatibility with human agency, responsibility, and long-run coordination.

11.3. Institutions as carriers of meaning and constraints on power

If incentives shape action at the margin, institutions shape the very grammar of social interaction. Institutions are not merely rules or constraints; they are repositories of shared expectations, historically sedimented interpretations, and tacit knowledge. Property rights, contract law, monetary regimes, and constitutional constraints are not neutral technical devices but social achievements that structure how individuals understand their opportunities and obligations.

Throughout this book, we have argued that sound policy does not consist in discretionary intervention but in the establishment of general, predictable, and impersonal rules. This is particularly evident in the monetary sphere. Discretionary monetary policy, even when constrained by technocratic norms, suffers from intrinsic knowledge and incentive problems. It invites short-termism, politicisation, and narrative instability, undermining the very coordination function that money is supposed to perform. Embedding monetary policy within a rule-of-law framework restores predictability and limits the scope for arbitrary power, thereby reinforcing the interpretative stability necessary for entrepreneurial planning.

The same logic applies beyond money. Institutions that are general rather than particularistic, predictable rather than discretionary, and abstract rather than outcome-oriented create a stable horizon of expectations. They allow individuals to form plans, revise interpretations, and engage in cooperative ventures without requiring centralised direction. In this sense, institutions do not replace judgment; they make judgment possible by constraining the domain of coercion and uncertainty.

11.4. COMPLEXITY, EMERGENCE, AND THE LIMITS OF POLICY DESIGN

One of the most damaging legacies of technocratic political economy is the illusion that social systems can be optimised through sufficient data, computational power, or expert knowledge. Complexity theory has decisively undermined this illusion by demonstrating that social systems are adaptive, non-linear, and characterised by emergent properties that cannot be inferred from their components alone.

From a hermeneutical perspective, complexity reinforces rather than weakens the case for humility. Policy interventions are not external shocks applied to a passive system; they become part of the system itself, altering incentives, expectations, and learning processes in unpredictable ways. Every intervention changes the narrative context within which future actions are interpreted.

The contribution of complexity-oriented policy analysis lies not in offering new tools for control, but in redirecting attention from outcome optimisation to process robustness. Sound policy, in a complex system, is not policy that "solves" problems once and for all, but policy that allows for error correction, feedback, and adaptation. This requires decentralisation, institutional diversity, and tolerance for experimentation rather than uniform solutions imposed from the centre.

Hermeneutical political economy converges here with the idea of applied mainline economics, which emphasises institutions over personalities, rules over discretion, and processes over targets. Policymakers are subject to the same cognitive limitations and incentive constraints as everyone else. Treating them as benevolent maximisers with privileged knowledge is not only unrealistic but dangerous.

11.5. HUMILITY AS A POLICY VIRTUE

Humility is often misunderstood as passivity or indecision. In a hermeneutical framework, humility is neither. It is an active virtue grounded in the recognition of fallibility, ignorance, and unintended consequences. To be humble is not to refrain from action, but to act with an awareness of limits, to prefer reversible rules over irreversible commands, and to design institutions that constrain one's own power.

Humility also has a moral dimension. Policies justified solely by measured outcomes risk eroding the moral agency of individuals by treating them as variables to be managed rather than persons to be respected. A hermeneutical approach insists that policy legitimacy cannot be reduced to effectiveness. It must also respect the dignity of choice, the plurality of ends, and the irreducibility of human meaning.

This does not imply relativism or policy nihilism. It implies a disciplined modesty in claims, a preference for general frameworks over detailed prescriptions, and a willingness to learn from failure without resorting to ever-greater control. Humble policy accepts that social order is largely the result of human action but not of human design, and that the role of the policymaker is to safeguard the institutional conditions under which this order can emerge and renew itself.

11.6. Policy as stewardship, not engineering

The central message of this book can now be stated clearly. Policy is not an exercise in social engineering but an act of stewardship. It is concerned less with directing outcomes than with maintaining the institutional ecology within which interpretation, coordination, and creativity can flourish. Getting policy right, therefore, means resisting the temptation to replace judgment with measurement, prudence with technique, and responsibility with control.

A hermeneutical political economy does not promise certainty or optimality. What it offers instead is a framework for thinking about policy that is intellectually honest, morally grounded, and institutionally robust. It reminds us that economic life is lived forward but understood backward, that knowledge is dispersed and contextual, and that freedom is not the absence of rules but the presence of good ones.

In an age increasingly dominated by technocratic ambition and narrative simplification, reclaiming humility in policy is not a retreat from reason but a defence of it. It is an invitation to rediscover political economy as a moral and interpretative discipline, oriented toward human flourishing rather than administrative control. In this sense, getting policy right is inseparable from getting economics right—and both ultimately depend on our willingness to accept the limits of what we can know and the responsibility of what we choose to do.

Concluding Note And Guide
To Further Readings

This textbook has been conceived as a continuous intellectual journey rather than as a conventional academic compendium. In order to preserve the unity of exposition and to maintain a smooth and readable narrative, in-text citations and constant references have been deliberately avoided. The choice was not motivated by disregard for scholarly standards, but by the conviction that excessive technical apparatus often interrupts the flow of reasoning and distracts the reader from the deeper conceptual and interpretative issues at stake. The ambition of this book is to invite reflection, not to overwhelm the reader with footnotes.

This stylistic decision should not be mistaken for an absence of intellectual roots. On the contrary, the book is the outcome of a long process of study, interpretation, and dialogue with a wide body of economic, philosophical, and methodological literature. Every chapter rests upon foundations laid by authors who have shaped the way we understand markets, institutions, knowledge, entrepreneurship, policy, and the limits of economic engineering. Their ideas inform the arguments developed here, even when they are not explicitly cited page by page.

For this reason, the concluding section offers a curated list of readings that represents the main intellectual scaffolding of the book. These works are not meant to be exhaustive, nor are they intended as a rigid canon. Rather, they should be read as points of orientation—texts that have provided inspiration, conceptual tools, and critical perspectives throughout the writing of this volume. Together, they form the background against which the arguments of the book have been developed and refined.

Readers who wish to deepen their understanding, verify interpretations, or pursue alternative perspectives are encouraged to engage directly with these sources. Doing so will not only enrich the reading of this textbook but will also reveal the broader conversations within which it is situated. The list that follows therefore serves a dual purpose: it acknowledges the intellectual debts underlying the book and offers an open invitation to continue the inquiry beyond its pages.

Alchian, A.A. (2006), *The Collected Works of Armen A. Alchian*, Volume 1: *Choice and Cost under Uncertainty*, Indianapolis, Liberty Fund.

Boettke, P.J., Salter, A.W. and Smith, D.J. (2021), *Money and the Rule of Law. Generality and Predictability in Monetary Institutions*, Cambridge, Cambridge University Press.

Blanchard, O. (2017), *Macroeconomics*, New York, Pearson.

Brennan, G. and Buchanan, J.M. (1980), *The Power to Tax. Analytical Foundations of a Fiscal Constitution*, Indianapolis, Liberty Fund, 2000.

Buchanan, J.M. and Wagner, R.E. (1977), *Democracy in Deficit. The Political Legacy of Lord Keynes*, Indianapolis, Liberty Fund, 2000.

Cairney, P. (2020), *Understanding Public Policy. Theories and Issues*, London, MacMillan.

Colander, D. and Kupers, R. (2014), *Complexity and the Art of Public Policy. Solving Society's Problems from the Bottom Up*, Princeton and Oxford, Princeton University Press.

Cowen, T. and Tabarrock, A. (2013), *Modern Principles: Macroeconomics*, New York, Worth Publishers.

——— (2015), *Modern Principles: Microeconomics*, New York, Worth Publishers.

Ferlito, C. (2025a), *Beyond Price Stability: The Role of Monetary Policy for Sustainable Growth and Social Welfare*, CME Policy Paper, 7, Subang Jaya, Center for Market Education.

——— (2025b), *Products, Processes and Policies (PPP): CME's Neo-Schumpeterian Approach to Innovation*, CME Policy Brief, 8, Subang Jaya, Center for Market Education.

——— (2026), *Economics: An Interpretative Science of Human Flourishing*, Jakarta, Universitas Prasetiya Mulya Publishing.

Friedman, M. (2007), *Milton Friedman on Economics. Selected Papers*, Chicago and London, The University of Chicago Press.

Friedman, M. and Friedman, R.D. (1980), *Free to Choose. A Personal Statement*, New York and London, Harcourt Brace Jovanovich.

Garrison, R. (2001), *Time and money. The macroeconomic of capital structure*, London and New York, Routledge.

Hayek, F.A. von (1929), *Monetary Theory and the Trade Cycle*, New York, Kelley, 1966.

——— (1931), *Prices and Production*, New York, Kelley, 1967.

——— (1933), *Price Expectations, Monetary Disturbances and Malinvestments*, in *Profits, Interest and Investment and Other Essays on the Theory of Industrial Fluctuations*, Clifton, Augustus M. Kelley, 1975, Chapter IV.

——— (1937), *Economics and Knowledge*, «Economica», 4, 13, pp. 33-54.

——— (1945), *The Use of Knowledge in Society*, «The American Economic Review», 35, 4, pp. 519-530.

——— (1946), *The meaning of competition*, in *The Collected Works of F.A. Hayek*, Volume XV: *The market and other orders*, Chicago, The University of Chicago Press, 2014, pp. 105-116.

——— (1968), *Competition as a discovery procedure*, «Quarterly Journal of Austrian Economics», 5, 3, 2022, pp. 9-23.

Hearn, J. and Ferlito, C. (2021), *The cause of inflation, its link to unemployment and the need for sound monetary control*, CME EduPaper, 8, Subang Jaya, Center for Market Education.

Lachmann, L.M. (1971), *The Legacy of Max Weber*. Berkeley, The Glendessary Press.

———— (1986), *The Market as an Economic Process*, Arlington, Mercatus Center at George Mason University, 2020.

Mankiw, N.G. (2011), *Principles of Economics*, Nashville, South-Western.

Mises, L. von (1920), *Economic Calculation in the Socialist Commonwealth*, Auburn, Ludwig von Mises Institute, 1990.

———— (1936), *The "Austrian" Theory of the Trade Cycle*, in R.M. Ebeling (Ed.), *The Austrian Theory of the Trade Cycle and other essays*, Auburn, Ludwig von Mises Institute, 1996, pp. 25-35.

———— (1949), *Human Action. A Treatise on Economics*, Auburn, Ludwig von Mises Institute, 1998.

Mitchell, D.M. and Boettke, P.J. (2017), *Applied Mainline Economics. Bridging the Gap between Theory and Public Policy*, Arlington, Mercatus Center at George Mason University.

Phaneuf, E. (2020), *The problem of knowledge and economic calculation. Can governments intervene in the market in a rational way?*, CME EduPaper, 4, Subang Jaya, Center for Market Education.

Schumpeter, J.A. (1911), *The Theory of Economic Development: An Inquiry into Profits, Capital, Credit, Interest, and the Business Cycle*, New Brunswick and London, Transaction Publishers, 1983.

———— (1939), *Business Cycles. A Theoretical, Historical, and Statistical Analysis of the Capitalist Process*, 2 vols., Chevy Chase and Mansfield Centre, Bartleby's Book and Martino Publishing, 2005.

Wagner, R.E. (1989), *To Promote General Welfare*, Arlington, Mercatus Center at George Mason University, 2019.

Yeager, L.B. (1997), *The Fluttering Veil. Essays on Monetary Disequilibrium*, Indianapolis, Liberty Fund.

www.ingramcontent.com/pod-product-compliance
Lightning Source LLC
Chambersburg PA
CBHW071348280326
41927CB00039B/2214